Eco-Terrorism

Eco-Terrorism

Radical Environmental and Animal Liberation Movements

DONALD R. LIDDICK

PRAEGER

Westport, Connecticut
London

Library of Congress Cataloging-in-Publication Data

Liddick, Don.
  Eco-terrorism : radical environmental and animal liberation
movements / Donald R. Liddick.
    p. cm.
  Includes bibliographical references and index.
  ISBN 0-275-98535-0 (alk. paper)
    1. Ecoterrorism—United States—History. 2. Environmentalism—
United States—History. 3. Animal rights movement—United States—
History. 4. Animal rights movement—Moral and ethical aspects—
United States. I. Title.
GE197.L53 2006
363.325'933370973—dc22   2006024499

British Library Cataloguing in Publication Data is available.

Library of Congress Catalog Card Number: 2006024499
ISBN: 0-275-98535-0

First published in 2006

Praeger Publishers, 88 Post Road West, Westport, CT 06881
An imprint of Greenwood Publishing Group, Inc.
www.praeger.com

Printed in the United States of America

∞™

The paper used in this book complies with the
Permanent Paper Standard issued by the National
Information Standards Organization (Z39.48–1984).

10   9   8   7   6   5   4   3   2   1

Contents

Introduction: Criminality in the Environmental and Animal Rights Movements

> When hopes and dreams are loose in the streets, it is well for the timid to lock doors, shutter windows and lie low until the wrath has passed. For there is often a monstrous incongruity between the hopes, however noble and tender, and the action which follows them. It is as if ivied maidens and garlanded youths were to herald the four horsemen of the apocalypse.
>
> —Eric Hoffer, *The True Believer*

Criminality and terror stemming from radical environmentalism and animal rights extremism is largely a modern phenomenon, developing in the last decades of the twentieth century. It is a movement far removed from the elite conservationist and animal welfare movements of the nineteenth century and the mainstream environmental and animal protection groups that emerged later. Often drawn from the same pool of concerned individuals that comprises the memberships of groups such as Greenpeace, the Wilderness Society, and People for the Ethical Treatment of Animals (PETA), some disaffected environmentalists and animal rights advocates have turned from political lobbying and lawful protest to direct action in the form of vandalism, theft, arson, and even violent attacks against people.

The growth and severity of so-called eco-terror and animal rights criminality from the 1970s to the present day is noticeable and significant. Attacks on research facilities, farming operations, construction companies, timber companies, fishing operations, fast-food restaurants, building sites, and sport-utility vehicle dealerships are well reported through media accounts and various Internet sites either endorsing or denouncing these activities. An emerging trend, especially in Great Britain, is the targeting of individuals. Research scientists, corporate officials, and their families have been the subject of threats and assaults by animal rights extremists. Law enforcement and government officials have recognized the increasing threat: the U.S. Congress has held numerous hearings on the subject, while the Federal Bureau of Investigation has declared these forms of violence to be the most serious domestic terrorism threat in the United States.[1]

The stated position of extremist groups such as the Earth Liberation Front (ELF) and the Animal Liberation Front (ALF) is that human beings are never targeted or harmed. However, it is also true that their methods of property destruction create substantial risks. In fact, the literature and statements produced by some radicals demonstrate that human welfare is typically viewed as secondary to the health of the planet and its non-human inhabitants. The following quote from Dave Foreman, a cofounder of the radical environmental movement Earth First!, embodies the mind-set:

> In everything we do, the primary consideration should be for the long-term health and native diversity of Earth. After that, we can consider the welfare of humans. We should be kind, compassionate, and caring with other people, but Earth comes first.[2]

Unfortunately, the position that environmental and animal rights activists should be "kind, compassionate, and caring with other people" has ostensibly fallen out of favor with some radicals. Animal rights terrorists in particular have become more radical and violent in recent years, targeting people for harassment and physical attacks. The *Intelligence Project*, a publication of the Southern Poverty Law Center, reported in its Fall 2002 issue that employees of various companies have had their homes vandalized and have faced death threats, firebombs, and physical assaults. In 2002 animal rights protestors stormed the offices of Arkansas-based Stephens Inc. and attacked workers, kicking them and breaking office equipment. Huntingdon Life Sciences, an international company that tests pharmaceuticals on animals, has in recent years witnessed an ongoing campaign of terror and violence—employees have been beaten with clubs, sprayed in the face with acid, and subjected to death threats directed at their children.[3] When a British journalist created a documentary critical of the animal rights movement, members of the Animal Liberation Front (ALF) kidnapped him and branded the letters *ALF* on his back.[4]

Neither does the stated commitment to nonviolence extend to the rhetoric emanating from the radical leadership. Craig Rosebraugh, a former spokesperson for the Earth Liberation Front, advocates the overthrow of the American government and has stated that "revolution in the United States must be comprised of a variety of strategies" and that "it cannot be successful without the implementation of violence."[5] When the managing director of Huntingdon Life Sciences was severely beaten by three animal rights activists wielding baseball bats, ALF cofounder Ronnie Lee said that the victim "got off lightly."[6] Edward Abbey, who authored *The Monkey Wrench Gang* (a work of fiction that has become something of a bible to the radical environmental movement), said: "I think we are morally justified to resort to *whatever means are necessary* [emphasis added] in order to defend our land from destruction, from invasion."[7]

Extreme rhetoric is evident on the animal rights side of the fight as well. In a 1990 book, Michael W. Fox, then vice president of the Humane Society of the United States, held that "the life an ant and that of my child should be granted equal consideration."[8] At other times equality of species does not go far enough, and misanthropy reigns; Ingrid Newkirk, president of People for the Ethical Treatment of Animals (PETA), believes that "humans have grown like a cancer. We're the biggest blight on the face of the earth."[9] In an infamous and oft-used argument, animal rights activists liken factory farming and the use of animals for food to slavery and the Jewish Holocaust. Even when statements like these do not explicitly endorse violence against humans, the effect of the moral philosophy adopted by radical environmental and animal rights activists has not been to extend equal consideration to the Earth and its nonhuman inhabitants but to devalue human life.

If the official position of these underground movements is that human beings are not to be harmed, it is also clear that the ideological framework for justifying human casualties has been forged. Developed by Norwegian philosopher Arne Naess, deep ecology is a philosophy that stresses biocentrism over anthropocentrism; rather than human beings enjoying special status in the natural world, all objects in nature are viewed as having intrinsic worth. The ideology of the radical environmentalist creates a milieu of moral equivalence between sentient and non-sentient objects, where humans, mountains, and protozoa all deserve equal consideration.[10] With the establishment of this moral equation, illicit acts, including violent crimes, apparently become justified in the minds of some radical environmental and animal rights activists.

The centerpiece of all radical environmental groups is that an environmental apocalypse is imminent—thus the justification for immediate direct action, including widespread property destruction. Environmental extremists are invariably shaped by some blend of anarchistic, apocalyptic, and millenarian thinking, striving to hasten the downfall of modern civilization so as to realize a better world where man will live in harmony with the natural world. In effect, this means that to restore and preserve the health and diversity of the planet, a significant decrease in the human population is necessary.[11] With this outlook, the ultimate threat from so-called eco-terrorism becomes evident: Might not a motivated animal rights or environmental extremist, believing the safety of the planet demands it, use an infectious biological agent to kill thousands, perhaps millions of people? Certain fringe elements in the mass movements discussed in this book would answer in the affirmative.

A Brief Overview of Radical Environmental
and Animal Rights Groups

Perhaps the best known of the truly radical (and sometimes criminal) environmental groups to emerge in the late twentieth century is Earth First! Founded in 1979, Earth First! was the brainchild of five disaffected mainstream environmentalists. The organization (or movement) grew exponentially throughout the 1980s and today consists of an unknown number (at least 10,000 by the late 1980s) of activists all over the world who demonstrate, practice civil disobedience, and in some cases perpetrate acts of "ecotage" (ecologically motivated sabotage). Earth First!'s official website and its newsletter state that the movement neither condemns nor condones illegal acts of property destruction. However, while many members no doubt limit themselves to peaceful demonstrations such as tree sitting, some have been far more militant in their defense of the Earth.[12]

An Earth First! splinter group called EMETIC (the Evan Mecham Eco-Terrorist International Conspiracy, sarcastically named after a former governor of Arizona) perpetrated a number of major attacks in the late 1980s. Consisting of five members inspired by Earth First! cofounder Dave Foreman, EMETIC caused $20,000 in damage to the bolts that anchored power lines on the Fairfield Snowbowl ski resort in Arizona in 1987. A year later the group destroyed power lines feeding uranium mines near the Grand Canyon, costing Energy Fuels Nuclear $200,000. In October 1988 they hit the Fairfield Snowbowl a second time, cutting through a pole supporting the chair lift with an acetylene torch. In May 1989 several EMETIC members were caught near Wendon, Arizona, cutting through a tower support that delivered electricity to a nearby substation. By the time of that attack the group had been infiltrated by an undercover FBI agent—a law enforcement success that led to the convictions of all five EMETIC members. The investigation revealed that EMETIC had been conspiring to simultaneously attack power transmission lines at three nuclear facilities in Arizona, California, and Colorado.[13]

The Earth Liberation Front (ELF) is an international underground movement that originated in the United Kingdom in 1992 and became active in North America in 1996. Essentially a spin-off of Earth First!, ELF has been responsible for well over $100 million in property damages since 1997. The loose-knit organization is bound together by a common set of core guidelines, published on the ELF website:

- To inflict economic damage on those profiting from the destruction and exploitation of the natural environment
- To reveal and educate the public on the atrocities committed against the earth and all species that populate it
- To take necessary precautions against harming any animal, human and non-human[14]

Modeled after its sister organization, the Animal Liberation Front, ELF comprises an unknown number of individual cells consisting of one or several people who act autonomously. With no official membership, leadership, or central organization, ELF activists remain anonymous to the public and one another, maximizing the security and fluidity of the movement. The group maintains an official website where it posts press releases touting acts of economic sabotage and property destruction, and it publishes a how-to guide for its most notorious method of attack, arson.[15] What follows is a partial list of recent ELF attacks.

- October 15, 2001: ELF took credit for setting timed incendiary devices at the Bureau of Land Management's Litchfield Wild Horse and Burro Facility in Susanville, California, causing a fire that resulted in $85,000 in damage.
- June 13, 2001: ALF and ELF acted together in attacking five Bank of New York buildings on Long Island. Activists glued locks and ATM machines, spray-painted slogans, and smashed twenty-five windows. (The Bank of New York has a relationship with Huntington Life Sciences, an animal testing company.)
- June 1, 2001: ELF burned an office and thirteen trucks at Jefferson Poplar Farms in Clatskanie, Oregon. Simultaneously ELF activists burned the office of Toby Bradshaw at the University of Washington; Bradshaw was working on tree gene research. The fires caused a total of $3 million in damage.
- February 20, 2001: ELF set a fire at the Delta & Pine Land Co. research cotton gin in Visalia, California. The activists were protesting the company's sterile seed program.
- July 21, 2000: ELF cut down thousands of experimental trees at the U.S. Forest Service's Forest Biotechnology Laboratory in Rhinelander, Wisconsin. The action, directed against bioengineering, resulted in $1 million in crop destruction and property damage.
- December 31, 1999: Arson at the offices of Catherine Ives at Michigan State University caused $900,000 in damage. ELF was protesting "work being done to force developing nations in Asia, Latin America, and Africa to switch from natural crop plants to genetically engineered sweet potatoes, corn, bananas, and pineapples."
- December 26, 1998: ELF set fire to US Forest Industries, Inc., offices in Medford, Oregon, causing $700,000 in damages.
- October 18, 1998: In the act that first brought ELF to national attention, activists burned three buildings and four ski lifts at a Vail, Colorado, resort, causing $26 million in damage.[16]

ELF cells have remained quite active in areas across the United States in recent years. In August 2002, ELF set fire to the United States Forest Service Northeast Research Station in Irvine, Pennsylvania, causing $700,000 in damage and destroying seventy years worth of research. And in the most expensive act of eco-terrorism in U.S. history, members of ELF in 2003 destroyed an unfinished condominium complex in San Diego, causing $50 million in damage.[17]

The sister organization of ELF is the Animal Liberation Front, which began in Great Britain in 1976. ALF first appeared in North America in 1979, when members "liberated" two dogs and a cat from the New York University Medical Center. Like ELF, ALF is a loosely structured collective of autonomous cells that have little interaction. ALF cells are dedicated to "animal liberation" and to ending the cruel treatment of animals. Their methods include vandalism, arson, and animal rescue operations directed against research laboratories, meat processors, taxidermists, fur retailers, farms, circuses, zoos, rodeos, and fast-food outlets. ALF has conducted criminal actions in at least twenty-five countries. It has claimed credit for:

- Raiding the University of Pennsylvania Head Injury Clinic in 1984, causing $60,000 in damage
- Releasing 1,000 animals from the University of California at Riverside in 1985, causing $700,000 in damage
- Setting fire to an animal diagnostic facility under construction at the University of California at Davis in 1987, causing $4.5 million in damage (the most expensive act of terrorism perpetrated by an animal rights group on U.S. soil)
- Releasing animals and setting fires at the University of Arizona in 1989, causing $500,000 in damage
- Setting fire to the Alaskan Fur Company in Minnesota in 1996, causing $2 million in damage
- Releasing 10,000 mink from the Arritola Mink Farm in Mt. Angel, Washington in 1997, causing $750,000 in economic losses when many of the animals died in the ensuing melee
- Setting fire to the Coulston Foundation's White Sands Research Center in New Mexico in 2001, causing $1 million in damage[18]

Environmental and animal rights criminality is not limited to the major groups discussed above. Other groups that have recently claimed responsibility for criminal actions in defense of the environment and non-human animals in North America include Animal Liberation–Tactical Internet Response Network, Bakers for Animal Liberation, Coalition to Save the Preserves, Concerned OSU Students and Alumni, the Frogs, Guerilla Advertising Contingent, Kangaroo Wilderness Defense, the Lawn Liberation Front, Pirates for Animal Liberation, and Santa and His Elves. In recent years the Animal Rights Militia (ARM), the Justice Department, and Stop Huntingdon Animal Cruelty (SHAC) have been especially active and violent in both the United States and Great Britain.[19]

Purpose and Scope

The primary objective of this work is to provide a comprehensive and up-to-date description of the extreme environmental and animal rights movements—their methods, motives, actions, and ideologies. The focus will be on the impact the various groups have on the United States; however, because the more significant movements are transnational in nature, the international dimensions of the problem will also be explored. The method for developing this core of information will involve a complete literature review, an exhaustive search of past and current media accounts from online sources, and an examination of relevant Internet sites. (Many groups of interest such as Earth First!, ALF, and ELF maintain their own web pages and press offices—a treasure trove of data.) Aside from the detailed historical and contemporary description of the radical environmental and animal rights movements, this work seeks to advance our knowledge of the phenomenon by providing relevant criminological analyses of eco-terrorism. Surveys of activists at several environmental and animal rights conferences, correspondence from imprisoned activists, and a database of criminal actions will be used to generate original data. The goal of assessing the extent and severity of the threat will guide the overall project.

A Word on Definitions and Objectivity

This is an academic study of a social phenomenon. Therefore, no political or philosophical position will be advanced, either for or against the groups/movements examined. Naturally, the author's preconceptions and biases will be set aside as much as is humanly possible. With that said, the phenomenon to be studied is inextricably linked to matters of public policy and private criminal behavior; in short, radical environmentalism and animal rights activism are at the epicenter of a highly charged political debate. Therefore, extra care will be taken to pursue and present research findings in an evenhanded manner.

Even the language and labels used in connection with radical environmental and animal rights activism reveal biases for and against actions taken. Environmental radicals and animal rights activists call what they do "direct action," while the government has called their behavior "eco-terrorism." The often quoted dictum "one man's terrorist is another man's freedom fighter" exemplifies the dilemma. Even the term *radical* should be carefully applied—after all, parameters of acceptable behavior are relative. The last point having been acknowledged, however, it is fair to apply the label of *radical* to the criminal actions in question, since a majority of the people who consider themselves environmentalists or in favor of the extension of rights to animals typically stop short of criminality.

A cursory examination of the criminal actions taken by the groups in question indicates that the vast majority are property crimes, many of which are properly classified as acts of vandalism. Except for the minority of actions that directly target human beings for attacks or threats, the application of the term *terrorism* does not seem to be warranted. That the U.S. government has labeled this type of criminality as eco-terrorism and animal rights terrorism for political and tactical reasons is obvious: terror-ists qualify for prosecution under the Racketeer-Influenced and Corrupt Organizations Act (RICO) and other laws that provide for lengthy prison terms. In essence, those responsible for nonviolent crimes, perhaps even relatively minor property crimes, could be prosecuted for engaging in a "pattern of criminal activity," which carries heavy penalties.

On the other hand, the moniker *direct action* fails to capture the crimi-nal nature of the observed behaviors. The oft-laid charge that actions like arson and tree spiking (inserting metal or ceramic into trees to deter log-ging) risk injury and death to humans is also reasonable. Firefighters responding to arson are placed at risk, and security guards patrolling empty laboratories and offices could be inadvertently caught in the smoke and flames. The issue is one of intent. Terrorists, by all definitions posited, target people indiscriminately, playing to a broader audience to instill fear and bring about social and/or political change. Environmental extremists and animal rights activists certainly aim to bring about radical change, but are fundamentally different from terrorists in several ways. First, so called environmental and animal rights terrorists specifically select targets related to their objectives: they vandalize SUVs that contrib-ute to air pollution, burn luxury homes that are a part of urban sprawl, and place metal in trees to inflict damage upon logging companies. In other words, their choice of targets is not indiscriminate. Certainly envi-ronmental extremists play to the media to bring attention to their cause, but their actions are explicitly targeted—they seek to instill fear and inflict economic damage directly on their perceived adversaries. More-over, as noted, radical environmental and animal rights activists do not usually target people. In criminal law terms, the mens rea (mental intent) of these criminals is not purposeful or knowing, but reckless and/or neg-ligent: that is, in the event that someone is injured or killed, the perpetra-tor either consciously or unconsciously created a substantial and unjustifiable risk of harm, without purposefully intending to harm an individual. Of course, under felony murder statutes, an activist responsi-ble for an "environmental" or "animal action" resulting in the death of a human being, although less culpable than a killer who plans and carries out a murder, would nevertheless likely be charged with first degree mur-der (felony murder is when someone dies as the result of the commission of a felony, such as an arson). In any event, the purpose here is to argue that most of the crimes perpetrated by environmental and animal rights radicals are not properly labeled as terrorism. On the other hand, those criminal actions that do threaten and injure humans (just over 10% of all the crimes observed for this study) in the name of environmental justice or animal liberation are more consistent with common academic defini-tions of "terrorism."[20]

Given the problems associated with labeling and definition, a classifi-cation scheme that delineates between types of behaviors associated with environmental and animal rights extremism is obligatory. The development of an appropriate typology will provide a gauge for measuring the severity of the problem. This classification scheme and accompanying analyses will be provided in chapter six.

Map

A brief outline of the remainder of the book is now appropriate. In chapter two the history and philosophy of the environmental movement is provided. Starting with the conservation movement, the development of the environmental movement will be traced from its innocuous beginning to the formation of more radical and proactive organizations such as Greenpeace. Noting the progressive radicalization of the movement coupled with an overview of environmental philosophy (including "deep ecology") will provide a stepping-stone for the exploration of criminal environmental groups. Chapter three will explore the history and philosophy of the animal welfare, animal rights, and animal liberation movements, with the aim of establishing a contextual foundation for the description and analysis of animal rights–related criminality in later chapters.

Chapter four provides a detailed description of criminality in the animal rights movement, most notably actions perpetrated by the Animal Liberation Front, the Animal Rights Militia (ARM), and Stop Huntingdon Animal Cruelty (SHAC). The role of People for the Ethical Treatment of Animals (PETA) in the animal rights movement will also be examined. Chapter five looks at criminality in the radical environmental movement, with a detailed look at Earth First! and the Earth Liberation Front. Both chapters four and five include comprehensive details of the histories, events, personalities, and motives of the various groups examined. International dimensions of the movements will be included as well.

Chapter six looks at the structure and modus operandi of the radical animal rights and environmental movements. A cursory examination of media accounts leaves one with the distinct impression that environmental and animal rights activism is becoming more extreme, with an ongoing increase in the frequency and severity of attacks. This is certainly the position that the U.S. government has taken, with its proclamation that environmental and animal rights extremism represents the number one domestic terror threat. As previously noted, attacks on human beings are apparently becoming more common. This issue will be directly examined through the cataloguing and classifying of actions reported from 1956 through 2005. Although minor acts of vandalism and civil disobedience may very well slip beneath the radar, detailed information on most attacks is widely reported by the media and on numerous websites representing both sides of the conflict. By developing a typology of environmental and animal rights crimes, it will be possible to conclude with a reasonable amount of quantitative certainty the degree to which activists employ various methods of attack.

Chapter seven will explore the characteristics of environmental and animal rights radicals, especially cognitive processes that may shed light on the epidemiology of this particular type of criminality. Some limited survey data in this area do exist, and this material will be presented. However, the main thrust of the chapter will be the exploration of a new thesis—the idea that a specific criminological theory may explain the social-psychological development of environmental and animal rights criminals. Gresham Sykes and David Matza introduced "neutralization theory" in 1957 as way of explaining the mental processes juvenile delinquents use to reconcile their antisocial behavior with societal expectations. Differing from some criminological theories (such as subculture theories) that posit criminals' rejection of societal values, neutralization theory suggests that the criminal experiences dissonance when he or she fails to conform to norms still viewed as legitimate. This conflict, according to Sykes and Matza, is resolved when the criminal assuages feelings of guilt by using one or more "techniques of neutralization,"—such as denying that the victim is injured, denying personal responsibility, appealing to a higher loyalty (such as allegiance to a group or movement), or condemning the victim (e.g., justifying burning down a corporate office on the grounds that the corporation is destroying the environment). Since its introduction, neutralization theory has been used to explain other types of criminality in addition to juvenile delinquency, including white-collar crime.[21] The contention here is that neutralization theory is also relevant to understanding the motivations, psychology, and epidemiology of environmental and animal rights crimes.

Neutralization theory will be applied in this study by examining the writings and statements of radical/criminal animal rights and environmental activists. A huge volume of such writings exists, much of it posted on organization websites or published in electronic journals. A few organizations have even published their thoughts in book form. In addition, unstructured interviews of known animal rights and environmental radicals will yield narrative accounts that can be similarly analyzed. The interviews (in the form of correspondence with imprisoned activists) should also provide additional insights, such as the presence of apocalyptic and millennial aims. It may be that a new technique of neutralization will be introduced: the radical activist's rationale, "I did it to save the planet."

Chapter eight will examine the likely future of eco-terrorism, animal rights criminality, and the broader social movements of which they are a part. The chapter will then position the subject in a broader discussion of terrorism and the problem of weapons of mass destruction—issues relevant to fringe radicals who advocate massive reductions in the human population. In addition, the efficacy and danger of leaderless resistance and one-person cells will be discussed against the backdrop of law enforcement and security countermeasures. The chapter will conclude by examining how much support exists in the broader environmental and animal rights communities for the illegal and sometimes violent actions undertaken by radicals. Many terrorist organizations ultimately fail to achieve their objectives because they do not enjoy broad support. (Even within the more radical populations, the history of the environmental and animal rights movements is replete with ideological rifts and splinter groups.) The goal here is to assess the depth of support for those relatively few extreme elements that actually carry out illegal actions.

Daniel T. Oliver, a researcher at the Capital Research Center, has documented the degree to which "long-established humane organizations" like the American Society for the Prevention of Cruelty to Animals and the Humane Society of the United States have evolved from animal welfare organizations to organizations that more closely support the radical position of the animal rights movement. By co-opting traditional humane associations, animal rights extremists promote their radical agenda under an umbrella of ostensible respectability.[22] Still, the radicalization of formerly mainstream groups might reflect merely changes in leadership and not broad support among the memberships. Surveys of participants at several mainstream environmental and animal rights conferences will aim at answering this question. Participant agreement with radical attitudes or endorsement of the methods of animal rights and environmental extremists would suggest a certain degree of support within the broader movements.

Chapter 2

History and Philosophy of Radical Environmentalism

Throughout early American history the dominant view was that the natural world was mankind's to exploit at will. By 1840 the ideology of Manifest Destiny had become a matter of public policy, and Congress passed legislation after the American Civil War inviting rapid expansion into the American West. The Industrial Revolution ushered in an era of increased industrialization and urbanization with little or no thought to environmental consequences.

In America, the first intellectual effort to recognize the inherent value of the natural world was advanced by the transcendentalists. Writers Ralph Waldo Emerson and Henry David Thoreau, inspired by eighteenth-century Romanticism, exalted nature and attempted to transcend material culture by introducing the notion of the "oversoul"—a divine moral force that is a part of every living thing. The Earth was seen as possessing a spirit of its own, with humans representing just one component of a diverse, natural world.[1] Foreshadowing cries for "ecotage" by environmental activists a century later, Thoreau worried about the consequences of a dam on the Concord River: "Who hears the fishes when they cry? I for one am with thee, and who knows what may avail a crowbar against Billerica dam."[2] Moreover, the transcendentalist idea espousing the interconnectedness of natural systems and the inherent value of sentient and non-sentient forms was a direct precursor to modern environmental philosophy and deep ecology—the ideological framework underlying much of contemporary eco-terrorism.

Organized concern for the natural environment began with the conservation movement of the late 1800s. In his 1864 book *Man and Nature*, George Perkins Marsh outlined the principles of conservation, stressing the idea that man's power to transform the natural environment should carry with it a sense of responsibility.[3] Although the notion of conserving natural resources was a radical idea for that time, many elites expressed concern over the environmental damage caused by the Industrial Revolution. In contrast to the broad grassroots support of the modern environmental movement, the early conservation movement has been described as a "fraternity of the upper-middle class," composed of powerful men such as Theodore Roosevelt and Gifford Pinchot.[4] By 1872 Yellowstone had been designated the first national park in the world; President Roosevelt later would expand the national forest system to 172 million acres and spur Congress to create six new national parks, fifty-one national wildlife refuges, and eighteen national monuments. As head of the U.S. Forest Service under Roosevelt, Gifford Pinchot championed conservation as a public policy that promoted human advancement by managing the use of natural resources. It should be noted that, consistent with the goals of conservation, national forests were used for a wide range of activities, including logging, mining, hunting, and recreation.[5]

Dissatisfaction with the goals of conservation bred the idea of preservation—placing off-limits to development large areas of wilderness. In 1892 John Muir created the Sierra Club with the idea of preserving untainted the beauty of California's Sierra Nevada mountain range.[6] Like Muir, Aldo Leopold criticized conservation policy and as an employee of the U.S. Forest Service came to champion the cause of preservation. Leopold cofounded the Wilderness Society in 1935 and helped lay the philosophical foundation for modern environmental and animal rights debates. Ethics, he believed, should be extended beyond human societal relations to the integrity of the entire "biotic community," including the land and the organisms that live on it. As opposed to conservationists, preservationists began to recognize a value to the natural world independent of human influence or exploitation.[7] The Franklin Roosevelt administration adopted some preservationist leanings, creating the U.S. Fish and Wildlife Service (FWS) and directing the Forest Service away from the broad uses of conservation. Upon its creation the FWS designated 160 new wildlife refuges.[8]

While World War II and the postwar era saw reduced concern for environmental causes, two significant events in the 1950s energized the movement. The first episode was an environmental success: the efforts of David Brower and the Sierra Club stopped the construction of dams in Colorado's Dinosaur National Monument. The second event, the construction of Glen Canyon Dam and the subsequent formation of Lake Powell in 1956, was an environmental failure but nevertheless precipitated an invigorated and politically sophisticated environmental lobby.[9] The development of environmentalism as a mass movement can perhaps be traced to the publication in 1962 of Rachel Carson's seminal work, *Silent Spring*. By the end of that year forty bills intended to regulate the use of pesticides, about which Carson had warned, had been introduced in state legislatures. Major acts of federal legislation were introduced and passed in subsequent years, including the Clean Air Act of 1963 and the Wilderness Act of 1964. The Wilderness Act in particular was a major victory for the philosophy of preservation; millions of acres were set aside and virtually closed to development or resource extraction.[10] During this era memberships in the Sierra Club and the Wilderness Society grew exponentially (the Sierra Club grew from 16,000 members in 1960 to 114,000 in 1970), culminating in the official birth of an environmental mass movement with the sponsorship of the first Earth Day in 1970. On April 22, 1970, twenty million people at thousands of colleges and schools across the country participated in events, and 250,000 people marched in Washington, D.C. Responding to broad public awareness and concern, the Nixon administration created the Environmental Protection Agency and implemented a revised Clean Air Act in 1970, the Clean Water Act in 1972, and the Endangered Species Act in 1973.[11] By the 1980s the larger mainstream environmental groups had become professionalized (the number of environmental lobbyists in Washington, D.C., grew from two in 1969 to eighty-eight in 1985).[12] Meanwhile, local grassroots organizations proliferated, and the movement took on global dimensions with the rallying cry of environmental justice.

Radicalization of the Environmental Movement

The explosion of the environmental movement in the 1960s and 1970s met with a marked backlash in the 1980s. The conservatism of the Reagan administration favored industry interests and property rights, a trend that continued through the first Bush administration. Regulations that benefited business over the environment were hardly countered in the Clinton-Gore years, and by the turn of the century new concerns such as Islamic terrorism and war in the Middle East pushed environmental concerns to the rear of mainstream political agendas (in 1997 Greenpeace even closed some offices). Opposition to the environmental agenda meanwhile had become highly coordinated, artfully pitting trees and owls against the rights of Americans to earn a living and dispose of their private property as they wished.[13] Especially after 1980, waning public concern over environmental issues, centrism in mainstream environmental groups, and government policies favoring industry over nature precipitated a more radical and motivated class of environmental activist.

Out of the late 1960s arose perhaps the best known and the first truly proactive environmental group. Greenpeace was begun by a handful of Canadian activists, the Don't Make a Wave Committee, who opposed the U.S. government's underwater nuclear tests near Alaska's Aleutian Islands. The cause quickly gathered steam, and in September 1970 6,000 protesters blocked the U.S.-Canadian border at Blaine, Washington, as an act of protest. A year later twelve volunteers set sail for Amchitka Island

Table 2.1
Founding Dates of Major Environmental Organizations

Sierra Club	1892
National Audubon Society	1905
National Parks Conservation Association	1919
Izaak Walton League	1922
The Wilderness Society	1935
National Wildlife Federation	1936
The Nature Conservancy	1951
Friends of the Earth	1969
Environmental Action	1971
Greenpeace	1972
Redwood Alliance	1978
Surfrider Foundation	1984
Rainforest Action Network	1985

aboard an eighty-foot halibut boat called *Greenpeace*. Bad weather and the U.S. Coast Guard turned the ship back, and a new ship called *Greenpeace Too* failed to reach the island prior to the planned test. Nevertheless, the publicity created by the activists led to a review of the situation by the U.S. Supreme Court and the eventual designation of the testing site as a bird sanctuary. In 1972 the Don't Make a Wave Committee foundered but reformed as the Greenpeace Foundation.[14]

Since its inception Greenpeace has expanded its targets, most famously disrupting whaling and seal-hunting operations. The group has always advocated nonviolent protest, choosing to disrupt and confront in the tradition of nonviolent civil disobedience. On the other hand, Greenpeace activists have themselves met with violent attacks on several occasions. While protesting nuclear testing in the South Pacific, the vessel *Greenpeace III* was rammed by a French military vessel. When the ship returned the following year, French commandos boarded the vessel and severely beat the captain. In 1985, agents of the French government used explosives to sink the Greenpeace vessel *Rainbow Warrior* in the harbor of Auckland, New Zealand, killing a photographer on board.[15]

Over the years Greenpeace has grown closer to the mainstream environmental movement, adopting the traditional methods of political lobbying and public relations. In 2000, the group purchased 140,000 shares of Shell Oil in an attempt to persuade the company to invest in a solar panel factory. In a similar move, Greenpeace organized BP Amoco shareholders to oppose a planned oil pipeline in the Arctic. By the 1990s the group had expanded its target list to include companies that create genetically engineered foods, arguing that they pose unknown risks to human health and the natural environment.[16]

An offshoot of Greenpeace, the Sea Shepherd Conservation Society (SSCS), was formed in 1977 when Greenpeace expelled activist Paul Watson for throwing a seal hunter's club into the ocean (firmly establishing Greenpeace's modus operandi of non-aggressive civil disobedience). Unlike Greenpeace, Watson's SSCS believed that animal life must take precedence over machinery and that the destruction of private property, although criminal, was an acceptable means to preserve life. Nevertheless, Watson set down specific rules of engagement, including a prohibition against the use of explosives, weapons, or any activity that had "even a remote possibility of causing injury to a living thing."[17] After obtaining money from the organization Fund for Animals, Watson bought a ship and set about harassing commercial drift-net fishing, whaling, and seal-hunting operations. By the early 1980s the SSCS had gained the reputation of being the naval arm of the fledgling Earth First! organization. Watson also gained celebrity support for his cause: After his arrest for disrupting a Canadian seal hunt in 1983, actor Mike Farrell of *M*A*S*H* fame posted his $10,000 bail. The group's most successful exploit occurred in 1986, when two SSCS activists caused $1.8 million in damage at a Reykjavik, Iceland, whale-processing plant and proceeded to sink two whaling vessels, causing an additional $2.8 million in damage. The SSCS has remained active, attacking two Japanese fishing vessels in July 1992 by cutting their nets and hurling incendiary devices.[18] The group also created headlines in 1998 when it disrupted a Makah Indian whale hunt—a virtual clash of politically correct interest groups, with multiculturalism on one hand versus the rights of animals on the other. To date the SSCS is credited with sinking nine fishing or whaling vessels, ramming at least a dozen others, and blockading the Canadian sealing fleet.[19]

In reality the radicalization of the environmental movement was long in the making, pre-dating Paul Watson's Sea Shepherd Conservation Society by at least two decades. By 1958 Edward Abbey was sawing down billboards in New Mexico; he would later pull up survey stakes to thwart federal Park Service road-building projects. In the early 1970s two pseudonymous radicals made headlines: The Arizona Phantom sabotaged coal-mining operations in Black Mesa by tearing up railroad tracks and destroying heavy equipment. Around Chicago, The Fox campaigned against polluters, plugging waste drains at a soap plant, capping a chimney at an aluminum plant, and dumping sewage in the executive offices of U.S.

Steel. At about the same time, the Billboard Bandits were sawing down billboards across Michigan, and the Bolt Weevils were toppling high-voltage towers in Minnesota. A group calling itself Eco-Commando Force '70 was briefly active around Miami, using yellow dye to track the passage of sewage into Miami waterways and the Atlantic Ocean. Another radical group active in the early 1970s was the Tucson-based Eco-Raiders, who cut down billboards; wrecked vacant newly constructed houses; pulled up survey stakes; and dumped thousands of cans and bottles at the doorstep of the Kalil Bottling Company. The authorities later apprehended five college-aged men "fed up with rampant development in Arizona."[20] The Eco-Raiders would become the model for the gang of activists in Edward Abbey's influential work *The Monkey Wrench Gang*.

Several important publications during the early 1970s gave a voice to the growing radical sentiment within the environmental movement and outlined what would become the modus operandi of radical groups including Earth First! and the Earth Liberation Front. A year after the first Earth Day, organizers of that event formed the group Environmental Action, which published the *Earth Tool Kit* in 1971. The book urged both violent and nonviolent actions designed to generate sympathy among the public and to pressure corporations responsible for environmental degradation. A year later Environmental Action published *Ecotage*, a how-to guide for activists. Although *Ecotage* espoused mostly innocuous methods such as letter-writing campaigns, it also encouraged criminal activity, such as sabotaging construction equipment, pulling up survey stakes, and destroying billboards.[21]

In 1975 Edward Abbey published *The Monkey Wrench Gang*, a fictional account of environmental saboteurs wreaking havoc in the southwestern United States. Based on the actions of the Eco-Raiders, Abbey's work is to the radical environmental movement what Peter Singer's *Animal Liberation* is to animal rights activists—a bible at the top of the movement's required reading list. In Abbey's writings can be seen the later anti-capitalist, apocalyptic, anarchistic, and millenarian doctrines that characterize the contemporary radical environmental movement. Abbey once wrote, "Representative government in the USA represents money, not people, and therefore has forfeited our allegiance and moral support."[22] According to Abbey, the thoroughly corrupted federal government was to be replaced by anarchy, in which civil society would be based on the Jeffersonian ideal of individual liberty, and societal arrangements would be shaped by a "decentralized, equally-distributed, fairly-shared" allocation of power and resources.[23] That Abbey's book provided the operational model for later groups such as Earth First! and the Earth Liberation Front is unmistakable: in one scene in *The Monkey Wrench Gang* activists discuss plans for a disorganized movement composed of small groups of anonymous cells that perpetrate economic sabotage across the nation. In another scene the activists agree that their actions must shape their ideology, an approach that Earth First! founder Dave Foreman would later adopt.[24]

The Philosophy of Radical Environmentalism

The ideological framework underlying what has come to be called eco-terrorism comprises a rich stew of ideas birthed from the zeitgeist of the 1960s. Social upheaval stemming from the war in Vietnam, battles over civil rights, and the feminist movement coalesced around philosophies such as Marxism, socialism, feminism, postmodernism, and Eastern religions. These ideas and their progeny were in polar opposition to mainstream notions of capitalism, patriarchy, and Judeo-Christianity, and were quite naturally adopted by defenders of the environment. Radical environmentalists saw the Earth as being raped and exploited by *man*kind in a pattern of oppression repeated over and over, in much the same way that prevailing power structures victimized minorities, women, and other marginalized societal players.[25]

If the ideologies surrounding the radical environmental movement are diverse and sometimes conflicting, it is also true that there is a central core of ideas embodied in the notion of deep ecology. Posited by Norwegian philosopher Arne Naess, deep ecology is a philosophy that promotes the idea of biocentrism as opposed to anthropocentrism, removing human beings from the philosophical center of the world. Instead, deep ecology considers all elements of the ecosystem when formulating a moral calculus regarding right actions. In fact, the concept of biocentric equality—a premise central to the deep ecology framework—insists that all life forms, from protozoa to humans, are of equal value.[26]

The basic tenets of deep ecology as enumerated by Naess follow:

1. The well-being and flourishing of human and non-human life on Earth have value in themselves (synonyms: intrinsic value, inherent worth). These values are independent of the usefulness of the non-human world for human purposes.
2. Richness and diversity of life forms contribute to the realization of these values and are also values in themselves.
3. Humans have no right to reduce this richness and diversity except to satisfy vital needs.
4. The flourishing of human life and cultures is compatible with a substantially smaller human population. The flourishing of non-human life *requires* a smaller human population.
5. Present human interference with the non-human world is excessive, and the situation is rapidly worsening.
6. Policies must therefore be changed. These policies affect basic economic, technological, and ideological structures. The resulting state of affairs will be deeply different from the present.

7. The ideological change will be mainly that of appreciating life quality (dwelling in situations of inherent value) rather than adhering to an increasingly higher standard of living. There will be a profound awareness of the difference between bigness and greatness.
8. Those who subscribe to the foregoing points have an obligation directly or indirectly to try to implement the necessary changes.[27]

As can be seen, deep ecology is truly a radical ideology calling for radical changes (a massive decrease in the human population), contrasting sharply with the "shallow ecology" of mainstream environmentalism, which acts from anthropocentric motives. Unlike mainstream environmentalists, who seek to protect the environment in order to foster the health and well-being of humans, deep ecologists recognize that all of nature has intrinsic worth, including non-sentient forms such as mountains and rivers, implying that people should give the Earth and the objects in it equal consideration when developing and implementing public policies. Mother Earth, or Gaia, is typically viewed as sacred. Indeed, followers of deep ecology, including many members of Earth First!, see their work in religious terms, viewing themselves as the anointed ones who must shepherd mankind into a post-apocalyptic society in which the interests of Nature transcend those of humans. In short, the Earth comes first.[28]

The adoption of deep ecology as a set of guiding principles implies truly radical changes in how humans participate in the natural world. In fact, Naess called for a fundamental change in human consciousness in order to accommodate a biocentric view. Because all objects in the biosphere have an equal right to live and flourish, the implementation of deep ecology principles requires that human society be returned to a pre-industrial state, where centralized bureaucratic authority and advanced technology are banished. The radical environmentalist who espouses deep ecology's basic tenets predicts an environmental apocalypse but also envisions, in a millenarian way, a post-apocalyptic primitive society in which people organize into small communities and live in harmony with nature. For example, after the inevitable collapse of industrial civilization, Earth First! cofounder Dave Foreman foresees a world dominated by wilderness, where humans exist in primitive hunter-gatherer collectives and use only those natural resources required to exist in the simplest of fashions. Hierarchical power relations, class stratification, competitive capitalism, patriarchal exploitation, most machines, and the rape of the natural environment will have no place in this new world, characterized by the spiritual melding of mankind with the natural environment.[29]

If ideas are dangerous, then the propositions at the heart of deep ecology bode ill for the future of most human beings. The principle of biocentric equality mandates that the interests of crustaceans (or, for that matter, viruses) be considered alongside the interests of human beings—and, if the interests of the crustacean are seen to outweigh those of humans, deference must be given to the crab. This is misanthropy taken to its limit. When Christopher Manes (author of *Green Rage*) infamously suggested that the AIDS epidemic just might be a viable solution to the overpopulation problem, not everyone in Earth First! was outraged (Dave Foreman, for one, agreed with Manes).[30] Indeed, the only hope for Mother Earth, in the view of the deep ecologist, is for a drastic reduction in the human population—only then can the post-apocalyptic, millenarian, primitive, earth-centered utopia come into being. It follows that if an environmental apocalypse is inevitable, imminent, and *necessary*, then some motivated deep ecologists may seek to hasten that apocalypse—hence the true threat of eco-terrorism.

History and Philosophy of the Animal Rights Movement

The animal rights movement and the criminal acts associated with it did not develop in a social or political vacuum. Understanding the development of the modern animal rights movement and the radicals who have adopted direct action as their modus operandi requires that they be placed in context. The history of significant events in the animal welfare and animal rights movements and the development of the ideology that has provided an intellectual foundation for extreme actions are especially relevant.

The Philosophy of Animal Welfare and Animal Rights

Philosopher Peter Singer notes that Western attitudes toward animals are founded on ancient Judeo-Christian and Greek traditions. The Hebrew Old Testament of the Bible provides for mankind's dominion over animals, including their use by humans for food, clothing, and labor (and in modern times, presumably, experimentation and entertainment). The Bible clearly notes that God made humans in his image, and therefore humans enjoy a special position within nature.[1] While some Eastern religions teach that all life is sacred, Christianity contains no such explicit admonition. God's care for animals and plants is mentioned in the New Testament but always juxtaposed against His far greater regard for mankind. The ancient Greeks give us a mixed heritage. The thought of Plato and then Aristotle assigned eminence to humans: as rational animals who were justified in exploiting unreasoning animals. On the other hand, Celsus argued in second-century Greece against the Judeo-Christian view that people are morally superior to animals. Celsus suggested that God may in fact be partial to the lower animals, since they can live in nature without the need for sowing seed or manufacturing clothing. Pythagoras practiced vegetarianism and espoused treating animals with respect.[2]

Morality in the Roman Empire did not extend to slaves and animals. Plutarch, Ovid, Porphyry, and Seneca all advocated the kind treatment of animals and/or endorsed vegetarianism, but, in general, the Roman and then the Christian tendency was to place animals outside the bounds of moral consideration. Still later, the great reconciler of Aristotelian and Christian thought, St. Thomas Aquinas, said that animals were irrational, unthinking beings and therefore did not deserve the same degree of moral consideration as humans. Aquinas's view lasted: in the middle of the nineteenth century, Pope Pius IX prohibited the opening of an office of the Prevention of Cruelty to Animals in Rome. One prominent exception to the official Catholic policy of indifference toward animal welfare was St. Francis of Assisi, whose moral concern for birds and beasts is legendary.[3]

Renaissance humanism did little to further the cause of animal welfare, as human beings were elevated even above God, and certainly above the "lower animals." Noted animal lovers Leonardo da Vinci and Michel de Montaigne were famous exceptions to the Renaissance rule. Leonardo wrote in his notes, "The time will come when men such as I will look upon the murder of animals as they now look upon the murder of men"; Leonardo's contemporaries, meanwhile, ridiculed his vegetarianism.[4] Rene Descartes wrote that animals were like machines—without consciousness or a soul. Descartes published several influential essays in the 1600s that were used to justify the practice of vivisection. In fact, vivisection became commonplace in seventeenth- and eighteenth-century Europe; articles from the period describe the howls of live dogs nailed to tables in anatomy classrooms.[5]

Probably nothing laid the intellectual foundation for the equal consideration of animals more than Darwin's theory of evolution and the publication of his *Descent of Man.* As Peter Singer has put it, after Darwin "only those who prefer religious faith to beliefs based on reasoning and evidence can still maintain that the human species is the special darling of the entire universe, or that other animals were created to provide us with food, or that we have divine authority over them, and divine permission to kill them."[6] (That such "reasoning and evidence" have led many intellectuals and philosophers not away from but closer to religious faith should be mentioned, but is tangential and will not be pursued here!) Darwin's theory and the thrust of science is that mankind enjoys no special status—or at least none so special as to give humans carte blanche authority to exploit nature with no thought of consequences beyond those that concern human welfare.

With the Enlightenment came the obvious notion that animals do suffer, and therefore deserve at least some consideration. John Locke wrote that children should be taught from an early age that hurting or killing any living thing is despicable, while David Hume argued for gentle treatment of animals. Jean-Jacques Rousseau felt that killing animals for food was murder, and Alexander Pope opposed vivisection. These sentiments were far from universal during the Enlightenment, however. Immanuel Kant told his students that humans have no direct duties toward animals because they cannot reason; nevertheless, he argued that cruelty to animals should be avoided—for the sake of *human*kind. The utilitarian philosopher Jeremy Bentham answered Kant with a proposition that has become the underlying ideological premise of the entire animal rights movement: the real question, Bentham said, is not whether animals can reason but whether they have the capacity to suffer. If animals can suffer and feel pain, then, according to Bentham and the proponents of animal rights, people have a responsibility to extend animals moral consideration—consideration perhaps equal to that extended to humans. Bentham also was the first to liken the plight of animals to that of black slaves, a controversial comparison repeated many times since by those in the animal rights movement.[7]

Peter Singer adopted utilitarian reasoning[8] in his influential 1975 book (referred to as the bible of the animal rights movement), *Animal Liberation*. Singer wrote that the benefits of eating animals and using them in biomedical research are minimal compared with the suffering of animals. Later, Peter Carruthers and R. G. Frey responded that such an application of utilitarian philosophy is inappropriate because equating animal suffering with human suffering is abhorrent and goes against common sense. Frey specified that animals have no expectations, wants, desires, or memories and therefore no interests or rights.[9] Frey's argument, called the full-personhood view, has been aggressively attacked by Singer and other animal rights advocates using the case of "marginal humans." Severely mentally disabled humans, infants (including the unborn), and people in persistent vegetative states or comas with no hope of recovery also lack "expectations, wants, desires, memories" as well as any hope of a conscious, self-aware future. According to the full-personhood view, then, these humans possess no rights—in fact, many non-human animals command far greater powers of reasoning and self-awareness.[10] (This line of thought has led to some infamous philosophical positions, including Peter Singer's statement that it may be morally correct to euthanize marginal humans but not dogs.) Animal rights advocates say that if sentience is the benchmark to be used for the extension of rights or moral consideration then to grant this consideration to marginal humans but not to animals is nothing short of *speciesism*—the same type of discrimination historically directed against women and minorities.[11]

The ethical dilemma created by using sentience as the benchmark for the extension of rights is addressed by the concept of *contractarianism*. Both Kant and John Rawls are associated with this school of thought, according to which "moral agents" voluntarily agree to abide by agreed-upon rules of morality in the interest of society and individuals.

Kant said that these moral codes reflect what moral agents would choose under ideal circumstances. Rawls went further and said that right actions are those that moral agents would choose if they were unaware of their own prejudices and biases. Rational moral agents in this view have direct rights and direct duties that extend to marginal cases such as babies, small children, and the mentally challenged. Following this reasoning, Carruthers suggested that people bear only indirect duties toward animals (the right to be treated humanely for the sake of humankind) because animals are not rational agents. Similarly, Tibor Machan says that animals are instinctively driven beasts and do not weigh moral consequences, and therefore cannot be a part of any moral social contract.[12]

The notion of animal rights received its fullest articulation in the work of Tom Regan. Unlike Peter Singer, who essentially argues that animals should be granted moral consideration, Regan states that animals have inherent value and are therefore deserving of moral equality.[13] Regan's position is most closely aligned with the modern animal liberation movement, which argues against the use of animals for any reason. Lawrence and Susan Finsen summarize the important distinction between the animal welfare/humane movement and animal rights:

> The humane movement promoted kindness and the elimination of cruelty without challenging the assumption of human superiority or the institutions that reflect that assumption. The animal rights movement, on the other hand, does not seek humane reforms but challenges the assumption of human superiority and demands abolition of institutions it considers exploitative. Rather than asking for a greater (and optional) charity toward animals, the animal rights movement demands justice, equality, fairness, and rights.[14]

While Tom Regan doesn't specifically identify which animals are worthy of rights, he and most animal rights advocates include mammals and, usually, vertebrates. Once again, the common benchmark is sentience or the ability to process sensory inputs. (The exclusion of plants from this scheme is a source of conflict with the deep ecology position, discussed in chapter two.)[15]

The animal rights view does not necessarily hold that humans and animals have identical rights, but that animals certainly have the right to life and to freedom from bodily interference. For example, the Animal Legal Defense Fund (ALDF) has published the following "Animal Bill of Rights":

1. To be free from exploitation, cruelty, neglect, and abuse.
2. Not to be used in cruel or unnecessary experiments.
3. Farm animals have the right to be in an environment that satisfies their basic physical and psychological needs.

4. The right of companion animals to a healthy diet, protective shelter, and adequate medical care.
5. The right of wildlife to a natural habitat, ecologically sufficient to a normal existence and self-sustaining species population.
6. The right of animals to have their interests represented in court and safeguarded by the law of the land.[16]

Of course, speciesism also has its defenders. Carl Cohen says that the concept of rights is a human concern, and that the capacity to suffer and experience pain does not grant animals rights. Moreover, people confuse rights and obligations: a human obligation to treat animals humanely does not mean that animals have rights. Cohen says that obligations involve what we ought to do, while rights are things that others may justly demand that we do.[17]

In any event, the philosophical debate over rights for animals will continue in academic circles. For the purposes of this work, however, it is clear that in the minds of some radicals a firm enough ideological foundation (based not on emotion but reason) has been laid to justify illegal direct actions.

Animal Welfare to Animal Rights: History of the Movement

The development of the animal welfare and environmental movements in the nineteenth century and their resurgence in the latter half of the twentieth century must be viewed in historical context and juxtaposed with the prevailing sentiments of the times. Moral concern for animals and the environment grew side by side with broader social trends, exemplified by heightened awareness of and compassion for the relatively powerless in society. The nineteenth century was a significant era for the growth of human rights, exemplified most notably by the women's suffrage movement and the movement to abolish slavery. In fact, the extension of moral consideration to animals at this time was directly linked to the compassion and empathy evident in the leaders of the women's rights and abolitionist movements.[18] In many cases the ranks of suffragists, abolitionists, and animal welfare advocates were drawn from the same pool of concerned individuals. For example, charter members of the American Society for the Prevention of Cruelty to Animals (ASPCA) were well-known for their opposition to slavery. Horace Greeley, the abolitionist editor of *The Tribune*, openly supported women's rights and vegetarianism. Suffragist Frances Power Cobbe founded the anti-vivisectionist Victoria Street Society. And Henry Bergh, who founded the ASPCA, took the lead in prosecuting the foster parents of a child abuse victim in 1874; the child was removed from the home and the foster parents punished under the authority of the ASPCA. (Only after this well-publicized event was the American Society for the Prevention of Cruelty to Children established.)[19]

It is no coincidence that the modern animal rights and radical environmental causes developed concurrently with the civil and women's rights movements of the 1960s. Whether one is speaking of the 1860s or the 1960s, the impetus for the humane treatment of animals and arguments favoring the extension of rights to nonhuman animals may be viewed as part of a broader historical trend characterized by heightened awareness of and mobilization against institutional oppression. Hence, today we have a rich stew of ideologies and philosophies (sometimes conflicting) in the animal rights and environmental movements, exemplified by groups with names like Gays and Lesbians for Animal Rights and Feminists for Animal Rights.[20]

By the early nineteenth century sentiment and concern for animals was translated into organized efforts to decrease their maltreatment and suffering. First in Great Britain and then in North America, animal protection societies were formed to introduce and enforce legislation, build shelters, and educate the public. Rapid advancements in nineteenth-century science and medicine, however, also accelerated the practice of using animals in experimental laboratories. By the late 1800s, anti-vivisectionists organized to oppose the use of animals in medical and scientific research. Although the humane movement was slow to take issue with the use of animals for food and goods, the ideological link to vegetarianism (and eventually veganism) was inevitable, and in 1847 the Vegetarian Society was founded in England. By the turn of the century vegetarianism had become accepted among a significant minority of the middle class and was advanced by the likes of Henry Salt, Henry David Thoreau, Percy Shelley, George Bernard Shaw, and later Mohandas Gandhi.[21]

Intellectual progress in the eighteenth century precipitated early attempts to legislate against the abuse of animals, primarily in Great Britain. In 1822 an Irish landowner, Richard Martin, introduced and passed a bill in British Parliament that prohibited the abuse of certain domestic animals. To enforce the law, Martin and a group of humanitarians formed the first animal welfare organization: the Royal Society for the Prevention of Cruelty to Animals (RSPCA). Parliament subsequently passed the Cruelty to Animals Act in 1849. That law and later amendments prohibited many common abuses of animals, established rules for the treatment of animals during impoundment and transport, and placed restrictions on the use of animals in research.[22]

The first animal protection law in the United States was passed in New York in 1828 and provided for the conviction of persons who maliciously beat and killed horses, oxen, cattle, and sheep. Similar laws were passed over the next decade in states throughout the Northeast and Midwest, although some protected only livestock and not domestic animals. In the United States, however, the animal welfare movement lacked any real power until 1866, when Henry Bergh founded the American Society for the Prevention of Cruelty to Animals (ASPCA). Fashioned after Britain's

RSPCA, the ASPCA had teeth and was granted authority to arrest and convict animal abusers. Similar societies soon appeared in Boston and Philadelphia.

Although it had been a common practice for many centuries, vivisection accelerated with advancements in medical science throughout the 1800s, and by the end of the century live domesticated animals were being subjected routinely to experiments and dissections, typically without anesthesia. Because the Cartesian view of animals as unthinking machines held sway in scientific circles at this time, little thought was given to the suffering of animal subjects. Vivisection was widely used in early American medical schools, including Harvard University. In Great Britain the RSPCA advocated abolishing painful experiments while permitting those that used anesthesia. Anti-vivisectionists viewed the RSPCA stance as too conservative, and in 1878 journalist and suffragist Frances Power Cobbe formed the Victoria Street Society (VSS).[23] When Stephen Coleridge took over the VSS in 1898 and moved for restrictions on vivisection, as opposed to its abolition, Cobbe left and formed the British Union for the Abolition of Vivisection, an organization still in existence. Legislation to restrict vivisection was passed in 1876, but lobbyists for the medical community weakened the Cruelty to Animals Act, eliminating the original prohibition against using cats and dogs in experiments. The medical establishment further mobilized against the anti-vivisectionists with the creation of the Association for the Advancement of Medical Research (AAMR), which persuaded British authorities responsible for licensing live-animal experimentation to give the AAMR power of review over applications; predictably, the number of licenses granted increased dramatically.[24]

Despite setbacks precipitated by the scientific and medical establishments, at the start of the twentieth century anti-vivisectionists enjoyed fairly broad support in Great Britain. Numerous societies had sprung up, including the National Antivivisection Society (descendant of the Victoria Street Society) and the Church Antivivisection League. Distrust of the medical community and identification among the poor with the plight of dissected animals brought the working class into the fray—strange bedfellows for the likes of notable anti-vivisectionists George Bernard Shaw and Queen Victoria, not to mention the many female suffragist/anti-vivisectionists. When the president of the National Antivivisection Society, Stephen Coleridge, was successfully sued for libel by a professor charged with animal cruelty, the readers of one of the many newspapers sympathetic to the anti-vivisection cause paid his fine. In the Brown Dog Riots of 1907, working-class men in London fought with medical students who were attempting to bring down a statue commemorating the death of a brown terrier at the hands of University College vivisectionists—once again indicating broad support for the anti-vivisection cause.[25]

While Great Britain had established and exported the animal welfare movement in the 1800s, support for the cause waned dramatically in the early twentieth century. The counterattack by the medical community was organized and effective, thwarting animal welfare and anti-vivisection legislation through powerful lobbying groups like Britain's AAMR and, in America, the National Academy of Sciences, the American Medical Association, and the Council on Defense of Medical Research. Appeals to observable advances in medicine such as inoculations to prevent diseases and antiseptic surgery were successfully cited by the medical community as just cause for using animals in research laboratories.[26]

As in Great Britain, early anti-vivisection societies in Illinois and the New England states were ineffective in halting the practice. With the passage of the Pure Food and Drug Act of 1938, animal testing of certain chemicals and drugs was mandated, and after World War II the use of animals in medical and scientific research accelerated. Subsequent animal procurement laws in many states met the demand for dogs and cats by permitting the acquisition of animals from pounds and animal shelters.[27]

Perhaps the main reason anti-vivisection fell out of favor was the schism that developed between the anti-vivisectionists and the mainstream humane movement in Great Britain and the United States. In their history of the animal welfare and animal rights movements, Lawrence and Susan Finsen note that "in Britain and the United States the humane movement withdrew from the institutional cruelties in farming, vivisection, and exploited wildlife."[28] The authors further suggest that the rich and powerful patrons drawn to organizations like the British and American SPCAs and the American Humane Association tended to blunt criticism of institutionalized animal cruelty; in 1900 an international conference of humane associations expelled all anti-vivisection societies. There was in fact an observable compromise with medical researchers as the leadership of the humane movement failed to address the underlying assumptions that made possible the use of animals in experiments. Vegetarianism and the notion that animals might have some worth beyond their use as resources hardly entered the debate during this period. The trend continued throughout the early twentieth century: in the 1950s the ASPCA began actively collaborating with the medical community to procure pound animals for research, and the Metcalf-Hatch Act in New York actually required municipal pounds to sell animals to research facilities.[29]

The decline of the anti-vivisection movement in the early twentieth century heralded a long era of diminished growth in the animal welfare cause. Two world wars and a global economic depression between them pushed issues like humane treatment for animals to the background. After World War II America entered a conservative political climate that rarely acknowledged arguments for human rights, let alone the extension of moral consideration to non-human animals. The idea that advancing

human health at the expense of animals might be too costly or that techniques for increasing the yield of animal flesh for consumption might be
inhumane were rarely articulated, let alone widely accepted. A rare legislative victory in this era was the Humane Slaughter Act of 1958 and the
Wild Horses Act of 1959, the former mandating that meat processors selling to the government anesthetize or stun animals prior to slaughter, and
the latter prohibiting the poisoning of wild horses and burros.[30]

The resurgence of animal welfare and animal rights issues in the 1960s
coincided with the civil rights and women's rights movements of that time.
By the 1970s an era of "progressive radicalization" had begun, where the
conservatism of humane associations precipitated the splintering of groups
into more aggressive factions. Groups grew dissatisfied with the goal of
improving conditions for exploited animals and sought instead an end to
animal exploitation. Changes in moral philosophy and genuine concern
over animal suffering triggered an explosion of animal rights and animal
welfare organizations in the latter half of the twentieth century. A list of
some of the more significant organizations is provided in Table 3.1.

The advocacy of animal welfare and animal rights has become a
worldwide movement, no longer confined primarily to Great Britain and
the United States. Every year since 1983 animal rights supporters have
sponsored a World Day for Laboratory Animals, marked by international
demonstrations, protests, and advertising campaigns.[31]

Efforts to end the use of animals for any purpose—typically advertising campaigns, grassroots promotions, and political lobbying—have met
with varying degrees of success. In Great Britain no experiment can be
performed on an animal without a license from the Secretary of State of
Home Affairs, and the Animals Act of 1986 mandates that the Secretary of
State weigh the costs and benefits of doing the particular research: if animal suffering is greater than any potential benefit, then the license must
be refused. British regulations now require that veal calves have enough
room to stretch their legs and turn around. In Australia, an Animal Experimentation Ethics Committee must approve animal experiments and scientists must use anesthesia in situations where normal veterinary or
medical practice would require it. In 1981 Switzerland began phasing out
battery cages for chickens (small wire boxes that confine up to seven hens
together with no room for movement); the Netherlands outlawed battery
cages in 1994. Sweden likewise has very strong laws that require commit-
tees to consider costs and benefits in animal experimentation. In 1987 the
European Parliament passed recommendations for the European Community that included ending the denial of iron and roughage to veal
calves and their solitary confinement in crates, phasing out all battery
cages for chickens, discontinuing sow confinement in individual stalls,
and ending livestock mutilations such as tail docking, beak trimming,
and castration.[32] In Great Britain, after many years of protest, the age-old
tradition of fox hunting with hounds was banned.

Table 3.1
Founding Dates of Significant Animal Welfare and Animal Rights Organizations

Animal Welfare Institute	1951
Humane Society of the United States	1954
Friends of Animals	1957
Beauty Without Cruelty	1959
Fund for Animals	1967
United Action for Animals	1967
Animal Protection Institute	1968
International Fund for Animal Welfare	1969
Greenpeace	1971
International Primate Protection League	1973
Animal Rights International	1976
Committee to Abolish Sport Hunting	1976
Sea Shepherd Conservation Society	1977
Animal Legal Defense Fund	1978
People for the Ethical Treatment of Animals	1980
Farm Animal Reform Movement	1981
Trans-Species Unlimited	1981
Mobilization for Animals	1981
Johns Hopkins Center for Alternatives to Animal Testing	1981
Feminists for Animal Rights	1982
National Alliance for Animal Legislation	1982
In Defense of Animals	1983
Humane Farming Association	1984
Physicians Committee for Responsible Medicine	1985
Last Chance for Animals	1985
Doris Day Animal League	1988
Ark Trust	1991

Source: Masters Evans, *Animal Rights*, 15–16, Table 1.2.

Regulations protecting animals are not so stringent in other European nations and the United States. Switzerland, the United Kingdom, Australia, Canada, Japan, Denmark, Germany, the Netherlands, and Norway all have stronger animal welfare laws than the United States regarding experimentation as well as factory farming. Still, as animal rights advo-

Table 3.2
Passage Dates of Significant U.S. Animal Welfare Legislation

Humane Slaughter Act	1958
Wild Horses Act	1959
Bald and Golden Eagle Act	1962
Endangered Species Act (ESA)	1966
Laboratory Animal Welfare Act	1966
Animal Welfare Act (AWA) amendments	1970
Marine Mammal Protection Act	1972
ESA amendments	1973
AWA amendments	1976
Horse Protection Act	1976
Fur Seal Act	1976
Metcalf-Hatch Act repealed	1979
AWA amendments	1985
Cambridge, Mass., Bans LD50 and Draize experiments	1991
International Dolphin Conservation Act	1992
Driftnet Fishery Conservation Act	1992
NIH Revitalization Act	1993

Source: Masters Evans, *Animal Rights,* 15–16, Table 1.2.

cates note, even the most liberal regulations are best characterized as providing merely for animal welfare and do not address the question of animal rights and exploitation. The dates of passage of significant U.S. animal welfare legislation are shown in Table 3.2.

Growth of the Animal Rights Movement

Beginning in the mid-1970s, the growth of the animal rights movement accelerated. A recurring pattern in the recent animal rights crusade has been the mobilization of public support around a single high-profile case that leads to a media feeding frenzy. Animal rights activists have picked their battles carefully, maximizing the potential for increased public awareness and the generation of sympathy for their cause. An early hero of the animal rights movement, Henry Spira, perfected the technique. Spira was a teacher and civil rights activist who organized protests against the New York Natural History Museum from 1975 to 1977. For twenty years, with funding from the National Institutes of Health (NIH), museum scientists had been conducting experiments on cats, destroying parts of the animals' brains to observe the effects on their sexual behavior. Naturally, the spending of taxpayer dollars to conduct painful and unnecessary experiments on lovable kittens played well for animal activists, and after eighteen months of protests the NIH withdrew its funding.[33] Spira and other animal rights activists continued to choose what they saw as soft targets, those practices most vulnerable to adverse publicity. A major success was the repeal of the Metcalf-Hatch Act, a law that had authorized the sale of pound animals to medical research laboratories. Spira also led the charge in publicizing and reducing the use by cosmetics manufacturers of the infamous Draize and LD50 tests (the Draize test involves placing irritants directly into the eyes of rabbits, while LD50 refers to the lethal dose of a product required to kill 50% of the animals tested).[34]

In 1984 another publicity success for the animal rights movement targeted the work of Thomas Gennarelli, a scientist at the University of Pennsylvania. Gennarelli received $1 million a year from the NIH to study head injuries. A raid on his lab by the fledgling animal rights group the Animal Liberation Front produced sixty hours of videotape that showed experiments in which baboons were subjected to precisely measured blows to the head. ALF turned the tapes over to the group People for the Ethical Treatment of Animals (PETA), which produced a thirty-minute video and lobbied the Department of Health and Human Services (HHS) to revoke Gennarelli's funding. The HHS refused to view the tapes, but numerous additional groups such as the American Antivivisection Society, the International Society for Animal Rights, and the Animal Legal Defense Fund joined the fight. After a year of protests, lobbying, and a three-day sit-in at the offices of the NIH, the HHS withdrew Gennarelli's funding. The melodrama gained the animal rights movement favorable coverage on NBC and CNN and in *The Washington Post* and *The New York Times*.[35]

Yet another dramatic case that propelled the animal rights cause forward and brought PETA nationwide attention involved an undercover investigation by PETA cofounder Alex Pacheco. Pacheco selected the Institute for Behavioral Research in Silver Spring, Maryland, for an investigation into laboratory conditions. Having acquired a volunteer position as a laboratory assistant, Pacheco gathered a large quantity of evidence of primate abuse in the lab headed by Edward Taub. PETA's undercover operative brought the evidence to Silver Spring police, who raided the lab and confiscated seventeen monkeys. The NIH subsequently cut off Taub's funding, and at trial the scientist was convicted on six counts of animal cruelty. However, five of the six counts were eliminated on appeal, and the remaining conviction was overturned after the Maryland Court of Appeals ruled that state anti-cruelty laws do not apply to researchers who receive federal funding. Still, the case was a success for the movement, bringing widespread attention to the animal rights cause and setting PETA on a path to becoming the most significant animal rights organization in the world.[36]

PETA was cofounded in 1980 by Alex Pacheco and Ingrid Newkirk. By using targeted campaigns for maximum media exposure and effect, PETA, a 501c tax-exempt nonprofit organization, has grown over the years to a large international organization with a multi-million-dollar operating budget and some 700,000 members. The PETA web page contains numerous links to other PETA sites, including a web page for kids, action alerts, news of ongoing campaigns, and numerous international offices, including PETA U.K., Germany, the Netherlands, France, and India. The goals of the organization are quite straightforward and radical, namely, ending the use of animals for whatever reason, whether for food, clothing, scientific advancement, or entertainment. While powerful opposition to date has prevented the full achievement of this goal, PETA has nonetheless succeeded in reducing animal suffering, educating the public, and forcing powerful industries to alter the manner in which they exploit animals.[37]

One of PETA's most successful tactics has been to use education and the media to draw attention to itself and the animal rights cause. PETA sponsors demonstrations, produces public-education materials including graphic documentaries, stages performances and street theatre (some featuring nude supermodels), produces and distributes educational and training materials for affiliated groups, and periodically runs a course on activism called Helping Animals 101 in cities throughout the world. Numerous celebrities have become supporters of PETA, including Paul McCartney, Pamela Anderson, Kim Basinger, and the late River Phoenix, to name a few.

PETA may be best known for its highly controversial advertising campaigns. It once ran a campaign claiming that beer was healthier than milk under the slogan "Got beer?"; the group Mothers Against Drunk Driving (MADD) was not amused. A broad cross-section of the general public was angered when PETA used a picture of popular former New York mayor Rudolph Giuliani in another anti-milk campaign called "Got cancer?" Claiming that diets high in meat and milk are linked to cancer, PETA was capitalizing on Giuliani's recent prostate cancer diagnosis. Aimed at children, "Unhappy Meals" and "Murder King" promotions targeting McDonald's and Burger King have featured images of dead cattle and toys in the shape of wounded farm animals. Whether protesting fishing by distributing a computer-generated picture of a border collie with a giant hook in its mouth or comparing the slaughter of chickens to the extermination of Jews in Nazi concentration camps, PETA has provoked widespread reaction and drawn attention to its cause.[38]

A testament to PETA's growth and power are the numerous lawsuits and boycotts it has sponsored against international corporate giants such as McDonald's, Procter and Gamble, Huntingdon Life Sciences, and Covance.

PETA has taken on what it calls animal exploiters in venues ranging from rodeos and circuses to the Australian wool industry. Over the years PETA has exposed animal cruelty in numerous product-testing companies, from a fur farm in Montana to General Motors. Often using undercover investigators to expose abuses, PETA has even forced companies such as Revlon, Procter and Gamble, Bristol-Myers, General Motors, Avon, and Gillette to change some of their practices. The release of videotapes made at a Gillette cosmetics testing lab in Maryland led to the shutdown of that lab in 1986. PETA has been at the forefront of attacks on factory farming and the consumption of meat, leading protests and boycotts against Wendy's, McDonald's, Burger King, and Kentucky Fried Chicken.[39]

PETA has also provided support to criminal animal rights activists. It has served as a media outlet for ALF and provided financial assistance to persons accused of or known to be involved in criminal activity. This aboveground-underground relationship will be explored more fully in chapter four.

Progressive Radicalization and Animal Rights Criminality

Dissatisfaction with the mainstream animal welfare movement and the slow, incremental improvement in the conditions afforded exploited animals has led many animal rights advocates to become more aggressive in their methods. In fact, the splintering of anti-vivisectionists and others from the mainstream humane societies and animal welfare groups is a pattern that has been repeated many times in both the animal rights and environmental movements. It is an observable sociological phenomenon: radical subgroups within broader movements break off and adopt more drastic methods, set more extreme goals, and espouse a more radical ideology. The process may be viewed as progressive radicalism.

Beginning in the 1960s, first in Great Britain and then in the United States, the idea that non-human animals not only deserved humane treatment but actually had rights, perhaps equal to those of humans, forever altered the course of the animal welfare movement. RSPCA head Richard Ryder coined the term *speciesism* in 1971, but the concept became firmly established in 1975 with the publication of Peter Singer's seminal work *Animal Liberation*.[40] Drawing on ideas originally voiced by Jeremy Bentham and Henry Salt, Singer suggested that racism, sexism, and speciesism are the same breed of human behavior, and that slavery, the Jewish Holocaust, the subjugation of women, factory farming, and vivisection all reflect unjustified discrimination. Singer based much of his argument on the concept of utilitarianism, a philosophical ideal that promotes the maximization of positive outcomes and/or the minimization of negative outcomes in a social order geared to the interests of all parties (including animals). In his book, Singer presented a large body of evidence to demonstrate that the suffering inflicted on animals by agribusiness and scientific experimentation far outweighed the benefits of those enterprises to humans.[41] In 1983, Tom Regan's *The Case for Animal Rights* more fully developed the notion of rights for animals and laid the ideological groundwork for liberating animals from human oppression.[42] Moreover, if the exploitation of animals amounts to a moral wrong equivalent to that of the Holocaust, as animal right advocates contend, it follows that drastic measures, perhaps even criminal actions, might be justified in the effort to rectify such a grave injustice.

New groups reflected this radical ideology in their methods, adopting direct action as their modus operandi. One of the first direct-action animal rights groups, the Hunt Saboteurs of Great Britain, were highly confrontational and uncompromising, and extended the animal rights movement to the working class. By the early 1970s the Band of Mercy (the precursor to the Animal Liberation Front) were setting fires and liberating animals in Great Britain. ALF later spread from Britain to North America, where it has since perpetrated hundreds of acts of arson and property damage against agribusiness, medical research facilities, and fur farmers.[43]

The process of progressive radicalization has been continuous in both the United States and Europe since the 1960s. While ALF officially denounces threats and violence against persons, ALF founder Ronnie Lee vocally supported the beating of a Huntingdon Life Science executive, and incidents of violence and threats, even against children, have become common.[44] Great Britain's Animal Rights Militia (ARM) sent letter bombs to Margaret Thatcher in 1982, and in 1988 Fran Trutt was arrested for planting a bomb outside the offices of the U.S. Surgical Corporation.[45] In May 2002 Volkert van der Graaf murdered Pim Fortuyn, a Dutch politician running for Parliament; Fortuyn had favored ending a ban on breeding animals for fur. The *Sunday Times of London* reported that van der Graaf was a member of a group called Environmental Offensive and as a teenager had founded a group called the Zeeland Animal Liberation Front. In 1999 an animal rights group calling itself the Justice Department mailed razor blades to eighty-seven American scientists working with primates; the blades were inserted so as to slice fingers when the envelope was opened. In yet another case, an undercover operative working for PETA infiltrated the Boys Town research facility in Omaha, Nebraska, triggering NIH and Agriculture Department investigations. During this time, Boys Town researchers were threatened with hate mail and phone calls; one letter read, "We will kill you and every member of your family in the exact same way you killed the cats, no matter where you hide! We will slice open your heads and cut the nerves in your brains while you are alive."[46]

Conclusion

Peter Singer notes in the preface to the second edition of *Animal Liberation* that the animal rights movement occupies the moral high ground in the animal welfare debate, and that activist violence sacrifices this crucial leverage. Singer goes on to cite Martin Luther King Jr., and Mohandas Gandhi as examples to be followed by animal rights activists.[47] And while there is no doubt that the vast majority of animal rights proponents are dedicated to protecting all animal life, human and non-human, the observed process of progressive radicalization is nevertheless producing a new fringe of extremists who, in likening factory farming and vivisection to the Jewish Holocaust and black slavery, have decided that the scale of non-human animal suffering is great enough to morally justify violent attacks against humans. In this extreme, the activities of some animal rights groups and individuals are properly labeled as terrorism.

Animal Rights Criminality

In 1990 the president of People for the Ethical Treatment of Animals (PETA), Ingrid Newkirk, said in a *Reader's Digest* interview, "Humans have grown like a cancer. We're the biggest blight on the face of the earth."[1] Statements like these are appropriately labeled as misanthropic; yet, in fairness, if trees and factory farm animals could talk, many would no doubt agree with Ms. Newkirk. PETA members and other animal rights activists, including members of the Animal Liberation Front (ALF), speak for animals—sometimes in a very loud, dramatic, and illegal manner.

Criminality associated with the animal rights movement has had a significant impact on numerous animal industries, from large international companies like Huntingdon Life Sciences to countless smaller family-owned fur farms. Moreover, the modus operandi of animal rights radicals has involved increasingly personal and violent attacks. Dr. Michael Podell at Ohio State University walked away from a tenured position and $1.7 million in research funding after PETA posted his experiments on its "action alert" list. Podell received a dozen death threats and was sent a photograph of a British scientist whose car had been bombed; scrawled on the top of the photo was the warning "you're next."[2] Another example of the increasingly violent nature of the movement is the five-year campaign waged against the Darley Oaks Farm, a breeder of guinea pigs located in Newchurch, Staffordshire. Farm owners, workers, and businesses associated with Darley Oaks (including a local pub and the farm's fuel supplier and domestic cleaner) have come under attack. Tactics in the Save the Newchurch Guinea Pigs campaign included throwing bricks through the windows of private residences, arson, death threats, and even threats against the children of employees. A local graveyard was desecrated, and the remains of the Darley Oaks owner's mother-in-law were stolen. (Darley Oaks eventually closed down.)[3]

Violence directly targeting humans is clearly becoming more accept-able among a fringe of animal rights extremists. Fugitive Daniel Andreas San Diego is wanted by law enforcement for detonating ten-pound shrap-nel bombs at two California biomedical research facilities in 2003; one device was set to explode an hour after the initial blast, in a clear attempt to murder first-responders.[4] The most sustained animal rights campaign has been conducted against Huntingdon Life Sciences, one of the world's largest product-testing laboratories. Over the last seven years personal attacks on company executives have financially devastated the company.[5] It would seem that more extreme methods are generating results. They have clearly reinforced and fueled further animal rights violence.

The Animal Liberation Front

The use of criminal means to advance the cause of animal rights began in Great Britain. An anti-vivisection youth group calling itself the Band of Mercy destroyed property in the 1800s, and criminality to support animal rights in the modern era began in 1963, when a twenty-one-year-old jour-nalist founded the Hunt Saboteurs Association (HSA). The HSA sabo-taged fox hunts by laying false scents, blowing hunting horns to divert hounds, and spooking animals to safety. A single, small cell quickly grew to a network of "hunt sab" groups across Great Britain, and with exten-sive media coverage and aboveground support from the League Against Cruel Sports, the HSA proved moderately successful. England outlawed the practice of hunting foxes with hounds (although it remains legal to shoot foxes). The Hunt Saboteurs Association is still in existence today.[6]

In an oft-repeated pattern, elements of the HSA, believing their meth-ods to be ineffective, broke off and formed a more radical group. Ronnie Lee and Cliff Goodman in 1972 formed the Band of Mercy (named after the nineteenth-century group) with the aim of attacking hunters directly. While initial actions typically involved disabling hunters' vehicles and leaving behind notes urging them to quit the sport, the group soon gradu-ated to more extreme methods while expanding its targets to include medical research facilities. In 1973 Band of Mercy members took credit for two separate acts of arson that destroyed the Hoechst Pharmaceutical building. Soon after, boats to be used in a seal hunt were burned, forcing the operator out of business. For two and a half years the Band of Mercy targeted hunters, farms, food producers, and research laboratories, burn-ing structures and liberating animals. In 1974 Ronnie Lee was caught while attempting to firebomb a medical facility and spent a year in prison. Upon his release in 1976, Lee and about thirty others started oper-ating as the Animal Liberation Front (ALF).[7]

In prison Ronnie Lee learned to mimic the Irish Republican Army (IRA), adopting the organizational structure of decentralized, small, autonomous cells. In its first year ALF caused damage amounting to a

quarter-million pounds sterling, attacking butcher shops, furriers, farmers, fast-food outlets, and animal breeders across Great Britain. ALF operatives even desecrated the grave of legendary British huntsman Robert
Peel and planted a bomb under the car of a cancer researcher. Within ten
years, ALF had grown to a movement of perhaps 1,500 activists causing
about 6 million pounds sterling in damage annually to British businesses
and research facilities. Lee himself was eventually convicted and sent to
prison for ten years for his part in firebombing department stores. By that
time, however, the movement had grown far beyond the influence of any
one person. By the mid-1980s more radical splinter groups such as the
Animal Rights Militia (ARM), the Justice Department, and the Hunt Retribution Squad had formed, and in 1989 alone fourteen attempted bombings were attributed to animal rights groups in Great Britain. Scotland
Yard has classified ALF as a terrorist organization in the same category as
the IRA and the Palestine Liberation Organization (PLO).[8]

Today, ALF has grown far beyond its British roots, becoming a significant international movement with an unknown number of members and
supporters worldwide. ALF cells are or have been active in the United
Kingdom, Canada, France, Germany, the Netherlands, Spain, Sweden,
Norway, Russia, Croatia, Italy, Australia, New Zealand, Iceland, Finland,
Denmark, Ireland, Austria, Belgium, Switzerland, and the United States—
more than twenty countries in all. Although no evidence suggests financial or operational connections between ALF cells in Great Britain and
those in the United States, it is clear that U.S. cells have followed operational and organizational patterns established in Great Britain, including a
demonstrated tendency toward more radical actions. According to a 1993
Justice Department study, the number of "hardcore" ALF members in both
Great Britain and the United States is thought to be one hundred or fewer,
although those who commit lesser acts of vandalism and animal liberation
are certainly greater in number (in the United States the Animal Liberation
Front Support Group claims a membership of 10,000).

The stated goal of the Animal Liberation Front is to stop animal suffering through "direct actions"—illegal activities involving the rescue/
release of animals from places of abuse and suffering—and by inflicting
economic damage on businesses and facilities that use and abuse animals.
The more devastating ALF attacks involve timed incendiary devices that
cause damage amounting to millions of dollars. In cases of burglary and
vandalism, perpetrators spray-paint walls with the ALF initials along
with graffiti, slogans, and threats.[9] Direct actions tend to be well organized and preceded by careful surveillance of the target; members infiltrate facilities by cultivating friendships or even becoming employees.
ALF cells often document their work on camera, and the videos usually
show one or several individuals destroying property then posing in ski
masks with the liberated animals.[10] Because of their illegal activities,
members work anonymously, either individually or in small cells of two

ALF has often targeted people in addition to property, and several spin-off groups have emerged with the explicit mission of bringing more extreme and violent attacks against industries deemed to exploit animals.[18] The FBI and other officials believe a significant overlap in personnel and support networks exists among ALF and related groups.[19] The move to target people for threats and violent attacks is one consequence of the process of progressive radicalization, the recurring trend within the broader animal rights movement in which radical factions, impatient with the lack of results, graduate to more extreme methods to achieve their aims.

ALF Splinter Groups

Founded in England in 1982, the Animal Rights Militia (ARM) is a splinter group of ALF that advocates a more proactive approach for the animal rights movement. ARM activists have mailed letter bombs to the British prime minister and to three party leaders (one exploded and injured an office worker). In Great Britain, ARM firebombed the cars and homes of employees of the British Industrial Biological Research Association and the Willcome Foundation. In the United States, it struck businesses in San Jose California, burning a warehouse owned by San Jose Valley Veal Inc. on September 1, 1987, causing $100,000 in damage, and torching the Ferrara Meat Company on November 26, 1987. ARM also perpetrated several hoaxes that caused significant economic damage to their targets. In 1984 activists claimed that they had poisoned Mars candy bars (Mars had been performing tooth decay experiments on animals), and in January 1992 in Canada, they engineered a similar hoax, falsely stating that they had injected Cold Buster Bars with oven cleaner, with the resulting recall costing the company $1 million. In other notable actions, ARM in 1994 was responsible for a Christmas turkey poisoning hoax in Vancouver, British Columbia, and the group attacked the home of a University of British Columbia faculty member, defacing the residence with red paint. In recent years ARM has torched leather shops in England. It remains very active in Sweden, where it mostly arranges animal liberations. ARM is perhaps most notorious for threatening to kill ten research scientists in the event of the death of imprisoned animal rights activist Barry Horne as a result of one of several hunger strikes.[20] (Horne didn't die on a hunger strike, but he did perish in prison due to liver failure; in any event, no scientists were assassinated.)

The Justice Department is a militant animal rights organization that sprang up in Britain in 1993 before expanding to the United States. Members of the group have claimed responsibility for hundreds of attacks in the United Kingdom; *The Independent* described its activities as "the most sustained and sophisticated bombing campaign in mainland Britain since the IRA was at its height." Structured in loose anonymous cells like ALF, Justice Department activists have also mailed letter bombs that injured several people. In 1996 the Justice Department claimed responsibility for mailing envelopes rigged with poisoned razor blades to over eighty primate researchers in the United States and Canada. A note inside the letters stated, "Dear animal killing scum! Hope we sliced your finger wide open and that now you die from the rat poison we smeared on the razor blade." In a razor blade–rigged letter sent to the University of California–Davis, a note read, "You have been targeted, and you have until autumn 2000 to release all our primate captives and get out of the vivisection industry. If you do not heed our warning, your violence will be turned back on you." A Justice Department manifesto is clear in its intent to target people for violent attacks: "The Animal Liberation Front achieved what other methods have not while adhering to nonviolence. A separate idea was established that decided animal abusers had been warned long enough . . . the time has come for abusers to have but a taste of the fear and anguish their victims suffer on a daily basis."[21]

Perhaps the most enduring and violent of the militant animal rights groups is Stop Huntingdon Animal Cruelty (SHAC). Greg Avery and Heather James started SHAC in Great Britain in 1999 after a video shot by PETA was aired on British television. The video showed the abuse of lab animals inside Huntingdon Life Sciences (HLS), one of the largest contract animal-testing laboratories in the world. In addition to e-mail campaigns, hacking of company computers, and harassing phone calls, SHAC's modus operandi involves direct action including "intimidation of HLS, its employees, its employees' families, its business partners, their business partners, their insurers, their caterers, and cleaners." SHAC further states that "anyone who delivers services to people who do business with HLS—even the owners of pubs employees visit, or the companies that deliver their milk in the morning—is regarded by SHAC as a legitimate target."[22] Unlike past forms of eco-terror and animal rights criminality that targeted impersonal corporate structures, SHAC operatives target in a very personal way individuals associated with HLS. Using the aboveground SHAC website, operatives have listed the home addresses and phone numbers of HLS employees, along with the declaration "wanted in collaboration with animal torture." Female HLS employees and associates have been threatened with sexual assault and followed home from work, while employees with families have received menacing e-mails asking, "Do you know where your children are?" To date, SHAC operatives have firebombed eleven privately owned cars and attacked numerous private residences. SHAC letter bombs have injured several people, including a furrier and his three-year-old daughter.[23] Brian Cass, the managing director of HLS, was wounded outside his home by three men wielding ax handles in February 2001. A neighbor who came to Cass's aid was sprayed with CS gas. Kevin Jonas of SHAC USA stated "I don't shed any tears for Brian Cass."[24] HLS marketing director Andrew Gay was attacked on his doorstep with a chemical spray that left him temporarily blinded and writhing on the ground in front of his wife and daughter.[25]

Executives of Marsh Inc., the company that insured HLS, were targeted until the company dropped HLS as a client. One Marsh executive's home was defaced with graffiti that said "puppy killer" and "we'll be back" in red paint. After a Marsh employee in Boston had his home address posted on the Internet, protestors surrounded his home, threatening to burn it down; a communiqué on SHAC's website had referenced the man's wife and two-year-old son.[26]

In 2000 SHAC obtained a list of HLS shareholders, including anonymous individuals and companies that had bought shares through a third party. The *Sunday Telegraph* published the list, and within two weeks an equity stake of 32 million shares was placed on the London Stock Exchange for one pence each. HLS quotes subsequently crashed, and the Bank of Scotland closed the HLS account. In December 2000 the New York Stock Exchange dropped HLS because of the share collapse, and on March 29, 2001, HLS lost its place on the main platform of the London Stock Exchange. HLS subsequently moved its financial center to Maryland and incorporated as Life Sciences Research, Inc. The company was actually saved from bankruptcy when it received a $33 million loan from the American investment bank Stephens, Inc. SHAC activists predictably responded with a campaign of threats, intimidation, and violence against Stephens offices and employees, and in 2002 Stephens sold its HLS shares at a loss.[27]

After the Stephens Inc. campaign, SHAC targeted Marsh Inc., the company that insured HLS. E-mails to SHAC supporters included a list of Marsh offices with phone numbers and home addresses of Marsh employees. One Marsh executive received a letter indicating that he had been "targeted for a terrorist attack." Other Marsh employees were threatened and harassed at home, and in July 2002 the release of smoke bombs at Marsh offices in Seattle forced hundreds of workers into the streets. By the end of 2002 Marsh announced that it would no longer insure HLS.[28]

In June 2001 a group calling itself Pirates for Animal Liberation tried to sink the yacht of a Bank of New York executive because of the bank's ties to HLS.[29] In June 2003 SHAC posted online the private information of employees of Chiron (another HLS affiliate), and later that summer two groups calling themselves the Animal Liberation Brigade and Revolutionary Cells set off pipe bombs at Chiron's Emeryville, California, offices. Only minor damage resulted, but an ominous communiqué posted to the SHAC website said, "You might protect your buildings, but can you protect the homes of every employee?"

Numerous Chiron employees, many of whom were never involved in animal testing, have been subjected to repeated late-night home visits from SHAC activists. They pound on front doors and shout obscenities through bullhorns, waking and scaring the young children of employees. Checking-account information is posted on the Internet, lewd and threatening phone calls and e-mails are sent, feces is smeared on homes, and spouses and children are threatened.[30]

In September 2003 the Animal Liberation Brigade and the Revolutionary Cells took credit for another bombing, this time at the offices of Shaklee Inc. in Pleasonton, California (Shaklee's parent company is an HLS associate); an anonymous e-mail claiming responsibility reiterated that HLS customers and their families were legitimate targets. Another communiqué from the Animal Liberation Brigade said that it was "time to bring the bomb and the gun back into amerikan politics," while the Revolutionary Cells taunted the Chiron chairman: "Hey, Sean Lance and the rest of the Chiron team, how are you sleeping? You never know when your house, your car even, might go boom. Who knows? That new car in the parking lot may be packed with explosives, or maybe it will be a shot in the dark."[31]

In September 2005 Leapfrog Day Nurseries, a major British childcare provider that offered childcare vouchers to HLS employees, received letters from animal rights activists threatening force: "Not only you but your family is a target. Sever your links with HLS within two weeks or get ready for your life and the lives of those you love to become a living hell." Leapfrog cut its ties to HLS.[32]

The Legacy Trading Company, the only remaining market maker for HLS by 2005, frequently has been attacked by SHAC, including actions directed against executive Skip Boruchin and his family. In addition to spray-painting his home and vandalizing the Legacy offices, SHAC targeted Boruchin's mother-in-law: the ninety-year-old woman's phone number and assisted-living address were posted on the SHAC website, and activists were instructed to send her sex toys and to have an undertaker visit the home to pick up her "dead body."[33]

In October 2005 the U.S. Senate Committee on Environment and Public Works devoted an entire hearing to SHAC and the HLS financial situation. John Lewis, a deputy assistant director of the FBI, stated that about one hundred companies had stopped doing business with HLS as a result of SHAC intimidation, including Citibank, Merrill Lynch, Charles Schwab, and Deloitte & Touche.[34]

ALF activists have joined with SHAC in the campaign to run HLS out of business, issuing a warning in May 2005 on the ALF website: "If you support or raise funds for any company connected with Huntingdon Life Sciences we will track you down, come for you and destroy your property by fire."[35] In June 2005 a Vancouver brokerage house, Canaccord, announced it had dropped its client Phytopharm PLC as a result of the May 2005 firebombing of a car belonging to executive Michael Kendall. ALF claimed credit for the attack, which involved entering Kendall's garage to place a timed incendiary device under his car while Kendall and his family slept.[36] In September 2005 the home of Paul Blackburn, corporate controller of GlaxoSmithKline—an HLS customer—was attacked with a device containing two liters of fuel and four pounds of explosives. Blackburn's wife and child were home at the time of the attack. An ALF communiqué claiming responsibility for the attack stated, "GSK, we realize that this may not be enough to make you stop using HLS but this is just the beginning, we have identified and tracked down many of your senior executives and also junior staff, as well as those from other HLS customers. Drop HLS or you will face the consequences. For all the animals inside HLS, we will be back."[37]

Carr Securities withdrew from making a market in HLS shares after a New York yacht club was covered in red paint by ALF activists; the club's membership included Carr employees. ALF announced, "Let this be a message to any other company who chooses to court HLS in their . . . entrance in the NYSE. If you trade in Life Science Research shares, make a market, process orders, or purchase shares you can expect far worse treatment. The message is simple, don't touch HLS!" On September 7, 2005, the New York Stock Exchange asked Life Sciences Research to delay its listing, and in October 2005 company after company divested their portfolios of HLS stock, which continued to plummet in value.[38]

By late 2005 the SHAC campaign had cells and operations in numerous countries, including Britain, the United States, New Zealand, Switzerland, Australia, and Ireland.[39] The FBI also believes that British SHAC operatives are funded by organizations and individuals in the United States. HLS remains in serious financial trouble at the time of this writing, and authorities fear that the success of the SHAC campaign will reinforce and fuel the trend in the animal rights movement of targeting humans for attack.[40]

The Animal Rights Money Trail and the Role of PETA

Although the methods of groups like ALF tend toward leaderless resistance and underground direct actions, some highly public individuals also play important roles. Academics such as Tom Regan, Steven Best, and Peter Singer provide the groups with their ideological arguments. In addition, support in the form of media exposure, education, public relations, and funding is arranged by a class of professional advocates that includes Ingrid Newkirk, Alex Pacheco, and Neal Bernard. In short, there is, in fact, a significant *aboveground* leadership in the animal rights movement.

Another significant trend in the animal rights movement has been the takeover and radicalization of traditional animal welfare organizations. For example, a PETA consultant in 1987 gained control of the Toronto Humane Society (THS); one of the new THS director's employees previously had been arrested for possession of explosives and vandalizing a restaurant that served meat. In another corporate takeover move, PETA acquired control of the New England Anti-Vivisection Society (NEAVS). The wife of PETA executive Gary Francione purchased 300 voting memberships for $3,000, and hundreds of applications for voting memberships arrived at the New England headquarters in bulk. PETA's Alex Pacheco set up the Action Campaign Fund to subsidize or pay full airfare to voting activists all over the country, and Pacheco, Ingrid Newkirk, and Dr. Neal Bernard of the Physicians Committee for Responsible Medicine (a PETA ally) were soon voted onto the NEAVS board of directors. Their election gave PETA access to an $8 million fund balance. The fund was subsequently drained by PETA to less than $6 million, and in 1998 the Massachusetts Superior Court ruled that the PETA board members and allies had "breached their fiduciary responsibilities" as NEAVS executive board members.[41]

The Animal Liberation Front was more confrontational when it gained control of the British Union for the Abolition of Vivisection in 1985: radicals bussed in two hundred "black-clad young people of anarchist aspect" to vote out conservative members, a journalist was threatened, microphones were turned off, and older anti-vivisectionists were reduced to tears by a flood of abusive language. In 1987 ALF supporters forced out nine directors and eighteen employees of the London-based National Antivivisection Society and replaced them with ALF sympathizers.[42] Other traditional animal welfare groups have also become aligned with the more radical animal rights movement in recent years, including the American Society for the Prevention of Cruelty to Animals (ASPCA) and the Humane Society of the United States (HSUS—not to be confused with local humane societies that run animal shelters). HSUS employee Miyun Park was named as a benefactor to ALF's *No Compromise* magazine and was the subject of six federal wiretap warrants in 2005. The HSUS also employs J. P. Goodwin, outspoken ALF supporter and former director of the radical group Coalition to Abolish the Fur Trade.[43]

PETA provides most of the aboveground leadership for the ALF. Aside from rather innocuous program activities like running "Helping Animals 101" seminars in cities throughout the world, PETA has from its inception provided vocal support and a range of critical services for underground direct-action operatives, including funding. In fact, a good deal of money flows to animal rights causes from a variety of foundations. These funds trickle down from legitimate sources to animal rights activists through the management of a group of interlocking nonprofit organizations such as PETA and the Physicians Committee for Responsible Medicine (PCRM).[44]

Consider the following network of animal rights supporters. PETA's Ingrid Newkirk is also a director of the Foundation to Support Animal Protection (FSAP). Dr. Neal Bernard, founder of the PCRM, is also a member of FSAP. Between 1988 and 1999, PETA contributed $185,026 to PCRM, and the FSAP funneled an additional $592,524 to PCRM in 1999–2000. The PCRM supports Stop Huntingdon Animal Cruelty and even co-signed a letter with SHAC USA's Kevin Jonas—formerly an ALF spokesperson—urging customers to boycott Huntingdon Life Sciences. The Helen Brach

foundation gave $30,000 to PCRM between 1998 and 2000, $15,000 to
United Poultry Concerns (UPC) in 1998–99 (Ingrid Newkirk is on the UPC
advisory board), and $10,000 to PETA in 1995. The Park Foundation gave
$10,000 to PCRM in 2000, $200,000 to PETA from 1997 to 1999, and $10,000
to UPC in 1998. The Benjamin J. Rosenthal Foundation contributes to PETA
and the Ruckus Society (the Ruckus Society was created by Earth First!
cofounder Mike Roselle and was behind much of the rioting at the 1999
WTO conference in Seattle). Other major contributors to PETA, PCRM, and
related nonprofits include the Judi and Howard Strauss Foundation, the
Geraldine R. Dodge Foundation, the Glaser Family Foundation, the Komie
Foundation, the Philanthropic Collaborative, the Pond Foundation, the San
Francisco Foundation, and the Lynn R. and Carl E. Prickett Foundation.[45]

While much of the money contributed for the animal rights cause is
used for lobbying, advertising, and political demonstrations, at least
some of it indirectly (if not directly) supports criminal activities. PETA is
the principal conduit, and in some cases the organization explicitly
defends and, in effect, sponsors criminal actions. PETA failed to disclose,
as required by law, the destination of approximately $1 million in dona-
tions in 1997 and 1998. Although it is impossible to say if any of that
money went to animal rights activists, PETA's financing of illegal operatives has been well documented. Following a 1986 raid at the University
of Oregon, PETA paid over $60,000 in legal fees and fines for ALF mem-
ber Roger Troen. PETA also paid Rod Coronado's legal bill ($45,200) and
sent another $25,000 to Coronado's father. In 1988, after Fran Stephanie
Trutt of Friends of Animals tried to kill Leon Hirsch of the U.S. Surgical
Company with a radio-controlled nail bomb, PETA provided $7,500 for
her legal defense. In 2000, PETA contributed $5,000 to the Josh Harper
Support Committee; Harper is an Oregon-based ALF member who advocates the downfall of industrial civilization and has been charged with
assaulting a police officer. PETA also gave David Wilson, an ALF spokesperson, $2000 in 1999.[46]

PETA's contributions also include a donation of $1,500 to the Earth Lib-
eration Front (ELF) for "program activities." Statements from PETA representatives provided numerous, conflicting accounts of what the
contribution was for, and news of a payment from a 501c(3) organization
to a group considered by the FBI to be a major domestic terror threat
became the subject of a congressional hearing in February 2002. It turned
out that the $1,500 actually went to the legal defense of Craig Rose-
braugh, an ELF spokesperson from 1997 to 2001. Appearing before the
committee chaired by Representative Scott McInnis, Rosebraugh repeatedly pleaded the Fifth Amendment right against self-incrimination. Later
Rosebraugh would answer fifty-seven written questions from the committee, expressing support for property destruction as a means of defending the environment. The McInnis Committee also asked PETA about the
Rosebraugh donation. A PETA attorney answered seven questions in

writing and marked them "confidential." PETA maintains that the hearings were merely a politically motivated witch hunt intended to revoke the group's tax-exempt status.[47]

PETA has also taken out full-page ads endorsing ALF criminality. One PETA publication states, "ALF's activities comprise an important part of today's animal protection movement. . . . Without ALF break-ins, many more animals would have suffered."[48] PETA publishes a guidebook called *Becoming an Activist: PETA's Guide to Animal Rights Organizing*, which explicitly instructs members how to articulate a defense of illegal action. In another pamphlet, called *Activism and the Law*, PETA notes that "no struggle against exploitation has been won without illegal actions." Essentially, PETA publishes legal counsel for those contemplating criminal actions.[49] PETA's Bruce Friedrich sums up the group's position on ALF: "If we really believe that animals have the same right to be free from pain and suffering at our hands, then of course we're going to be blowing things up and smashing windows. I think it's a great way to bring about animal liberation, considering the level of suffering, the atrocities. I think it would be great if all of the fast-food outlets, slaughterhouses, these laboratories, and the banks that fund them, exploded tomorrow."[50]

PETA cofounders Alex Pacheco and Ingrid Newkirk have repeatedly expressed support for ALF criminality. Pacheco said that "arson, property destruction, burglary and theft are acceptable crimes when used for the animal cause,"[51] and Newkirk has expressed remorse that she does not personally have the "guts to light a match."[52] Pacheco, who has left PETA and presently works as a fundraiser for the animal rights cause, has acknowledged that PETA serves as a public relations firm for the ALF. In fact, when ALF raided and set fire to a research facility at the University of Arizona, PETA issued press statements and distributed videotapes taken during the raid. After a raid at the Texas Tech University Health Sciences Center that caused $55,000 in damage, PETA issued press releases on behalf of ALF and subsequently filed a lawsuit based on information obtained from the burglary. When arson at the University of California–Davis caused $4.6 million in damage to the Veterinary Diagnostic Laboratory on April 16, 1987, PETA issued a press release and a videotape of the raid the following day. When documents were stolen from the office of Dr. Adrian Morrison at the University of Pennsylvania on January 14, 1990, PETA almost immediately had copies. In 1989 news of a $1 million Texas Tech fire that destroyed research into sleep disorders and Sudden Infant Death Syndrome was publicized by PETA, which again issued a press release on behalf of ALF.[53] Following a 1991 three-alarm fire at a food co-op, PETA explicitly endorsed ALF criminality, stating, "They [ALF] act courageously, risking their freedom and their careers to stop the terror inflicted every day on animals in the labs."[54]

In some cases, PETA action alerts and undercover investigations precipitate ALF crimes, with ALF activists carrying out direct actions against targets publicized by PETA. One such incident involved two PETA investigators who secured jobs as security guards at the Boys Town National Research Hospital in Omaha, Nebraska. The undercover operatives videotaped the lab's operations, providing information that PETA used to file a complaint with government regulators. Although no major violations were noted, the publicity from the incident forced the lab to stop using kittens in experiments. The two principal scientists running the lab were subjected to numerous death threats, bomb threats, and harassing phone calls. In 1996 PETA's Michele Rokke infiltrated Huntingdon Life Sciences, secretly taped lab activities, and stole 8,000 pages of documents. Although Rokke's actions precipitated a lawsuit against PETA, the effort nevertheless served as the genesis for the Stop Huntingdon Animal Cruelty Campaign.[55]

The connection between PETA and ALF involves more than just animal rights rhetoric, media relations, and payment of legal expenses for activists. In fact, it may be fair to say that the border between PETA and ALF is amorphous, and that the notion that they are separate at all is a fiction intended to shield PETA from law enforcement. There is good reason for law enforcement officials to believe that a distinct overlap of PETA and ALF memberships exists. The links between PETA and ALF's Rod Coronado, for example, are substantial. Immediately before and after the 1992 burglary and fire at Michigan State University, two Federal Express packages were sent to a Bethesda, Maryland, address from an individual identifying himself as Leonard Robideau. PETA president Ingrid Newkirk had a PETA employee, Maria Blanton, pick up the first package, but Federal Express employees intercepted the second package. Handwriting analysis confirmed the sender of the second package was Coronado. Ingrid Newkirk had arranged for the packages to be mailed prior to the arson. The second package contained documents stolen from MSU's Dr. Richard Aulerich and a videotape of a perpetrator disguised in a ski mask. Evidence seized from Blanton's home included surveillance logs, code names for Coronado and PETA cofounder Alex Pacheco, burglary tools, two-way radios, night vision goggles, phony identification for Coronado and Pacheco, and animal euthanasia drugs. Federal authorities believe that the evidence shows Coronado and Pacheco also planned a 1990 raid and burglary at Tulane University's Primate Research Center.[56]

On occasion PETA members themselves have crossed the boundaries of legality, carrying out ALF-like direct actions. Protesting the fur trade in support of PETA's ongoing dispute with *Vogue* magazine editor Anna Wintour, activists walked into a restaurant and dropped a dead raccoon on her plate. Typical PETA activist assaults include hurling tofu pies and splashing fur coats with red paint. PETA activists disrupt business at fast-food outlets and light fires at political demonstrations. In March 2000, Chrissie Hynde of the rock band the Pretenders and other PETA activists were arrested for destroying leather clothes at a New York Gap store.[57]

PETA cofounder Alex Pacheco was himself active in the British anti-vivisectionist movement in the 1970s, including time aboard the *Sea Shep-herd*, which rammed fishing and whaling ships. Pacheco was briefly imprisoned after one such ramming incident. Upon his release, he joined the Hunt Saboteurs Association, the predecessor of ALF, still intact today. Pacheco also became acquainted with Kim Stallwood, an alleged ex-ALF member and friend of ALF founder Ronnie Lee. After PETA was formed by Pacheco and Ingrid Newkirk in 1980, Stallwood became the organization's first executive director.[58] Another explicit example of PETA-ALF cross-membership is Gary Yourofsky, who was convicted in Canada of an ALF farm burglary. Yourofsky, who has expressed "unequivocal support" for the death of medical researchers in ALF arsons, was hired by PETA to speak to school children on animal rights issues.[59]

Conclusion

The problem of animal rights criminality has grown far beyond liberating rabbits and guinea pigs from research laboratories. Dr. Jerry Vlasak, a heart surgeon from Los Angeles and member of the radical group Animal Defense League (his wife is the head of SHAC-USA), stated at a 2003 animal rights conference that the assassination of biomedical scientists would save millions of animal lives. "I think violence is part of the struggle against oppression. If something bad happens to these people, it will discourage others. It is inevitable that violence will be used in the struggle and that it will be effective." Vlasak also said, "I don't think you'd have to kill too many. I think for five lives, 10 lives, 15 human lives, we could save one million, two million, 10 million non-human lives."[60] While Dr. Vlasak was positing a hypothetical scenario, an issue of real concern in the biomedical research community must be whether animal rights extremists will choose to test his theory. Also, if the murder of billions of broiler chickens is the moral equivalent of the Jewish or Armenian genocides, would not an animal rights activist understandably view Vlasak's statement as a suggested course of action?[61]

The rationale underlying animal rights criminality taken to its logical conclusion does not bode well for human animals—ALF and SHAC legal disclaimers aside. If humans are indeed the "biggest blight on the face of the earth," then a truly sincere animal rights advocate might not hesitate to release, say, a biological agent (like the newly reconstructed 1918 flu virus) to wipe out tens of millions of people. From the view of an animal rights extremist, such an occurrence would certainly be beneficial for the planet and its non-human inhabitants. In fact, if one accepts the premise that underlies and justifies animal rights criminality, then justice for animals dying in the present "holocaust" would seem to require such action.

Criminality in the Radical Environmental Movement

The development of the first truly radical environmental organization is typical of the process of "progressive radicalization," where efforts such as political lobbying and protest fail to bring about desired change, leading to criminality in the name of the given cause. Just as Paul Watson's departure from Greenpeace precipitated the more proactive and confrontational Sea Shepherd Conservation Society, Dave Foreman began his activism in the environmental mainstream as a conservationist and lobbyist for the Wilderness Society before cofounding Earth First!. Foreman, a one-time staunch conservative and Republican, quickly became disillusioned with Washington politics when he witnessed corruption among fellow environmental lobbyists and the sellout of the cause by Carter administration officials who, he believed, were more concerned with reelection than with the health of the environment. When from 1977 to 1979 the Forest Service's Roadless Area Review and Evaluation II (RARE II) opened up 36 million acres of pristine wilderness for commercial development, Foreman saw this as the complete failure of the mainstream environmental movement and the inability (or unwillingness) of government to protect the natural world.[1]

The beginning of Earth First! is shrouded in myth, but an amalgamation of several existing versions involves a week-long hike by Dave Foreman and four like-minded environmentalists in New Mexico's Pinacate Desert.[2] Regardless of the specifics, the story of the group's founding exemplifies themes central to Earth First! specifically and to the radical environmental movement generally: disaffected activists take a leave from modern technological society and, in a state of removal reminiscent of Native Americans chewing peyote and communing with nature (during the Pinacate hike beer drinking was a central activity), achieve enlightenment of a spiritual nature.[3] In the Earth First! organization's first official action, Foreman and eight others hiked into New Mexico's Gila

Wilderness and erected a plaque in honor of an Apache warrior who had destroyed a mining camp to protect the wilderness from the "destructive activities of the white race."[4] A female Earth First!-er declared the group's position in a subsequent interview: the enemy is not capitalism, socialism, or communism, but corporate industrialism.[5]

The Earth First! founding members were all former mainstream environmentalists who were fed up with the political system and believed that radical action was necessary to avert the imminent environmental crisis. Dave Foreman was joined by a core of environmental activists including Mike Comola, former president of the Montana Wilderness Association; Randall Gloege, a former representative to Friends of the Earth; Susan Morgan, a former education coordinator for the Wilderness Society; Howie Wolke, another former representative to Friends of the Earth; Mike Roselle, a "veteran of many radical, left-wing groups"; and Ron Kezar, a former member of the Sierra Club. At the first annual Round River Rendezvous in DuBois, Wyoming, this core group met with about sixty others to hash out the organizational details and ideological positions of the fledgling movement. The "Circle of Darkness" was created, made up of twelve core members who would decide policy, approve memberships, and generally run the organization.[6] The 1980 Round River Rendezvous also defined Earth First!'s ideology and goals. A memo from Dave Foreman outlined the following principles:

- Wilderness has a right to exist for its own sake.
- All life forms, from a virus to the great whale, have an inherent and equal right to existence.
- Humankind is no greater than any other form of life and has no legitimate claim to dominate Earth.
- Through overpopulation, anthropocentrism, industrialization, excessive energy consumption/resource extraction, state capitalism, father-figure hierarchies, imperialism, pollution, and natural area destruction, humankind threatens the basic life processes of Earth.
- All human decisions should consider Earth first and humankind second.
- The only true test of morality is whether an action—individual, social, or political—benefits Earth.
- Humankind will be happier, healthier, more secure, and more comfortable in a society that recognizes humankind's true biological nature and is in dynamic harmony with the total biosphere.
- Political compromise has no place in the defense of Earth.
- Earth is Goddess and the proper object of human worship.[7]

Although the last item was soon dropped, the religious (and feminist) themes are apparent. By 1984 "deep ecology" (discussed in chapter two) quite naturally became an integral part of Earth First!'s ideology, stressing biocentrism and the equality of all species. Dave Foreman encapsulated the deep ecology mindset taken to its logical extreme when he said, "Gooding's

Onion . . . has a history, has a pedigree on this planet just as long as mine is, and who's to say I have a right to be here, and it doesn't?"[8]

Although Earth First!-ers typically shun philosophy and rely on intuitive feelings and empirical evidence to support their position (early Earth First! newsletters were notably lacking in philosophical discussions), they have no problem identifying the "enemy." American government and corporations are seen as a manifestation of human greed, enabling a destructive cycle of overconsumption and resource depletion. Earth First!-ers have a clear conception of an imminent environmental apocalypse, and they have strong ideas about what needs to be done in order to save as much wilderness as possible for an envisioned postapocalyptic world. The early Earth First! political platform called for a massive increase in designated wilderness areas, the dismantling of all nuclear weapons, the complete cessation of strip mining and uranium mining, a ban on the use of automobiles, and the elimination of dams, roads on public lands, and power plants of any kind. The underlying ideology and resulting politics of Earth First! are uncompromising and require extreme and fundamental changes to modern technological society. Earth First! goals are embodied in another Dave Foreman quote: "If we take the tenets of civilization, psychic, social, sexual and spiritual, and stand them on their head, then we would have a decent basis for a respectable and creative existence."[9] Earth First!-ers do not think of themselves as radicals, but instead view themselves as preservers of all that is good. Their belief system is ultimately millenarian, defining the Earth First! movement as a mission of historic importance, one that will save for future generations what remains of the natural world after the pending environmental catastrophe.[10]

From its inception Earth First! was financially self-sustaining, accepting contributions, distributing a newsletter, and selling t-shirts and other merchandise to support program activities. The Earth First! Foundation was established and touted as a separate entity, and even received tax-exempt status from the IRS. Because hierarchy and entrenched bureaucratic authority were seen as producing the environmental crisis in the first place, the loose coalition of Earth First!-ers that developed across the United States (and eventually the world) rejected a rigid organizational structure or formal constraints on members; rather, the group, or movement, was shaped largely by a shared culture manifested in symbols, stories, and song. The *Earth First! Newsletter* (later just *Earth First!* and then the *Earth First! Journal*) was crucial in developing the membership, providing lists of contacts in regions throughout the United States. A grassroots infrastructure soon developed and made possible the first Earth First! Roadshow in 1981. Leaders such as Foreman and Bart Koehler (performing as "Johnny Sagebrush") toured the nation, staging performances, music, and films with the aim of recruitment, organization, and publicity. Creative traditions became an integral part of the movement—poetry, song, dance, and storytelling contributed to an evolving folklore that was communicated through roadshows, the newsletter, and the annual Round River Rendezvous. This unique Earth First! subculture provided a sense of community and a shared belief system that bound activists together.[11]

The movement was always quite militant in tone, uncompromising in its push to undo civilization—"Back to the Pleistocene!" is one Earth First! slogan.[12] And always coupled with militancy was spirituality: Earth First!-ers were "eco-warriors" engaged in something very much like a holy war, where "ecotage" became a sacrament. Folklore and hyperbole, which were played out dramatically at roadshows and the Round River Rendezvous, propelled the movement forward. These elements are evident in a speech Dave Foreman gave at the 1983 Round River Rendezvous:

> Look at me! Sired by a hurricane, dam'd by an earthquake, half-brother to the cholera, nearly related to the smallpox on my mother's side! Why I could eat 19 oil executives and a barrel of whiskey for breakfast when I'm in robust health, and a dead bulldozer and bushel of dirt-bikers when I'm ailin' . . . I crack Glen Canyon Dam with a glance. The blood of timber executives is my natural drink, and the wail of dying forest supervisors is music to my ears.[13]

The spread of the movement was also fostered by publicity; like most controversial protest movements, Earth First! used high-profile stunts coupled with elaborate props to generate media attention. In the spring of 1981 about seventy-five Earth First!-ers gathered on the Colorado Bridge to protest the existence of Glen Canyon Dam. As the demonstration proceeded, five people scaled a fence and unfurled a three hundred–foot piece of plastic down the face of the dam, producing what appeared to be a huge crack. Edward Abbey, author of *The Monkey Wrench Gang* and the movement's guru, spoke at the event and advocated the razing of the dam and, in a more general way, the subversion of the political-economic system that manufactured the obstruction of the Colorado River. Ecotage, or "monkey wrenching," became an official tool of the movement, with the stated objective of raising public awareness and inflicting economic damage to industries destroying the environment. The destruction of property was seen as necessary, so when "the floundering beast finally, mercifully chokes in its own dung pile, there'll at least be *some* wilderness remaining as a seed bed for planet-wide recovery."[14]

Typical methods of ecotage employed by Earth First!-ers include pulling up survey stakes, dumping sugar in the gas tanks of construction vehicles, and placing metal or ceramic in trees to deter logging; "tree spiking" has been an especially controversial tactic since it poses a physical threat to loggers. On at least one occasion an industrial saw exploded in shrapnel when it hit an embedded spike, seriously injuring an operator. (Although tree spikings are often publicly announced as a warning, the use of ceramic spikes in order to avoid metal detectors is an ominous development.) Other common Earth First! actions include simple trespass and acts of civil disobedience such as "tree-sits," burying oneself up to the neck to prevent the building of a road, or chaining oneself to a piece of construction equipment. Monkey wrenching tactics are featured in the journal *Earth First!*, and Dave Foreman himself wrote a how-to guide called *Ecodefense*. Foreman, affectionately referred to in the movement as "Uncle Digger," long remained a unifying force, writing under pseudonyms in *Earth First!* and generally committing the loose coalition of activists to tactics that included law violation.[15]

Regional Earth First! chapters proliferated in the early and mid-1980s, and the movement soon boasted as many as ten thousand members. Between 1984 and 1987 Earth First! claimed responsibility for hundreds of demonstrations and acts of civil disobedience. The activists were typically quite dedicated, and some campaigns to save wilderness areas lasted for months. Notable actions included major tree spikings in Washington's Wenatchee Forest and Virginia's George Washington National Forest.[16] Other tree spikings were claimed in Oregon by ad hoc groups calling themselves the Hardesty Mountain Avengers and the Bonnie Abbzug Feminist Garden Club.[17] Some international campaigns were undertaken as well, including sustained protests against Central American and Australian deforestation precipitated by the beef industry. In some cases more destructive actions were undertaken, such as the arson of a woodchipping site in Hawaii. In March 1986 a group of Earth First!-ers destroyed the logging equipment of a small Montana company, and in May of the same year a group of saboteurs cut the power lines leading to the Palo Verde nuclear plant near Phoenix.[18]

Although public consciousness was perhaps raised during this time period, little wilderness was protected, since the Reagan administration was especially intractable when it came to more ambitious environmental positions. The overall lack of success coupled with the growing and pluralistic membership eventually fractured Earth First! into two groups. The split was the result of evolving and fundamental differences in the movement's ideology and vision. In one camp was Dave Foreman and like-minded individuals who retreated from the notion that the creation of a postapocalyptic biocentric society was a realistic goal. Those Earth First!-ers in Foreman's corner were misanthropic, saw no hope that human nature could be changed, and merely endeavored to save as much wilderness as possible until the environmental meltdown occurred. In opposition to the Foreman group, which steadfastly valued the natural world over any human concerns, was the faction best represented by another Earth First! founder, Mike Roselle. Earth First!'s social justice faction linked human concerns with environmental needs and embraced the millenarian concept of creating a perfect socially and environmentally responsible society to follow the apocalypse. Throughout the late 1980s the conflict became more pronounced, often played out in the pages of *Earth*

First! and at the Round River Rendezvous. When Foreman suggested eliminating immigration to the United States and returning illegals, the social
justice faction labeled him an "eco-fascist," "redneck," and "right-wing
thug." To Foreman, the social justice group were "West Coast hippies"
adhering to a "woo-woo" culture—a derisive term for the mystical–
pagan–eco-feminism that had co-opted Earth First!. A series of articles
published in *Earth First!* written by Christopher Manes (under the pseudonym Miss Ann Thropy) amplified the debate; Manes suggested that the
global AIDS crisis just might present a viable solution to the human overpopulation problem.[19] Massive decreases in the human population (especially *disadvantaged* persons) did not resonate well with the social justice
camp, however beneficial it might be for the planet.

The final split of Earth First! occurred in 1990 after the death of Edward
Abbey in 1989 and the arrest of five Earth First!-ers in a major FBI sting.
Beginning in 1987, a small cell of Earth First!-ers calling themselves the
Evan Mecham Eco-Terrorist International Conspiracy (EMETIC) began a
campaign against the commercial development of sacred Navajo and
Hopi land. The group attacked the Fairfield Snow Bowl ski resort twice,
severing bolts on chair lift towers and cutting the lift's main support
pylon. In another action, EMETIC cut twenty-nine power poles at the
Grand Canyon Uranium Mine, costing the company $200,000. What
EMETIC didn't know was that they were the subject of a million-dollar
FBI investigation and had been infiltrated by an undercover agent who
had emotionally manipulated a female member of the cell. On May 31,
1989, the group set out to cut power lines that fed the Central Arizona
water lift project but was stopped when agent Mike Fain released a signal
flare, triggering the descent of fifty FBI officers. Although he was not
present at the action, Dave Foreman, the true target, was later indicted for
allegedly financing the project and distributing copies of *Ecodefense* to the
group. Four EMETIC members ended up with jail sentences, but Foreman
negotiated a guilty plea to a felony conspiracy charge and was given five
years probation. The FBI infiltration, the ideological schism, and the
death of the man who had created the prototype for the movement
proved to be too great a strain, and Foreman and his followers officially
departed from Earth First! on September 22, 1990.[20]

After the split, Earth First! continued to grow, now solidly controlled
by the millenarian social justice faction. A 1990 CBS *Sixty Minutes* episode
highlighted both Foreman and Darryl Cherney; on national television
Cherney infamously proclaimed, "If I knew I had a fatal disease, I would
definitely do something like strap dynamite on myself and take out
Grand Canyon Dam." Subscriptions to the *Earth First! Journal* subsequently soared.[21] Judi Bari became a leading activist in the new Earth
First!, organizing the Redwood Summer campaign in 1990 to protest logging in Northern California. Moving away from the "macho, beer-
drinking tradition," Bari eschewed sabotage and tree spiking, even finding

common ground with loggers by forming an alliance with the radical labor group Industrial Workers of the World. One of the most publicized chapters in Earth First! history occurred in May 1990 when a bomb exploded under a car carrying Bari and Daryl Cherney. Judi Bari was seriously injured, suffering a broken back and shattered pelvis. The FBI arrested Cherney and Bari, but eventually dropped the charges and declined to investigate further. The two Earth First!-ers then filed a civil rights action against the FBI, and were vindicated at a 2002 trial when a jury awarded them $4.4 million (posthumously for Bari, as she succumbed to cancer in 1997). Evidence at the trial clearly showed that FBI agents fed false information to the Oakland police that was later used to obtain search warrants and make unlawful arrests. The car bombing remains unsolved.[22]

From the early 1990s on, Earth First! evolved into a large, international ecological movement, far removed from the small, insular entity envisioned by Dave Foreman in 1980. Moreover, despite claims that Earth First! has no organizational structure, membership, or leadership, the broad movement includes numerous incorporated organizations, such as Daily Planet Publishing (which puts out the *Earth First! Journal*), the Fund for Wild Nature (previously the Earth First! Foundation), the Trees Foundation, and the Earth First! Direct Action Fund. These tax-exempt foundations rely on private donations to finance a broad variety of Earth First! projects and campaigns, including the establishment of spin-off groups such as Mike Roselle's Rainforest Action Network (RAN) and the Ruckus Society.[23] The current Earth First! website has links to numerous regional and international EF! chapters, including EF! Cascadia, EF! Britain, EF! Melbourne, EF! Netherlands, EF! Prague, and Sierra Nevada EF!, with additional chapters in Poland, Nigeria, Mexico, and the Philippines (a partial list). Coordination and leadership within the movement occur at dozens of regional Earth First! chapters, a structurally sound approach that provides activists with the flexibility to respond to local needs.[24] There may be as many as several hundred Earth First! entities in America, with at least fifty in other nations. A precise tally is impossible, as many groups are ad hoc, forming and disbanding as regional issues and campaigns arise. The Earth First! movement includes many affiliated groups in addition to those local chapters that adopt the EF! moniker.[25] See Table 5.1 for a partial list of organizations the Earth First! website lists as contacts or affiliates.

The "big tent" approach adopted by the social justice faction has indeed enlarged the Earth First! movement, drawing in a diverse crowd of activists. Recent Earth First! letter-writing campaigns exemplify the broad social justice orientation of the movement, and include anti–Iraq war petitions as well as efforts such as "Save the Barents Sea," "Stop Office Max," "Impeach Bush Now," and "Stop the Seal Pup Slaughter." The eco-feminist influence seems to be particularly strong. Mission statements emphasize the social justice and feminist orientation of the movement,

Table 5.1
Earth First! Affiliates

Biodiversity Liberation Front	Blue Mountains Biodiversity Project
Cascadia Forest Alliance	Cascadia Forest Defenders
Church of Deep Ecology	Coastwatch
Cold Mountain/Cold Rivers	Cove Mallard Coalition
Daily Planet Publishing, Inc.	Direct Action Fund
Earth Defense Education Project	End Corporate Dominance
Environmentally Sound Promotions	Foghorn
Fairfax Action Team	Friends of the Wolf
Flagstaff Activist Network	Lawrence Grassroots Initiative
Forest Ecosystems Action Group	Lost Cause Collective
Green Vigilance	Mountain Eco-Collective
League of Wilderness Defenders	Pink Planarians
Mass Direct Action	Project Harmony
New Mexico Direct Action	Rustic Revolt
Popular Power	Slingshot
Redwood Action Team	Tornado Alley Resistance
Shuksan Direct Action	Warrior Poets Society
Stone Soup Collective	Wilderness Defense
Unci Maka Uonihanpo	
Wild Wasatch Front	
Zero Xtract from Public Lands	

Source: http://www.activistcash.com

stressing the importance of fighting patriarchy and oppression right along with racism, the plight of indigenous peoples, and the degradation of the environment.[26] A fall 2005 issue of the *Earth First! Journal* featured an article about the rape of a female activist, and a recent letter-writing campaign targeted Nigerian authorities who sentenced a woman to death (by stoning) for adultery. Recent statements in the Earth First! literature generally note the importance of elevating environmental concerns to the level of human interests[27]—a subtle but significant shift, since this implies that Earth no longer necessarily comes first. So although a broad social justice orientation undeniably expanded Earth First! into an international mass movement, the question of whether it is effectively promoting its original biocentric goals is debatable. Certainly Earth First! at present little resembles the entity Dave Foreman and a small group of activists began in 1980. In fact, it may be more appropriate to describe today's Earth First! as a collection of social movements loosely tied together under a familiar banner.

Not everything in Earth First! has changed over the years. The Round River Rendezvous tradition continues—in 2005 the twenty-fifth anniversary event included a week-long party in the woods, with a range of activities and workshops (including "action planning and civil disobedience training") that culminated in a final day set apart for "actions!". Similar annual meetings are held in other countries, and "action camps" and related training and orientation seminars abound. Earth First! continues to promote using "all the tools in the toolbox," from lobbying and litigation to protest and monkey wrenching. Civil disobedience in the form of tree sitting and physically blocking logging roads continues to be very popular (and sometimes effective) among Earth First! activists. The sense of urgency and militancy within the movement has not waned. A recent *Earth First! Journal* article decrying the war in Iraq proclaimed, "By every means necessary we will bring this and every other empire down! Mutiny and sabotage in defense of Mother Earth!" Concerning informants, another *Journal* contributor wrote, "A snitch is no longer entitled to basic expectations of safety. As such, it is righteous to hurt them, burn down their house or do similarly naughty things to them." A 2002 *Journal* piece listed the names and addresses of employees who worked for the biotechnology company Monsanto, explicitly endorsing intimidation and harassment of those "eco-terrorists."[28] Other Earth First!-ers have expressed support for methods employed by the animal rights group Stop Huntingdon Animal Cruelty (SHAC), which expands the environmentalists' toolbox to include threats and violence against people.[29]

The effectiveness of Earth First! has been piecemeal, with the group typically halting some commercial development but never altering public policies in a meaningful way. One thing that Earth First! has accomplished is to make previously labeled "radical environmental" organizations such as Greenpeace and the Sierra Club seem politically moderate. Dave Foreman's mentor, David Brower, said, "The Sierra Club made the Nature Conservancy look reasonable. I founded Friends of the Earth to make the Sierra Club look reasonable. Then I founded Earth Island Institute to make Friends of the Earth look reasonable. Earth First! now makes us look reasonable. We're still waiting for someone else to come along and make Earth First! look reasonable."[30] Brower would not have to wait very long.

Earth Liberation Front (ELF)

The Earth Liberation Front (ELF)[31] is a radical spin-off of Earth First! that describes itself as "an international underground organization that uses direct action in the form of economic sabotage to stop the exploitation and destruction of the natural environment."[32] Unlike Earth First!, ELF activists do not generally have plans for a postapocalyptic world; they are geared toward preventing the environmental apocalypse from happening. The organization is believed to have started in Brighton, England, in 1992 when Earth First! activists decided to distance themselves from illegal activities. The idea of "decoupling" aboveground from underground operations took hold in the United States shortly thereafter. In a 1994 *Earth First! Journal* article U.S. Earth First! activist Judi Bari wrote, "England Earth First has been taking some necessary steps to separate above ground clandestine activities. . . . If we are serious about our movement in the U.S., we will do the same. . . . It's time to leave the night work to the elves in the woods."[33] The rationale underlying ELF actions and the group's modus operandi are summarized succinctly on the first page of the "frequently asked questions" section of the North American Earth Liberation Front Press Office (NAELFPO) website:

> The ELF realizes the profit motive caused and reinforced by the capitalist society is destroying all life on this planet. The only way, at this point in time, to stop that continued destruction of life is to by any means necessary take the profit out of killing.[34]

In terms of structure and mode of operation, ELF models itself on its "sister organization," the Animal Liberation Front (ALF). There is no official membership or organizational hierarchy. However, there is one important aboveground organizational structure: the NAELFPO, centered in Portland, Oregon, publishes and distributes organization literature and a recruitment video, and reports on ELF actions and communiqués. ELF and ALF activists sometimes work together and claim joint responsibility for actions, and there is good reason to believe that many individuals are active in both movements. Radical icon Rod Coronado is a case in point, having participated in the Sea Shepherd Conservation Society, ALF, and Earth First!. Structurally, ELF operates in small, autonomous cells of two to five people. Anonymity is guaranteed by this loose, fluid, and ad hoc structure; members of one cell are unknown to members of other cells, so it is impossible to say just how many ELF activists there are.[35] ELF guidelines, published by the NAELFPO, are as follows:

1. To cause as much economic damage as possible to a given entity that is profiting off the destruction of the natural environment and life for selfish greed and profit

2. To educate the public on the atrocities committed against the environment and life

3. To take all necessary precautions against harming life[36]

Anyone who follows the guidelines is considered a member of ELF. Because of the anonymity necessary to thwart law enforcement, joining an existing ELF cell is difficult, if not impossible. "Wannabees" are simply encouraged to find some sincere, trustworthy companions and begin operations.[37]

The first ELF actions in the United States occurred in 1996, when on three separate occasions McDonald's restaurants had their locks glued and were spray-painted with slogans. Then in October 1996 a U.S. Forest Service pickup truck was torched in Detroit, Oregon, and arson destroyed a Forest Service ranger station in Eugene, Oregon, causing $5 million in damage.[38] An anonymous communiqué posted to the Internet in 1997 taunted law enforcers, claimed affinity with other movements, and announced ELF aims and ideology:

> Welcome to the struggle of all species to be free. We are the burning rage of a dying planet. . . . The war of greed ravages the earth and species die out every day. ELF works to speed up the collapse of industry, to scare the rich, and to undermine the foundations of the state. We embrace social and deep ecology as a practical resistance movement. We have to show the enemy that we are serious about defending what is sacred. Together we have teeth and claws to match our dreams. Our greatest weapons are imagination and the ability to strike when least expected.
>
> Since 1992 a series of earth nights and Halloween smashes has mushroomed around the world. 1000s of bulldozers, powerlines, computer systems, buildings and valuable equipment have been composted. Many ELF actions have been censored to prevent our bravery from inciting others to take action.
>
> We take inspiration from Luddites, Levellers, Diggers, the Autonome squatter movement, the ALF, the Zapatistas, and the little people—those mischievous elves of lore. Authorities can't see us because they don't believe in elves. We are practically invisible. We have no command structure, no spokespersons, no office, just many small groups working separately, seeking vulnerable targets and practicing our craft.
>
> Many elves are moving to the Pacific Northwest and other sacred areas. Some elves will leave surprises as they go. Find your family! And let's dance as we make ruins of the corporate money system.[39]

Since 1997 ELF has been responsible for numerous criminal actions ranging from vandalism to arson, causing over $100 million in damage. ELF actions have been claimed across North America, throughout Europe, and in South America, and have been perpetrated to highlight a variety of issues, including urban sprawl, deforestation, ecosystem destruction, the use of "slave labor" by corporations, and the production and distribution of genetically modified crops.[40] One of ELF's most infamous actions occurred on October 18, 1998, when activists simultaneously burned five buildings and four ski lifts at the Vail ski resort in Colorado, causing over $26 million in damage. The following communiqué accompanied these actions:

> On behalf of the lynx, five buildings and four ski lifts at Vail were reduced to ashes on the night of Sunday, October 18th. Vail, Inc. is already the largest ski operation in North America and now wants to expand even further. The 12 miles of roads and 885 acres of clearcuts will ruin the last, best lynx habitat in the state. Putting profits ahead of Colorado's wildlife will not be tolerated. This action is just a warning. We will be back if this greedy corporation continues to trespass into wild and unroaded areas. For your safety and convenience, we strongly advise skiers to choose other destinations until Vail cancels its inexcusable plans for expansion.[41]

An anonymous communiqué that accompanied a December 27, 1998, arson at the corporate office of U.S. Forest Industries in Medford, Oregon, was less cordial:

> To celebrate the holidays we decided on a bonfire. Unfortunately for U.S. Forest Industries it was at their corporate headquarters office. . . . On the foggy night after Christmas, when everyone was digesting their turkey and pie, Santa's ELFs dropped two five-gallon buckets of diesel/unleaded mix and a gallon jug with cigarette delays; which proved to be more than enough to get this party started. This was in retribution for all the wild forests and animals lost to feed the wallets of greedy fucks like [name deleted], U.S.F.I. president . . . and it's a warning to all others responsible, we do not sleep and we won't quit.[42]

ELF's most destructive action occurred on August 1, 2003, when activists burned down a condominium complex in San Diego and destroyed a 100-foot crane, causing an estimated $50 million in damage. A 12-foot banner bearing the ELF acronym read, "If you build it, we will burn it."[43]

Like its counterparts in the animal liberation movement, ELF has grown increasingly radical, with some activists expressing support for violence against people. After a 2002 arson that caused $700,000 in damage at a U.S. Forest Service research facility in Irvine, Pennsylvania, a communiqué claiming responsibility for the crime stated, "While innocent life will never be harmed in any action we undertake, where it is necessary we will no longer hesitate to pick up the gun to implement justice, and provide the needed protection for our planet that decades of legal battles, pleading, protest, and economic sabotage have failed so drastically to achieve."[44] ELF feels that its hand has been forced, and it is clear that the promise not to harm "innocent life" does not include any persons deemed guilty of harming the environment.

Like the social justice faction of Earth First!, ELF has increasingly linked its environmental cause with related "justice" endeavors. In addition to striking at those directly responsible for deforestation and ecosystem destruction, the ELF target list has expanded to highlight various issues, including the antiwar movement, urban sprawl, the exploitation of workers, and genetically modified crops. Nike retail outlets, SUV dealerships, unfinished housing projects, and university offices and labs have all become targets of ELF attacks. The destruction of a truck and spray-painted slogans on vehicles at a military recruiting station in Montgomery, Alabama, in March 2003 were later claimed by ELF to be a direct action to protest the ongoing war in Iraq.[45]

Politically, ELF activists lean toward anarchism or are themselves anarchists who see the destruction of the global capitalist economic system as a necessary prerequisite to saving life on Earth. Craig Rosebraugh and Leslie James Pickering, press officers for the NAELFPO from 1997 to 2001, went on to form Arissa, an organization dedicated to the violent overthrow of the U.S. government. Citing the founding fathers and events such as the Boston Tea Party, Rosebraugh and many other environmental and animal rights activists view themselves as patriots or freedom fighters who merely advocate the same violent methods to achieve their aims as did the men who engineered the American Revolution. (In an online statement protesting the Iraq war, Rosebraugh recommended urban riots and attacks on military, financial, and media centers as means to disrupt the war machine.)[46]

Appearing before a congressional hearing in 2002, Craig Rosebraugh explained the invocation of his Fifth Amendment right, saying, "In light of the events on September 11, my country has told me that I should not cooperate with terrorists. I therefore am refusing to cooperate with members of Congress who are some of the most extreme terrorists in history."[47] The cognitive elements in this statement are clear and exemplify the mind-set of activists throughout the radical animal liberation and environmental movements. The people burning down buildings are not terrorists; rather, the U.S. government and greedy corporations that are destroying the environment are the *real* terrorists. In what is seen as a just war to save the planet and its non-human inhabitants, those dedicated to direct action increasingly feel that the realization of their goals justify whatever means are necessary to achieve them.

Structure and Modus Operandi
of Radical Movements

A key to understanding any social phenomenon is to examine its structure and method of operation. Criminality associated with animal liberation and environmental extremism is not well organized, and the individuals and small groups who carry out illegal acts are not part of any formal organization with a rigid authority structure. In fact, the extremist mass movements called animal liberation and radical environmentalism lack agreed-upon goals, let alone features such as task specialization or a rational division of labor. Underground activists in ELF and ALF typically operate in small cells of two to five people, and sometimes they work alone. Moreover, these cells or individuals are completely autonomous, working independently of other groups. For security purposes, the members of different cells remain anonymous, so there is no communication among cell members. The criminal component that attacks research laboratories and liberates animals is but one small segment of a much larger social movement, many of whose members eschew criminality and are bound only loosely by the goals of wilderness preservation and the amelioration of animal suffering. Because underground activists remain anonymous and isolated, their success depends critically on aboveground members in the movement, who provide support and direction.

The method employed by the animal rights/liberation and radical environmental movements—and the much smaller segment devoted to criminal direct action—may be best characterized as leaderless resistance, in which small groups and individuals fight entrenched power through independent acts of criminality. The technique was popularized by Louis Beam as a means for white nationalists to continue their struggle against the government.[1] (Interestingly, leaderless resistance was first used effectively in the United States by right-wing single-issue terror groups such as the The Order, the Posse Comitatus, and The Covenant, the Sword, and the Arm of the Lord.) Leaderless resistance is effective in splitting a movement or organization into an aboveground sector that deals with propaganda and an underground portion that engages in criminal acts. The maintenance of aboveground operatives is especially important in providing at least a perception of legitimacy to the given movement and communicating agendas to underground operatives; in short, the aboveground sector is essential if there is to be any hope for political change. Hence, the Irish Republican Army (IRA) has Sinn Fein, and the Animal Liberation Front has PETA.

Although animal liberation and radical environmentalism are social movements devoid of organizational structure or formal leadership, organs *within* the broad stream of activism include incorporated organizations and public figures who may be viewed as ideological/motivational leaders. Groups like PETA, the Earth First! Foundation, and SHAC USA are nonprofit, tax-exempt organizations, incorporated to provide direction, disseminate information, inspire underground activists, and even provide financial support for direct action—all the while attempting to maintain plausible deniability by maintaining an arm's-length relationship with underground elements. This decoupling method has not been entirely successful (see chapter eight). Also, while there may be no official leaders in leaderless resistance movements, in the realm of animal rights and environmental radicalism there are nevertheless authors, public figures, and press officers who provide inspiration and ideological support; Ingrid Newkirk, Peter Singer, Steven Best, Edward Abbey, Paul Watson, Craig Rosebraugh, Leslie James Pickering, and Dave Foreman are just a few relevant examples. Movement icons are especially important and provide inspiration; Barry Horne, for example, engaged in several lengthy hunger strikes and died while incarcerated for animal liberation crimes, and Julia "Butterfly" Hill holds the record for the longest tree sit (about two years).

The central role of movement elites has been examined by social scientist Lyle Munro, who refers to the process of cognitive praxis. According to Munro, the core identity of a social movement, composed of prominent aboveground figures, fills the crucial role of a "knowledge-router and bearer of new ideas."[2] Other researchers support Munro's position: Ron Eyerman and Andrew Jamieson have concluded that movement intellectuals are crucial to the success of any social movement.[3] In any event, the animal liberation and radical environmental movements are represented by a relatively small cadre (perhaps only a few dozen) of high-profile elites who, at least in part, attempt to provide the appearance of legitimacy to social movements frequently characterized by criminality.

Wesley Jamison uses a stratification pyramid to conceptualize the structure of the animal rights mass movement. Jamison says that "influential members" compose the top 1%; the Peter Singers, Ingrid Newkirks, and Steven Bests of the movement have advanced philosophical notions, are uncompromising, and devote a significant amount of time and resources to the cause. "Active members," perhaps 4% to 5% of the entire movement, are less stable philosophically but are emotionally invested and devoted to the movement; these are the (usually younger) underground direct activists who perpetrate crimes. Jamison's third tier comprises what he calls "attentive members," who make up 10% of the movement; they have less stable political views, may not even distinguish between animal welfare and animal rights, and tend to be older and more pragmatic. Members of the third tier pay attention to what's going on, contribute money, and are concerned about the welfare of animals. "General members" are by far the largest group (85%) and fill the base of Jamison's pyramid; they are not very devoted to the cause, are unacquainted with underlying philosophical issues, and must be motivated to become involved or contribute money.[4]

In no way a part of the animal liberation and environmental movements, the news media plays an important role and is crucial to the success of any social movement. The media communicates agendas and strategies to anonymous and independent cell members. Actions widely covered by the media are copied by sympathizers, and highly successful operations that are publicized can be used to inspire potential recruits. In fact, generating favorable news coverage intended to influence the general public remains an important issue in both movements and, along with questions of morality, frames the debate as to which methods, including the use of violence, are appropriate to achieve animal liberation and environmental justice.

Direct Action and the Issue of Violence

A major debate continues in both the radical environmental and animal liberation movements as to the morality and efficacy of illegal direct actions as a means to achieve movement goals. A large number of folks, even within the more radical sectors of each movement, eschew violence against people and property destruction not only because it is morally questionable but also because illegal actions are seen as undermining their cause. Ultimately, for radical environmentalism and animal liberation to win the day, the majority in society must accept their fundamental premises as legitimate; obviously, threats, violence, and arson are behaviors that do nothing to promote societal legitimacy. In the other camp are those extremists who argue that anything less than a violent reaction to factory farming, vivisection, and environmental degradation amounts to speciesism or is a sellout. And so the argument continues, with divergent methods within the movements reflecting differences in opinion and moral calculus.[5]

Direct actions exist on a continuum, from legal actions at one pole, through acts of civil disobedience and open rescues (in which activists free animals but accept responsibility and pay for any damages to property), progressing finally to acts of property destruction, arson, and even violent attacks against people. In order to assess the methods employed by radical environmental and animal liberation activists, the following classification scheme delineates various direct actions on a continuum of criminality. (Legal methods such as lawful protest, outreach education, advertising, and political lobbying are not included here.)

> **Type I:** Minor crimes involving little or no property damage (less than $10,000, the limit to invoke federal law) and no threat of human injury
>
> **Type II:** Significant acts of property damage, including arson and bombings, whose damages exceed $10,000, no intended violence against humans but with an indirect threat of physical harm
>
> **Type III:** Threatening behavior directed against people, including minor physical assaults producing no injuries
>
> **Type IV:** Physical attacks against persons in which injury actually occurs or is intended

The types are not necessarily progressive in terms of criminal liability. Legal statutes, and most persons with an opinion on the topic, would not consider throwing a tofu pie in someone's face (Type III) to be more serious than a multi-million-dollar arson (Type II). In my scheme, Type I and Type II crimes should be viewed as a subgroup (united by the common element of not targeting human beings for threat or attack), and Type III and Type IV as a second subgroup (with the two types sharing the element of specifically targeting human beings). In this scheme, Type II is more serious than Type I (primarily in terms of the amount of property damage caused), and Type IV is more serious than Type III. All Type IV crimes fit the definition of terrorism, while only some Type III crimes do (bomb hoaxes, for example). Because Type II crimes do not involve the targeting of humans, labeling these actions as terrorism is debatable and would depend on the definition used (certainly the FBI would call arson in defense of animals terrorism). Type I crimes are not acts of terrorism, and at worst should be considered acts of ideological vandalism.

Using the most readily accessible online sources, a database has been prepared with the aim of providing a broad overview of the types of illegal actions performed by underground activists. Sources include http://www.directaction.info/library, the National Animal Interest Alliance website at http://www.naiaonline.org, http://www.animalliberation.net, the "Diary of Actions" at http://www.earthliberationfront.com, and the *2001 Year-End Direct Action Report*. Ron Arnold's 1997 book *Ecoterror* contains an extensive chronology of events and was also used. Limitations in the database are evident, and in no way should it be viewed as exhaustive. Although numerous sources were accessed, it was impossible to determine if all reported actions actually occurred. Small-scale animal

Table 6.1
Typology of Criminal Actions

Type I	Type II
Civil disobedience	Destroying logging equipment
Trespassing	Torching sport utility vehicles
Protesting without a permit	Setting fire to research laboratories
Open animal rescue	Tree spiking
Hanging banners	Large-scale animal rescue
Blocking logging roads	Use of firebombs/incendiary devices
Pulling up survey stakes	
Tree sitting	
Spray-painting slogans	
Gluing locks	
Smashing windows	
Type III	**Type IV**
E-mail threats	Murder
Bomb hoaxes	Beatings
Placing harassing phone calls	Bombings
Rigging mail with razor blades	Actions causing personal injury
Publicizing personal financial data	Actions intended to cause personal
Staging demonstrations at private homes	injury
Defacing private homes with graffiti	
Splashing people with red paint	*Hypothetical*
Pelting people with tofu pies	Biological attacks
Leaving dead animals on dinner plates	Poisoning of aquifer

rescues and minor acts of vandalism are not widely reported in the media; reported actions on movement websites could be fabricated and damage estimates inflated. It is reasonable to assume that the database contains only a fraction of all animal liberation and radical environmental actions over the time period studied (some sources contained numerous actions for a given year, but had no data for other years). Minor Type I crimes were probably underreported in the sources and, if so, are under-represented in the database. Countless minor acts of civil disobedience in defense of the environment from around the world were not included; in fact, the database includes few reports of criminal environmental actions outside the United States, an omission that cannot be viewed as indicating a lack of radical environmental actions internationally. Many actions from Europe are included, but foreign media accounts were not used; the emphasis was on criminality in the United States. For this reason, reliable conclusions about the relative frequency and severity of acts between the United States and other countries are difficult to extrapolate from the data. In addition, some error likely occurred in classifying actions—in particular, where damage estimates were missing or vague, determining whether an action was Type I or Type II was difficult. One database not used, the New Scotland Animal Rights Index, documented 2,980 animal rights incidents in the United Kingdom from just 1990 to 1992. Because these figures were not included in the database (total actions for the United Kingdom were 278, or 9.8% of the total), it is fair to conclude, based on the best available evidence, that animal rights criminality has been more frequent in the United Kingdom than anywhere else (and, as will be seen, more willing to target human beings).[6]

The total number of illegal actions in the database is 2,836. Actions recorded date from 1956 to late 2005. As the following analysis demonstrates, the vast majority of crimes perpetrated by animal liberationists and environmental radicals are not properly classified as terrorism (although many of the actions do share the common element of coercion for the purpose of altering human behavior). The most common types of actions involved broken windows, glued locks, spray-painted slogans, and the removal of a few animals from a farm or lab. While some actions were as innocuous as liberating a mouse or a minnow, at the other end of the spectrum were acts of arson causing millions of dollars in damage, incendiary devices planted under the vehicles of research scientists, grave robbery, threats against children, physical assaults, and murder. (Contrary to the oft-repeated claim by activists, people have been injured, some seriously, and in 2001 a radical animal rights activist murdered Dutch politician Pim Fortuyn.) The total number of Type I acts of criminality, those that caused less than $10,000 in property damage and threatened no humans, is 1,813, or 63.9% of the total. The total number of Type II actions, those that caused more than $10,000 in damages to property and in some cases indirectly threatened human injury, was 664, or 23.4% of the total. A subcategory of Type II actions, arsons and bombings undertaken without intent to harm humans, composed 10.4% of the total. Threats and minor assaults against humans (Type III) constituted 9.7% of the total; and Type IV crimes, in which humans were injured or serious human harm was intended, composed 2.9% of the total.

Criminal actions were further coded as being either in defense of the environment or in defense of animals. The vast majority of observations were in defense of animals (88.6%), with actions in defense of the environment accounting for 11.4% of the total. Again, while radical environmental actions were almost certainly underreported internationally, it seems reasonable to conclude, based on the data, that animal liberationists are more energized compared with radical environmentalists, and that the radical environmental movement is most active in the United States. Although animal liberationists committed more actions than radical environmentalists across all four category types, proportionately the animal activists were less likely to engage in arson and bombings. Thirty-one percent of environmental actions were arsons or bombings, while only 7.8% of animal actions were in that category. On the other hand, animal activists were more likely to directly target human beings for threats and violence: 10.3% of animal actions were Type III, while only 4.9% of environmental actions were in that category. Three percent of animal actions fell into Type IV, while 2.5% of environmental actions were Type IV.

Geographically, the vast majority of all actions occurred in North America and Europe, with 47.5% occurring in the United States, followed by 9.8% in Great Britain. However, as previously noted, the New Scotland Animal Rights Index, which has catalogued thousands of animal rights crimes in Great Britain, was not included here. Obviously, Great Britain sees the greatest number of animal rights crimes. Using just the present data, we find that Great Britain also suffers a greater proportion of threats, physical attacks, and fire-bombings directed at humans: 37.1% of all Type III crimes occurred in North America compared to 51.3% in Great Britain, while 22.6% of Type IV crimes were recorded in North America compared to 66.7% in Great Britain.

A heavy concentration of animal rights activity was located in the Scandinavian countries, with Sweden leading with 9.5% of all records in the database. Other countries represented in the database include Finland, Canada, Norway, Austria, Belgium, Denmark, France, Germany, Ireland, Italy, the Netherlands, Poland, Slovakia, Spain, Australia, New Zealand, Israel, Switzerland, and Iceland. A few crimes were recorded in Brazil, and one unlawful PETA protest occurred in Beijing, China. Not included in the present database were actions by the Russian ALF.

While for a large number of records the group or individual responsible for the criminal action was not known, by far the single most prolific group was the Animal Liberation Front. Perpetrating crimes in nearly every country mentioned, ALF was responsible for 1,116 actions, or 39.3% of all events recorded. Other groups committing a significant but much smaller number of actions include the Earth Liberation Front, Earth First!, the Justice Department, the Animal Rights Militia, Stop Huntingdon Animal Cruelty (SHAC), the Paint Panthers, and the Wild Minks (a complete list of all groups represented in the database is presented in Appendix A).

Other Surveys

A survey of national forests by Forest Service Special Agent Ben Hull found that in an eighteenth-month period from 1987 to 1988 there were 219 serious acts of vandalism to Forest Service or contractors' property, amounting to $4.5 million in damage. In addition, forty-two letters were received threatening vandalism or sabotage of logging equipment, and thirty-two demonstrations temporarily halted logging operations, resulting in $201,000 in losses. In this survey, 75% of all illegal activity occurred in the Pacific Northwest or the Northern Rockies.[7]

The Animal Enterprise Protection Act passed by Congress in 1992 mandated the compilation and analysis of documented animal rights-related crimes in the United States. The U.S. Justice Department compiled a database of 313 individual acts of animal rights crimes committed between 1977 and June 30, 1993. The Animal Liberation Front was responsible for approximately 60% of the crimes recorded. The study found that numerous kinds of animal enterprises were targeted, led by university facilities (20%), fur retailers (16%), individuals/private residences (14%), butcher shops and delis (11%), food production facilities (9%), and private research facilities (7%). By far, the most common type of act was vandalism causing minor property damage (51%), followed by the theft or release of animals (25%), threats against individuals (9%), major property destruction (8%), arson (7%), bomb threats (5%), fire-bombings (4%), and bomb hoaxes (3%). Two incidents involving a personal attack or assault, and one assassination attempt numbered among the total of 313 incidents. During the sixteen-year time period animal rights crimes were recorded in twenty-eight states and the District of Columbia, 46% of the total occurred in California. Only a handful of acts occurred in the late 1970s and early 1980s, followed by a rapid increase in the late 1980s then a precipitous decline in the early 1990s. The authors of the Justice Department report concluded that the underreporting of animal rights–related crimes and limitations in the study's methodology meant that the true total of all incidents was far greater than the reported 313.[8]

How-to Guides

Supporting the animal liberationist and radical environmentalist's penchant for illegal actions is a fairly significant body of literature best characterized as direct action how-to guides. Animal rights terrorist manuals prepared in Great Britain include sophisticated details on how to form criminal cells, build and deploy bombs, cover trails, and utilize the media for maximum effect. A 1986 manual titled *Action for Animals* tells how to force cars off the road, gather intelligence, bypass security systems, bug phone lines, and cause maximum damage to research facilities. Advice for evading capture includes suggestions such as duct-taping sneakers, discarding clothes, and sharpening crowbars and bolt cutters to leave no traceable markings.[9] Publications readily available on the ALF website include *Arson Around with Auntie ALF, Setting Fires with Electrical Timers*, and *The ALF Primer*—all quite instructive. For example, *The ALF Primer* contains sections titled "Finding People to Work With," "Getting Started," "Planning," "Preparation," and "Security." The primer contains explicit instructions for illegal actions, ranging from gluing locks to setting fires to releasing animals from secure facilities. Much of the guide is rather facile, reflecting the nature of most animal rights–related attacks (relatively minor property crime).[10] The section titled "Windows" includes the following passage:

> Windows are probably the easiest target available in most situations, yet large windows can cost hundreds, making them an ideal target. Glass etching fluid (hydrofluoric acid) is available in some larger arts and crafts stores. Be sure to buy out of town on specialized items like this. Its [sic] a liquid cream that eats through the surface of glass. If you can get a hold of some, put it in some kind of squeeze bottle, one of those plastic lemon ones for instance, and off you go. If you get the cream it can also be applied with a paint brush, allowing slogans to be written on the window. Its [sic] potent stuff, so be careful not to get it on your skin. Working quickly at the target youll [sic] probably make somewhat of a mess with the bottle, so bring a plastic bag to throw it in after you are done. Its [sic] a quick and relatively safe way to cause some financial damage. A less expensive but much noisier method is simply smashing windows. It is loud, so get ready to run. Aside from throwing a brick or rock, a popular way to do this is with a sling shot. They are available in many sporting stores. You may have to patronize a store that sells hunting equipment to find one, but you can always offset this by returning at a later date and smashing their windows in turn.[11]

Other sections of *The ALF Primer* discuss using paint bombs, vandalizing cars, bypassing security shutters on storefronts, dismantling phone lines and security cameras, and clogging public toilets—hardly the stuff of terrorism. However, the primer does contain an extensive section on arson. In this section, as throughout the manual, the author's position remains consistent with the ALF tenet of causing no injury to animals or people. For constructing incendiary devices, the author warns followers away from other Internet sites, including The Anarchist's Cookbook, reportedly written by a "right wing individual" who purposefully used faulty recipes to injure and kill. The guide notes that arson carries the tag of terrorism and must "be used wisely as not to discredit the entire movement." The methods described for starting fires range from the simple to the complex, with explicit instructions for each type. Simple timed devices using plastic bottles filled with flammable liquid, sponges, candles, and matches are described. Placed between the bottles, the candles melt down to the matches and sponges, which burn and melt the plastic bottles. Lengthy and detailed sections describe more intricate devices. For example:

> A timed device used for vehicles is similar. It begins with the same box [a playing card box], card, bulb, and batter set up. Using pieces from a plastic bag, make a small bag, about 4 × 2.5 cm, containing a mixture of half sodium chlorate (weed killer) or potassium nitrate (saltpeter) and half white granulated sugar (use Jack Frost—it's vegan!). UHU or similar glue is used to seal the edges of the bag. The bag is placed along the filament . . . if you don't want to mess around with the bag, use the same firelighter set up as the 12 hour device [described in the previous section]. Instead of a watch being used

as a timer, this one uses a cooking timer which has a rotating arm. A nail is banged into the top of the timer, not far enough to affect the mechanism, and secured with glue. A piece of metal that can conduct electricity is bent into a letter L shape. This piece is glued to the arm, so that the L touches the nail when the timer reaches that point. The wires are attached to this arm and to the nail. The device is glued to a plastic bottle filled ¾ full with gasoline, and dish washing liquid is added. The dish washing liquid is used to sustain the flame. It does solidify the gasoline in around three days, so the device should be used within 24 hours. The device should be placed inside the truck, on the upholstery. If you can't open a door, you'll have to break a window or use it below the truck. Before using such a device it is absolutely necessary to check the truck to make sure the driver is not sleeping inside, as is often the case with larger commercial vehicles. Any product that repels dogs and cats can also be placed around the truck for safety, especially with longer timers. Again, make sure all fingerprints are completely gone before setting off for an action and only touch with gloves after that.[12]

Other significant publications include Dave Foreman's *Ecodefense: A Field Guide to Monkeywrenching* and Paul Watson's *Earthforce! An Earth Warrior's Guide to Strategy*. Although Watson's book strongly prohibits harming any living thing, other manuals are less innocuous. In 1991, Sydney and Tanya Singer, writing under the pseudonym Screaming Wolf, published a book called *A Declaration of War: Killing People to Save Animals and the Environment* (outlawed in Canada and the United Kingdom).[13]

Conclusion

The publication of manuals detailing criminal methods and the increasingly extreme rhetoric of some animal liberation and radical environmental leaders have been matched by violent direct actions, particularly in the underground animal liberation sector. Beginning in the United Kingdom and spreading to the United States, terrorist actions in defense of animals have increased, indicating a trend of progressive radicalization. As traditional methods for bringing about change fail, or do not bring change quickly enough, disaffected activists break off and form a new group or movement that advocates more extreme methods. Prominent examples exist in both the animal rights and radical environmental movements:

Progressive radicalization of organizations within the animal rights movement:

The Royal Society for the Prevention of Cruelty to Animals →Hunt Saboteurs Association →Band of Mercy →Animal Liberation Front →Stop Huntingdon Animal Cruelty.

Progressive radicalization of organizations within the environmental rights movement:

The Wilderness Society →Greenpeace →Sea Shepherd Conservation Society →Earth First! →Earth Liberation Front

Both examples demonstrate the progressively immoderate methodology adopted by animal rights and environmental activists, beginning with legal protest and lobbying, advancing to civil disobedience, and graduating to major acts of property destruction and violent attacks against people. Moreover, as the most extreme elements are pushed to the margins even within their own movements, this small body of hardcore activists is likely to become more violent.

_____ *Chapter 7* _____

A Profile of Eco-Warriors and Animal Liberationists

Members of the animal liberation and radical environmental movements are motivated by a belief that what they do is absolutely necessary and just. The exploitation of animals is no different from the abuse and extermination of Jews during the Holocaust, and crimes committed to end the abuse and to free animal "slaves" are every bit as noble as the actions taken by those abolitionists who ran the Underground Railroad in the American South. Activists see attacks on governments and corporations that defile nature as just actions in defense of the Earth itself; indeed, without radical actions, including crimes, they are convinced that much of life on the planet will cease to exist. The sincerity and depth of feeling among animal rights and environmental extremists should not be doubted, and it is exemplified by ALF activists who risk legal penalties and see value in freeing the smallest animal, be it a guinea pig, mouse, or snail. In fact, a current debate over tactics within the animal liberation movement is reconsidering the efficacy of arson, since countless mice, spiders, and smaller organisms suffer and are destroyed in the flames.

For most people, the idea of harming humans to liberate animals or prevent timber sales is unconscionable and misanthropic. The average person wonders how activists can justify threatening children in order to save guinea pigs. Aren't the medical and health needs of humans, for example, more important than the suffering of a rodent? Animal liberationists respond that most people are hopelessly blinded by speciesism and that animal suffering to benefit humans is morally wrong. Environmental "monkeywrenchers" adopt an equally radical stance; after all, what good are natural resource extraction, private property, and profit making if the Earth itself is destroyed by mankind? Earth First! cofounder

Dave Foreman framed the debate in stark and unequivocal terms when he used the following metaphor to justify criminal actions in defense of the environment: "If you come home and find a bunch of Hell's Angels raping your wife, your old mother, and eleven-year-old daughter, you don't sit down and talk balance with them or suggest compromise. You get your twelve gauge shotgun and blow them to hell. . . . there are people out there trying to save their mother [Mother Earth] from rape."[1]

Those people who commit crimes for the cause of animal liberation and environmental health are not easily categorized; attempts to dismiss them as "animal rights wackos" and "tree huggers" are overly simplistic, unfair, and probably dangerous. First, the degree of moral consideration due to non-human animals has become a serious philosophical debate, and the conclusions arrived at will have much to say about who we are and how we define ourselves as a civilization. Moreover, balancing the health and diversity of life on the planet with human consumption will likely be the single most important issue of the twenty-first century. Second, radical activists come from a broad array of backgrounds and have diverse beliefs about tactics, strategies, and goals. Earth First! split over differences in ideology, tactics, and the appropriate direction for the movement; a raucous debate over methods continues to rage in the animal liberation movement. The different types of direct actions employed by animal liberationists reflect divergent motivations and thought processes—those who engineer open rescues of animals and even replace damaged locks are motivated by love for animals, whereas those who burn down buildings (while perhaps loving animals) are clearly driven more by anger and hatred. The window-breaking and spray-painting of many young activists is akin to the ideological vandalism of the juvenile delinquent; in fact, it may be fair to say that much of the relatively minor criminal activity witnessed is perpetrated by those suffering from teenage angst who feel the need to run around and break things (calling themselves activists may be more of an afterthought, part of a cognitive process fulfilling the need to belong, and to justify).[2] Others who commit crimes in defense of animals and Earth have been at it for many years, have highly developed ideological positions, and have devoted their entire lives to the cause. Some, in the words of Eric Hoffer, are "true believers," seeking to remake the world.[3]

Although the ranks of animal liberationists are quite diverse, research does indicate some distinct patterns, which allow for generalization. In his study, Harold Guither states that about half of ALF activists are working-class and the other half middle-class, with a strong showing of teachers, lawyers, and civil servants.[4] Wesley Jamison and William Lunch surveyed 426 animal rights activists at the March for the Animals in Washington, D.C., on June 10, 1990. The survey respondents were 93% white and 68% female; 66% had some college (19% had an advanced degree); 66% lived in urban areas; mean income was $37,000; mean age was 29; 40% were professionals and 14% were students. In terms of political affiliation, 37% were independents, 35% were Democrats, 14% were Republicans, and 11% were "other."[5] In another study, Rebecca Richards and Richard Krannich conducted a mail survey of 1,020 subscribers to a major online animal rights journal, *Animals' Agenda*. The researchers found that 33% of respondents held an advanced degree; 97% were white; 39% had an income of over $50,000; 78% were female; 23% were under 29, 57% were between 30 and 40, and 20% were over 50 years of age. In addition, the study found that 40% of respondents were executives; 28% were in technical professions or sales; 73% lived in an urban area; and 84% had no children at home. Interestingly, this sample did not seem to have a problem with killing rats or cockroaches, suggesting at least some degree of speciesism.[6] In an unrelated 1984 *Animals' Agenda* survey, 65% of animal rights activists reported being atheists, and 56% opposed using animals in research even if they were not harmed.[7]

On the radical environmentalist side, Gary Perlstein and Kelly Stoner concluded in their study that most ELF members are teenagers or young adults, educated, and middle-class, with a history of environmental activism. The researchers also suggested that at least some ELF activists are technically proficient; operational practices during the commission of crimes include computer hacking and the encrypting of communiqués. In general, the best available evidence derived from limited arrest data (only a dozen or so ELF activists have been arrested to date) and the prodigious amount of materials posted to chat rooms and online zines indicates that so-called ecoterrorists are young white males, educated and bright, angry, politically far to the left and/or anarchist, vehemently anti–corporate America, antiwar, and often aligned with other social justice movements.[8]

The role of women should not be downplayed in the radical environmental and animal liberation movements. According to Ingrid Newkirk, the founder of ALF in the United States was a woman,[9] and Earth First! history tells us that women have always played an important part, sometimes assuming leadership or iconic positions, as in the cases of Judi Bari and Julia Hill. Women may very well constitute a majority in the animal rights movement. However, the smaller field of hardcore activists who set fires, destroy research laboratories, and on occasion threaten and attack other people seems to consist primarily of young men. The lack of non-white animal rights and environmental extremists as well as the dearth of persons of lower socioeconomic status among the ranks of direct activists is no doubt due to pragmatism: out of necessity, minorities and the poor spend more time thinking about ways to improve their own lot, with little time or will left over for animal liberation or environmentalism.

Letters from Prison

One good way to ascertain the mindset and character of animal liberationists and radical environmentalists is to talk to those persons who actually perpetrate the crimes. For obvious reasons this is not easily accomplished; however, a ready pool of known activists is available, confined in various jails and prisons throughout the world. By accessing various online prisoner support networks, I was able to obtain the names and addresses of imprisoned activists. Four of twelve individuals I contacted responded to letters containing the following questions:

- The stated objectives of groups like ALF and ELF is to cause economic damage to organizations that harm the environment and non-human animals. I'm interested in what you see as the long-range goal for those who participate in direct actions in defense of the Earth. Where do you see things going for the environmental and animal rights movements? Is there any hope for your movement, and the planet? Ultimately, how do you see things ending up?

- How did you become interested in the animal rights/environmental movement? Tell me something about your personal background (education, family, political beliefs, influences, etc.). Please feel free to elaborate.

- This question is hypothetical, and should in no way reflect any activities you have participated in, or plan to participate in. I am asking for your opinion—something that may be freely expressed and is protected by the First Amendment to the United States Constitution. . . . Do you feel that illegal direct actions are an acceptable way of trying to change behaviors relating to the environment and non-human animals? If you do feel that illegal actions are appropriate, how do you justify (in your own words) actions that are against the law?

The first respondent is Peter Young, convicted for releasing thousands of minks from fur farms in Iowa, South Dakota, and Wisconsin. Upon his arrest in 2005, he was prosecuted under the Animal Enterprise Protection Act of 1992. He pleaded guilty and was sentenced to two years in prison and $254,000 in restitution. Young wrote the following letter to me while in prison in late 2005:

> I would correct your assertion that the main objective of the ALF is to cause economic damage to animal exploitation industries. The main objective of the ALF is to save animals. Economic sabotage will always be an indirect way of saving animals. The economic damage of ALF actions is most often emphasized by the media who either does not understand, or censors outright, the motive of saving lives that lay behind such actions. Economic sabotage which forever shuts down an operation such as a fur farm or slaughterhouse will always be of greater benefit to animals than live liberation. Tactics such as

arson, as well as exposing atrocities with video footage to put pressure on labs and factory farms, are tactics which take a roundabout route to saving lives. But to be clear, saving animals is always the priority.

(1) The long-range goal of animal liberationists is to end animal exploitation industries, and ultimately, speciesism itself. The extreme atrocities committed against animals by human hands will always demand an extreme response. ALF actions will not end until every laboratory, factory farm, slaughterhouse, and fur farm is out of business or in ashes. This is the long-range goal.

In furtherance of this mission, I see the ALF continuing to hit weak links in the massive web of animal abuse industries, and in the process bringing the public an increased awareness of the suffering upon which their dietary and lifestyle habits rely. Momentum has and will continue to build slowly, as the animal liberation movement is still in its relative infancy. But as the collective experience of animal liberationists builds, and their knowledge is shared through anonymously authored primers on tactics such as burglary alarm bypassing, we will see the bar raised to new heights as ALF activity will increasingly resemble the work of skilled government spies or black-ops teams. As we learn from our successes and failures, it can only go in this direction. I see the days of amateur hour window breaking drawing to a close. Actions which exemplify this level of high skill will resonate through the entire movement, and serve as an example. This will increase momentum. Today, small-scale actions such as the targeting of fast food restaurants are rarely seen anymore, because the movement has evolved. These actions of questionable effectiveness have been delegitimized as ALF activity, opening ground for newer, more innovative and more effective actions. It is my hope to see clandestine animal liberation cells grow in numbers, their strikes increasing in frequency and potency, weakening the infrastructure of the animal abuse complex until it collapses. Whether this will come to pass, I cannot say. It's important to remember that animal liberation is unique in the realm of liberation struggles in that it is not an all or nothing fight. Every life saved is a success story, and as we work towards our ultimate goals, there can be many small victories along the way.

(2) I was raised in a fairly middle-class northern California household. The media has been incorrect about my background from the beginning —I am not from the Seattle area as has been stated, but was born in Los Gatos (Silicon Valley), CA on June 26, 1977, and did not move to Mercer Island, WA until I was 13. My family had no overt political bent, and I do not see any family members as having any influence on my current politics beyond their providing the open space for me to develop my own belief system. I am a high school graduate, and never attended college, although I have my entire adult life given the highest priority to self-education. I like to think I am educated, but not formally so. My first exposure to the plight of nonhuman animals came through my involvement in the straight edge hardcore music scene. Hardcore is a more abrasive faction of the punk rock scene, and tends toward being more message-oriented. Straight edge is a subfaction of hardcore, which is comprised of people who shun the drug and party culture, abstain from drug and alcohol use, and are usually vegan or vegetarian. It sounds like a fairly obscure subculture, but it is in fact very

well documented, with a history going back to the band Minor Threat in 1981, and it remains an active and vibrant subculture to this day. In the mid-90s, the straight-edge scene saw an emerging consciousness on the subject of our treatment of nonhuman animals, and many of the bands I was getting into at the time (most notably Earth Crisis and the intentionally provocative Vegan Reich) pushed the Vegan ethic through their lyrics. I found myself increasingly interested in this underground music scene and began taking the short bus ride a few miles west to Seattle to see touring straight edge hardcore bands play in basements and small venues. At first it was the message of nonconformity that attracted me, as well as the rejection of the party scene, which I saw as rather degenerate. As I began to give more thought to lyrical content, I began to find myself more appalled by what I was learning about what humans did to nonhumans for greed. My supplemental reading solidified my feelings that this was an injustice of the greatest scale, urgency, and magnitude. In 1994 I became vegan, and in 1995 began to get involved in activism, with a group at the University of Washington. In the mid-90s, kids from the straight edge hardcore music scene had a large presence in the animal rights movement, and many of the people recruited through this scene remain active to this day. If I could point to one song whose lyrics had the greatest impact, it would be "The New Ethic" by Earth Crisis. Their song "The Wrath of Sanity" was also inspirational. In remaining motivated for over a decade now, I would credit in no small way my rejection of the many numbing agents society throws at us which lead to apathy such as drugs, alcohol, television, and frivolous internet use.

(3) The only justification I need for illegal activity on behalf of sentient beings is that it works. If corporations are gong to murder, they must prepare for compassionate people responding with the urgency that preventing murder necessitates. People do not break into labs because it is fun. They do not burn down feed supply warehouses for the bragging rights, and they do not risk decades-long prison sentences for the thrill. People break the law for animals because it is necessary, and it works. This is the only justification needed. Synthetic man made laws will always yield to those higher. The justification comes in seeing a mink disappear from its cage into the forest. It comes in seeing a veal slaughterhouse close forever. And it comes in revealing to the public the atrocities that happen behind closed doors, doors that there are no legal ways to open. The ALF works because it doesn't ask for permission.[10]

Young also made the following statement to the court upon his sentencing:

This is the customary time when the defendant expresses regret for the crimes they committed, so let me do that because I am not without my regrets. I am here today to be sentenced for my participation in releasing mink from six fur farms. I regret it was only six. I'm also here today to be sentenced for my participation in the freeing of 8,000 mink from those farms. I regret it was only 8,000. It is my understanding of those six farms, only two of them have since shut down. I regret it was only two. More than anything, I regret my restraint, because whatever damage we did to those businesses, if those farms were left standing, and if one animal was left behind, then it wasn't enough. I don't wish to validate this proceeding by begging for mercy or appealing to the conscience of the court, because I know if this system had a conscience I would not be here, and in my place would be the butchers, vivisectors, and fur farmers of the world. Just as I will remain unbowed before this court—who would see me imprisoned for an act of conscience—I will also deny the fur farmers in the room the plea-sure of seeing me bow down before them. To the people here whose sheds I may have visited in 1997, let me tell you directly for the first time, it was a pleasure to raid your farms, and to free those animals you held captive. It is to those animals I answer to, not you or this court. I will forever mark those nights on your property as the most rewarding experience of my life. And to those farmers or other savages who may read my words in the future and smile at my fate, just remember: We have put more of you in bankruptcy than you have put liberators in prison. Don't forget that. Let me thank everyone in the courtroom who came to support me today. It is my last wish before prison that each of you drive to a nearby fur farm tonight, tear down its fence and open every cage. That's all.[11]

As can be seen, Young is very articulate, has a well-developed moral philosophy in the area of animal rights, and remains sincere and unapolo-getic about his cause and actions. Especially interesting is his reference to straight edge music, and the significant influence that art form and sub-culture had on the development of his personal ideology. Reference to his "restraint," the vision of sophisticated military-style operations, and the lyrics from the song "Wrath of Sanity" ("retribution from my hand . . . a bullet for every demon . . . images of your mutilated victims as I line you in my sight") suggests that he would support future direct actions prop-erly characterized as terrorism.

John Wade wrote to me as well. Wade is serving thirty-seven months at a federal institution in Petersburg, Virginia, for property destruction attacks on a McDonald's, a Burger King, and an SUV car dealership. He is a self-identified member of ELF. Wade wrote:

I have no problem participating in your study. I don't care if you use my name or don't. I am hopefully going to include a paper I wrote the other day that kind of sums up all my positive thoughts on radical environmen-talism. It came out a little bit more focused on capitalism than I would like—I am more concerned with people's real relationships with each other and the interconnectedness of all things than I am with abstract political and economic systems. Anyways . . .

1. Obviously ELF as a fringe group of a few angry environmentalists could do nothing to advance the environmental cause. However, ELF as part of a larger movement of popular support for less smog in the air, poison in the water, pavement in the woods, and more respect for life and

ourselves could be a beautiful thing. Right now I think a lot of people are getting sick of corporate greed and exploitation both where it concerns the environment and where it concerns communities, jobs, etc. The only difference between ELF and the Sierra Club is that we understand that the people in control aren't going to voluntarily give up their profits. Only by endangering their profits can we force them to act responsible and give up a little of their short-term profit for what is more important for everybody. I would say there is always hope but I am not optimistic. There are just too many people.

2. I am twenty years old and just celebrated my first year anniversary of coming to prison last May. My family is upper-middle class and my Dad and step-mom are both Republicans. However, my Dad is a "cob 1" Republican—he doesn't believe in the death penalty and is pretty reasonable on everything—our political differences arise more from perspectives, beliefs, etc. (subjective interpretations of facts) rather than from greed, bad logic, etc. He honestly believes in the free market. Anyways, as long as I can remember I have been a voracious reader. I have been against the death penalty since I was probably 13, and I wanted Gore to win when he was running against Bush because of Gore's stance on the Arctic National Wildlife Refuge. I guess I was 15 then. However, my real political awakening occurred right around the time I was 16. I started hanging out with a friend who was really involved in politics and who is also a genius, a term I don't use lightly. Anyways, I started volunteering for the democratic party, the ACLU, the Sierra Club, U.S, PIRG, Human Rights Coalition, Nature Conservancy, etc., etc. Because of my youthful (and characteristic) lack of respect for authority, open mindedness, and a thirst for justice (more on that later), I quickly started reading Edward Abbey (Desert Solitaire, the Monkeywrench Gang, etc.) and he made sense. Perhaps there was also some more negative motivations, (as there are many and different conflicting motivations for many actions)—frustration, anger, desire to play hero or martyr—but mostly my actions and beliefs were pure and genuine as perhaps only a child's can be. As far as the "thirst for justice," I realize that it is a bit melodramatic, but I don't get along with my step-mom and as a very young child always keenly felt the unfairness of her actions towards me and thus I am left with an unnatural sense of fair-play. My favorite authors are J.D. Salinger (not the Catcher in the Rye), Hunter S. Thompson (not Fear and Loathing in Las Vegas), Steinbeck, Vonnegut, Jorge Amado, Tolstoy, and Edward Abbey.

3. This was mostly answered in the paper but let me just say that I haven't given my allegiance to any government and I will stop breaking the law when the law stops breaking me. PEACE, John[12]

Like Peter Young, Wade is a young white male, proficient in his written expression, and, as a self-proclaimed member of ELF, unrepentant and totally dedicated to his cause. Wade was quite open and introspective; peer and cultural influences as well as participation in mainstream leftist political action groups seem to have played a major role in his development as an activist.

I also received a letter from Chris McIntosh, who was arrested, pleaded guilty, and was staring down the barrel of eight to ten years in prison when he wrote to me in late 2005. McIntosh was convicted of perpetrating arson at a McDonald's restaurant in Seattle. He said that he committed the crime on behalf of both ALF and ELF. McIntosh wrote:

> I tried to answer your questions as best I could. I've been in the hole for like 77 days now—It's got me kinda burnt out—plus I'm getting a little stressed because my sentencing is coming up—have a good one. P.S. I don't mind you using my name . . . Chris "Dirt" McIntosh.
>
> Well, as for long-range goals for direct actions, I think they vary because those who perpetrate direct actions don't necessarily have the same beliefs. . . . For me and others who share a green anarchist/anti-civilization belief system the long range goal of the actions we perpetrate are to eradicate the systems/corporations who seek to profit from this culture of consumption and environmental disregard, by destroying their property and otherwise making it unprofitable to operate. . . . Specifically, green anarchists seek to destroy civilization, civilization being the sole reason there are even targets to hit or even a reason to hit targets.
>
> I personally believe the greatest potential of ELF/ALF is to give the average person an outlet in which to strike back, and feel the empowerment that comes when a person leaps over the line from theory to action and damages those who are exploiting them, the animals, and their environment.
>
> Even in the face of the current government repression, I see the ELF/ALF gaining strength in the years to come, due mostly in part to the escalation of deprivations of a magnitude not seen before in the 10,000 years since civilization first sprang up. The frustration of the conscious has reached a boiling point worldwide and a battle-call has been sounded . . . luckily for the earth the call has been heeded. . . . With more and more people realizing that hope does not lie in impotent groups who disavow direct action and strive to make change through working with the system. There is a great amount of hope for the earth and the movement. People are angry and anger is the catalyst for true action.
>
> I became an anarchist when I was 14. . . . The earth/animal liberation struggle was just one part of a larger goal of liberation from the tendrils of civilization. . . . When you choose the anarchist path you choose a path of total liberation, not a compromised system in which some remain slaves while others walk free. . . . This extends especially to earth and animal kind who are largely helpless against the horrors being done to them. . . .
>
> I do feel "illegal" actions are acceptable. . . . I feel this way because I believe that the laws of this system were enacted solely to protect this system and its injustices. . . . Since "illegal" then is a term which the system does not have the right to inflict upon me or anyone else, it must be completely disregarded.
>
> Those who would have rebelled against the horrors of the Nazis would have been considered illegal by the people ruling over them—but they would have been right to do so. . . . So too are we correct in this struggle. Sometimes heroes aren't publicly heroes until after the fact—time will tell

whether the mainstream will one day vindicate those who fought against this holocaust. In short the laws don't apply to us because they never applied to those in the system—plus the system has no right to enact them. . . . The question is not how can we justify it—it's how can they condemn it![13]

In these three imprisoned activists we have a member of ALF, a member of ELF, and a green anarchist—a small but representative sample of those fringe elements in the animal rights and environmental movements who perpetrate illegal direct actions. They seem to have the common bond of anger toward the "system," as well as a sincere desire to change it. They are "true believers," motivated by a desire to administer what they genuinely feel is justice in an unjust world.

Theodore Kaczynski (the Unabomber) wrote to me as well; his letter is included in the final chapter, as he had much to say about the future of so-called eco-terrorism.

Cognition and Rationalization in the True Believer

One of the most intriguing aspects of so-called eco-terrorism and animal liberation criminality is the mind-set and beliefs of the persons involved. As previously noted, the sincerity of the activists should not be doubted—they are usually vegans or vegetarians, dedicated to turning back the clock to a time when wild nature was left untouched by humans. They are what sociologist Eric Hoffer called "true believers," devoting their lives to changing the world.[14]

Many activists are admittedly unsophisticated in their ideology. Dr. Steven Best, founding member of the Center for Animal Liberation Affairs and philosophy professor at the University of Texas at El Paso, has observed that many young activists simply "take a look around, say, this is bullshit, fuck it, and break shit."[15] Certainly much of what passes for eco-terrorism has the appearance of juvenile vandalism. But it is also clear that underground perpetrators of direct action are guided by previously established belief systems. Radical and criminal behaviors in defense of animals and the Earth are framed by a shared culture that is communicated through music, art, writings, online communications, and countless zines (amateur online publications that give a voice to green anarchists, animal liberationists, "earth warriors," and others—these are in addition to the "official" group publications, such as *Arkangel, Bite Back Magazine, Green Anarchy, Earth First! Journal, No Compromise,* and *Do or Die!*). Taken together, these various media spread the word and proselytize, planting and germinating shared belief systems that justify direct action. Budding activists can read books by university philosophers, listen to ideologically motivated music, attend PETA workshops and lectures, discuss movement literature, produce poetry, and communicate with one another and share ideas in a variety of forums. In short, this vast body of literature, music, and art is readily available for consumption and provides all of the cognitive fodder necessary to release individuals from internal and social constraints that would normally inhibit criminal behavior. These belief systems, according to philosophy professor Steven Best, are established prior to underground direct actions and provide, in the mind of the activist, justifications for breaking the law.[16]

Perpetrators of crimes in defense of animals and the Earth are faced with a dilemma of psychological dimensions. These people who break the law think of themselves as decent, moral human beings, waging their war for the most noble of causes. Yet the vast majority of people, including a significant proportion of those within the environmental and animal rights movements, decry their acts and call them criminals. The U.S. government calls them terrorists. This creates self-image problems for the eco-warrior and animal liberationist, a state of cognitive dissonance,[17] where the individual's concept of herself as a good person conflicts with the label being applied. Criminologists Henry Sykes and David Matza[18] argue that when faced with such attacks on the self-image, would-be criminals utilize various "techniques of neutralization" to preserve the concept of the individual as someone who adheres to societal norms, even when intended and overt behaviors suggest otherwise. The process is seen as disinhibiting: internal and external controls that would normally deter criminal behavior are neutralized by cognitions that justify the action in the mind of the perpetrator. Essentially, the cognitive process of neutralization enables criminal behavior.

Additional research on the subject of terrorism supports the notion that animal and environmental radicals go through a process of moral justification. In his introductory book on terrorism, Jonathan R. White cites Paul Wilkinson:

> They may argue that terrorism is a just revenge for social evils or that it is a lesser evil than the exercise of government power. Terrorism is often justified as being the only course of action available. Regardless of the argument used, Wilkinson demonstrates, *the terrorist group must develop its own parameters of ethical normalcy and go through a process of moral justification* [emphasis added][19]

H.H.A. Cooper also describes a process that terrorists undergo to justify their actions. Cooper argues, in what he calls the "doctrine of necessity," that terrorists come to believe that maintenance of the status quo is far worse than the violence they perpetrate;[20] certainly animal liberationists and environmental radicals fit this mold, strenuously arguing that the "holocaust" of factory farming and the steady destruction of the natural world is the real crime.

A perusal of animal liberation and radical environmental publications and statements made by aboveground and underground activists reveals that they frequently use techniques of "neutralization" to justify criminal behavior. The three techniques[21] commonly used by animal liberationists and environmental radicals are what Sykes and Matza called "denial of the victim," "condemnation of the condemners," and "appeal to higher loyalties." In the following section we will examine the verbatim statements of animal liberation and environmental activists. The quotations come from a variety of sources, including online journals, communiqués from activists claiming responsibility for crimes, and other publications. Some are statements made by those who merely lend vocal support for direct action, while others come from individuals who actually perpetrate so-called eco-crimes.

Movement literature (books, online journals, zines, etc.) frequently condemns its condemners as a rationale for engaging in direct action. With this neutralization technique, attention is diverted from the wrong-doing of the activist to the real or alleged wrongs committed by others. In fact, the wrongs perpetrated by those who condemn the activist are seen as far more serious (that the condemner's claims may be absolutely true is, of course, irrelevant—the fact remains that environmental and animal rights activists cite the wrongs of others to justify their own criminal actions). Consider the following statements made by aboveground and underground activists

- As ecowarriors see it, the human individuals, corporations, and state entities that promote or defend the exploitation of the natural world are the true violent forces and the real terrorists.[22]
- The state unleashes draconian rule with legislation such as the Patriot Act, but champions of animal rights and radical ecology are smeared for using intimidation tactics.[23]
- We should never feel like we're going too far in breaking the law, because whatever laws you break to liberate animals or to protect the environment are very insignificant compared to the laws that are broken by that parliament of whores in Washington. They are the biggest lawbreakers, the biggest destroyers, the biggest mass-murderers on this planet right now.[24]
- One of the central ironies of our time is that within the exploitative and materialistic ethos of capitalism, property and inanimate objects are more sacred than life, such that to destroy living beings and the natural world is a legal and (to all too many) ethically acceptable occupation, while to smash the things used to kill animals and plunder the earth is illegal, immoral, and even an act of "terrorism."[25]
- Torching a research or vivisection laboratory is considered more heinous than anally electrocuting foxes or conducting LD50 tests, which pour industrial chemicals into the bodies of animals until half of them die.[26]
- Critics whine about the possibility of physical violence by the ALF but fall silent before the actuality of state terrorism, animal massacres, and environmental destruction on a global scale.[27]

- This action was a snarl of rage directed towards the planet rapers [sic] who construct these unregulated petroleum guzzlers and the capitalist whores who pander to them and profit off the pollution caused by fuel emissions.[28]

The previous statements clearly demonstrate the manner in which direct activists and those who support them justify criminal actions and maintain a positive self-image. They are not bad people; research scientists and greedy corporations are the bad guys, the U.S. government are the *real* terrorists, and so on and on.

Perhaps the most frequently used neutralization technique is the "appeal to higher loyalties." Consider the following statements:

- Because something is illegal doesn't make it immoral.[29]
- The threat to the life of the planet is so severe that political violence must be understood as a viable option.[30]
- In pursuit of justice, freedom, and equal consideration for all innocent life . . . segments of this global revolutionary movement are no longer limiting their revolutionary potential by adhering to a flawed, inconsistent [sic] non-violent ideology . . . where it is necessary, we will no longer hesitate to pick up the gun to implement justice.[31]
- To assault the meatpacking industry is to mount a challenge to the mentality that allowed well over a million dehumanized humans to be systematically slaughtered by the SS *einsatzgruppen* in Eastern Europe during the 1940s, and the Nazis' simultaneous development of truly industrial killing techniques in places like Auschwitz, Sobibor, and Treblinka.[32]
- They are not violent aggressors against life; they are defenders of freedom and justice for any enslaved species.[33]
- In this endeavor, they unleash a frontal assault on the prevalent mentality that says animals are objects, resources, or property, and they advance the universalization of rights that is the key marker of moral progress.[34]
- In this conception, animal liberationists continue a hallowed line of heroic visionaries; the Suffragettes fighting in the early twentieth century, those in the 1960s engaged in the Civil Rights Movement, and, perhaps more fittingly, the courageous men and women who harbored Jews in Nazi-occupied Europe.[35]
- Animal liberation is the next logical development in moral evolution.[36]
- From the Boston tea party to the underground railroad, from the suffragettes to the civil rights movement, from Vietnam war resistance to the Battle of Seattle, key struggles in US history employed illegal direct action tactics— and sometimes violence—to advance the historical movement toward human rights and freedoms.[37]
- Whereas corporate society, the state, and mass media brand the ALF as terrorists, the ALF has important similarities with some of the great freedom fighters of the last two centuries, and is akin to contemporary peace and justice movements in its quest to end bloodshed and violence toward life and to win justice for other species.[38]

- The ALF is grounded in the principle that laws protecting animal exploitation industries are unjust, and they break them in deference to the higher moral principle of animal rights.[39]
- Following a basic tenet of civil disobedience philosophy, the ALF believes that there is a higher law than that created by and for the corporate state complex, a moral law that transcends the corrupt and biased statutes of the U.S. political system.[40]
- Most significantly, the aim of the liberationists is altruistic; they fight for the improvement of the lot of nonhuman animals.[41]

In their "appeal to higher loyalties," animal liberation and environmental activists compare themselves to Nazi resistors, Underground Railroad abolitionists, and freedom fighters the world over. They see themselves as not unlike the Sons of Liberty at the Boston Tea Party, exercising their right of civil disobedience and fighting a tyrant for a noble and just cause. Arson, property destruction—even violence against humans—is justified because their loyalties lie not with corrupt, self-serving man-made law, but with a higher moral law. Their motives are conceptualized as pure and good—the cognitive dissonance is balanced and positive self-image maintained.

The third common technique of neutralization used by activists is to deny the victim. The following statements exemplify this cognitive process.

- I don't feel any sympathy for people in England or America who have had their cars tipped or torched, because those cars were paid for out of blood money.[42]
- Dear animal killing scum! Hope we sliced your finger wide open and that you now die from the rat poison we smeared on the razor blade.[43]
- Monkey-wrenching is more than just sabotage, and you're goddamn right, it's revolutionary! This is jihad, pal. There are no innocent bystanders, because in these desperate hours, bystanders are not innocent. . . . Go out and get them suckers, fill 'em full of steel![44]
- Do not be afraid to condone arsons at places of animal torture. Matter of fact, if an animal abuser were to get killed in the process of burning down a research lab, I would unequivocally support that, too.[45]
- The animal liberation front has taken advice from our Commander in Chief to "smoke terrorists out of their holes." The target was Los Angeles number one terrorist [name of target deleted]. Military strength smoke grenades were detonated on the floor of this animal killer's abode. [Name of target deleted] you are a disgusting human being who takes pleasure in the murder of over 50,000 animals a year. You are a target. Sleep light.[46]
- Black hair ladies of the night were sent to the home of [name deleted] along with several hundred dollars worth of pizza and a coroner to collect the body. . . . Friday night a party was thrown at her house without her foreknowledge. Last but not least a 'gangbanger' looking for a 'gangwhore' was sent. Be careful, the next night might bring us. Resign bitch now, ALF.[47]
- This action was done on behalf of thousands of helpless animals killed by [name deleted] because she does not do her job. . . . She is a piece of scum

who hates animals. She should not be in charge of helping animals because all she knows how to do is kill them. You can't hide anymore. ALF.[48]

- With the click of a mouse we can cut off your insurance and you will get $0 dollars when we set fire to your car, which by the way, begs for it each time [name deleted: wife of target] parks it at the Oyster Bay Train Station . . . how is it that you can buy everything in the world . . . but can't seem to find a way of buying getting [name deleted: wife of target] pregnant? Could it be that you can't get it up because you feel so inadequate with who you have become? Or maybe you just like boys? Now here is the real trip. We have your whole life seized. This info is going to travel all over the world. How's about we begin with your finances, and then we will get into your family and friends.[49]

When utilizing the neutralization technique of denial of victim, environmental and animal liberation criminals are saying that the victim "deserved it." The statements above come from anonymous communiqués and some of the more militant spokespersons for ELF and ALF. In stark contrast to those activists who appeal to higher loyalties, these statements seethe with self-righteous anger. The activists deal out justice with a vengeance, striking with barely concealed pleasure, even mocking their victims, wallowing in the fear they produce. But it is justice, and they are heroes risking their very freedom to strike down evil "earth rapers" and "animal murderers."

Richard M. Pearlstein believes that political terrorists (an appropriate label for the most serious offenders of interest here) experience what he calls "narcissistic injury" or "narcissistic disappointment," where narcissism is defined as an "internal, intrapsychic, regulatory tool that enables the individual to defend the self from damage and harm."[50] Narcissistic injury is simply profound damage to self-esteem, while narcissistic disappointment refers to disillusionment with individuals or groups that espouse societal norms, and a "resultant disappointment in the self for ever having embraced those standards."[51] Pearlstein goes on to say that political terrorists engage in "autocompensatory violence" as a means of establishing and maintaining a new "pseudoidentity" that allows the individual to assume the "mask of omnipotence" and eschew the "mask of villainy" normally ascribed to criminals and terrorists. The key to this process is the "unremitting manipulation of objects in order to transform negative self-image or self-esteem into positive self-representation."[52] The process is, simply put, the "violent defense of the self." The following passage from Pearlstein's 1991 publication *The Mind of the Political Terrorist* recalls that technique of neutralization called "condemnation of the condemners," as well as what he calls the unifying and underlying "doctrine of necessity":

The actual psychopolitical dynamics inherent in this evasion or circumvention of negative identity are illustrated in George Orwell's characterization of political writing and speech as "the defense of the indefensible." Thus, through the promiscuous, yet careful, utilization of murky euphemism, the political terrorist is—again, from his own perspective—able to deflect ultimate responsibility for his own actions or, preferably, to assume a positive identity. In so doing, political terrorism becomes, to recall a familiar military dictum, *what the other guy does* [emphasis added]. At the same time, the political terrorist both perceives and publicly portrays his craft as a defensive us-against-them response to the other guy's actions.[53]

Pearlstein's framework is clearly applicable to environmental and animal rights activists who perpetrate crimes. The statements in the preceding pages involve the manipulation of external objects to satisfy the requirements of the self/ego. These criminals "eschew the mask of villainy" for the "mask of rhetoric," addressing the dissonance they experience between what society tells them is acceptable behavior and what they actually do. Sykes and Matza would say radical activists use techniques of neutralization to preserve a positive self-image. Observing the same process, Pearlstein suggests that activists repair narcissistic injury or disappointment through a process of venting their resultant "narcissistic rage." Whatever terminology is used, the cognitive processes described preserve a positive self-image, either releasing the individual from the constraints that prohibit direct-action criminality, or justifying criminal actions after the fact (or, quite likely, both).

In his seminal work, *The True Believer*, Eric Hoffer captured well the social-psychological processes involved in the essential defense of the self that occurs within mass movements like radical environmentalism and animal liberation: "To the frustrated a mass movement offers either substitutes for the whole self or for the elements which make life bearable and which they cannot evoke out of their individual resources."[54] Hoffer continues:

> The burning conviction that we have a holy duty towards others is often a way of attaching our drowning selves to a passing raft. What looks like giving a hand is often a holding on for dear life. Take away our holy duties and you leave our lives puny and meaningless. There is no doubt that in exchanging a self-centered for a selfless life we gain enormously in self-esteem. The vanity of the selfless, even those who practice utmost humility, is boundless.[55]

And finally, in a quote that does not bode well for moderation in the animal rights or environmental movement, Hoffer states:

> We can have qualified faith in ourselves, but the faith we have in our nation, religion, race, or holy cause has to be extravagant and uncompromising. A substitute embraced in moderation cannot supplant and efface the self we want to forget.[56]

It may well be that underground ELF and ALF activists, their brethren the green anarchists, and others with similar anti-civilization goals do what they do as much for themselves as for the animals or the earth. In their uncompromising quest for justice, grandiose eco-warriors and animal freedom fighters find meaning and purpose. As for justice, that is a relative term, and another matter.

The Future of Eco-Terrorism
and Animal Liberation

The future does not look bright for ELF, ALF, and the rest of the radical environmental and animal liberation movement participants. Although some dramatic and costly attacks have generated media attention and framed radical groups like PETA and Greenpeace as comparatively moderate, changes in societal use of animals and environmental protection have been incremental and slight. Yes, some cages are larger, fewer people are wearing furs, and security costs at biomedical research facilities are higher;[1] but such goals as ending the use of animals for any reason, setting aside massive tracts of wilderness on a global scale, and engineering the downfall of modern technological civilization remain remote and almost certainly unattainable.

The dim outlook for the radical environmental and animal liberation movements is due to a number of factors, not the least of which are the concerted governmental and law enforcement efforts unleashed against underground activists. The Animal Enterprise Protection Act of August 26, 1992, makes any attack causing more than $10,000 in damage to an animal enterprise a federal offense punishable by a year in prison. Attacks causing serious bodily harm or death may result in sentences of ten years to life. Between 1988 and 1992, thirty-two states enacted laws to protect animal enterprises.[2] A rider attached to the Drug Act of 1988 made tree spiking a federal felony offense.[3] In labeling environmental and animal rights radicalism the most dangerous domestic terror threat in the United States,[4] the U.S. government in recent years has set the stage for the application of the Patriot Act to the prosecution of so-called eco-terrorists.

As the federal government has applied its resources, arrests and convictions of animal liberation and radical environmental activists have accelerated in recent years. On January 25, 2001, Frank Ambrose became the first ELF activist arrested in North America (for a tree spiking in

Portland's Liberation Collective (a direct-action group dedicated to fighting a variety of issues from vivisection to globalization), Leslie James Pickering went on to become, along with Craig Rosebraugh, a press officer for ELF and ALF. From 1997 to 2001, and for a brief period in 2002, Pickering received anonymous communiqués from ELF and ALF activists. Forming the North American Earth Liberation Front Press Office in 2000, both Pickering and Rosebraugh reported on and defended direct actions. By 2002 Pickering's rhetoric had become increasingly violent, framing ELF actions as part of a larger revolutionary struggle. In 2003 Pickering and Rosebraugh founded the Arissa Media Group with the goal of eliminating from the world "one of the greatest terrorist organizations in planetary history, the U.S. Government."[15]

I asked Pickering the following question, to which he responded by e-mail in early 2006:

Q: What do you think the future holds for ELF/ALF? In a more general sense, how will all of this end up—will ALF achieve its goal of ending animal exploitation in all its forms? Will ELF influence state bureaucrats to place huge wilderness areas off-limits to commercial enterprises?

Pickering: I don't think influencing bureaucrats to place huge wilderness areas off-limits to commercial enterprises is a specific goal of the ELF. Maybe some members or supporters would see this as a minor improvement, but I don't see how sabotage of this scale would be effective in influencing government policy. If influencing government policy were the objective I would think an organization would either take more drastic action, like the FLN in Algiers for example, or would simply go through the existing processes like lobbying and courts.

As I've grown to understand it, sabotage efforts like we've seen with the ELF are more intended to build a radical or even revolutionary resistance movement to the existing power structure than they are intended to influence government policy. In this light, if the ELF loses it'd be because they failed to inspire people to unite and struggle for change, not because the government never set huge wilderness areas off-limits to commercial enterprises.

I would guess the future either holds growth or decline for the ELF and their larger movement. If they are successful, the resistance will grow and we will see more ELF activity and more people thinking and expressing the kinds of ideas the ELF represent. If they are not successful, they will fizzle out and will eventually be lost in history. We've also seen many examples that fall between these two outcomes. A number of resistance movements experience devastating repression and are destroyed as a result, but continue to be an inspiration to movements that sprout up in the generations that follow.

For the period that I had the privilege to serve as spokesperson, the ELF were clearly growing and building much public support. This is because they were taking frequent spectacular actions and consistently evading capture. They were very successful at gaining media attention and causing extensive economic damage to their chosen targets. For whatever reasons their activity seemed to cool off and now we are seeing more in the news about the government's actions against individuals suspected to have been involved in the ELF than anything the ELF might be up to now.

There was a shift in strategy at some point, which I was concerned about from the beginning. Targets changed from buildings housing corporate headquarters and government agencies to SUV dealerships and luxury housing developments. When large corporate and government buildings were burning down people were awed and there was a sense of separation between the targets of the ELF and the public. When car dealerships and housing developments were burning it was generally less impressive and the perceived separation between the targets of the ELF and the general public was not as clear. The media and the government worked to exploit this situation, as expected, and in general these smaller actions failed to gain the exposure that the multi-million dollar corporate and government attacks gained.

Good strategy is a direct result of theory. As spokesperson I often offered my personal understanding of ELF theory, as I could make it out, by analyzing their apparent strategy from my sympathetic standpoint. The later strategy of the ELF to target SUV dealerships and housing developments did not fit as well with my understanding of the group's theory. Of course my understanding of ELF theory may very well be inaccurate and there are a number of people who were very glad to see Hummer dealerships and McMansions aflame, but if their strategy was not a linear result of their theory, and more of a result of something like opportunity, then I would not be surprised if that strategy failed to lead the group where they hoped to go.

With the loose autonomous structure that the ELF embraces it wouldn't at all be surprising to see a non-linear relationship between strategy and theory, or even the fatal underdevelopment of theory and strategy prior to action. While this type of structure is in some ways very egalitarian and works to keep the membership out of prison, in this example it may have failed to foster a healthy development and relationship between strategy and theory necessary to lead the ELF to achieve their goals.[16]

Citing the "non-linear relationship between strategy and theory," Pickering suggests that ELF may be failing and offers a possible reason for this failure. One suspects that, given his work with Arissa, Pickering's feelings about the prospects of broader revolutionary change are more hopeful.

Another person well-positioned to draw conclusions about the likelihood of success for radical environmentalism is Theodore Kaczynski, the Unabomber. In 1978 Kaczynski began an eighteen-year one-man terror campaign—his mail bombs killed three people and injured twenty-three others. His last two victims, both of whom died, could be perceived as anti-environmentalists. Thomas Mosser was an executive at Burson-Marsteller, whom Kaczynski claimed in an anonymous letter to the *New York Times* was responsible for helping to clean up the image of the Exxon Corporation after the *Exxon Valdez* oil spill. Gilbert Murray, the president of the California Forestry Association, was also killed by a Kaczynski bomb (although the target had been William Dennison of the Timber Association of California). Ron Arnold, author of *Ecoterror,* documents evidence that suggests Kaczynski was influenced by Earth First! and chose at least one of his victims from *Live Wild or Die!* magazine's "Eco-Fucker hit list." Although Arnold cites a media account where Kaczynski is said to have voiced support for the 1998 ELF arson of a ski lodge in Vail, Colorado, in his letter to me Kaczynski disavows all connections to the radical environmentalists and even states that groups like ELF should be resisted (though not for the reasons offered by the law enforcement community or private commercial interests). Kaczynksi does share with green anarchists and some radical environmentalists a desire for the downfall of modern technological civilization. At any rate, his background qualifies him to offer an informed opinion on the future of radical underground environmental activism.[17]

In response to the same three questions I asked the ELF/ALF activists in chapter seven, Kaczynski wrote the following:

> I trust you've received my note dated December 16, 2005. Here I will give you my answers to the three questions that you sent me with your letter postmarked November 7, 2005.
>
> First I need to state my conviction that destructiveness toward the natural world is built into technological civilization. It may be feasible to palliate that destructiveness to a limited extent, but in the long run there will be no way of controlling it. Consequently, wild nature, or the biosphere (or whatever you choose to call it), cannot be saved by anything short of the dissolution of technological civilization. It follows that if we want to save the biosphere, then the only really effective actions we can take are those designed to promote the breakdown of technological civilization.
>
> Of course, every civilization breaks down eventually, and technological civilization will do so too. But if technological civilization lasts long enough, then there will be nothing left after it is gone. On the other hand, if technological civilization breaks down soon enough, much will be saved. So the objective must be to bring about the collapse of technological civilization at the earliest possible moment. This point of view underlies my answers to your questions.
>
> To answer your questions in order:
>
> 1. (a) You ask what I "see as the long-range goal for those who participate in direct actions in defense of the Earth." I take it you are asking about the long-range goal of ELF, ALF, and those who subscribe approximately to their ideology. Since I am not one of these people, I am not qualified to state their goal for them. But from what I know of this ideological sector, I won't be surprised if most of your respondents state goals that are fuddled, or unrealistic, or both. I also think that the *stated* goals of people who belong to this sector do not necessarily coincide with their *real* goals. I don't doubt that these people *believe* that their stated goals are their real goals, but I would argue that in many

cases their real goal is not to save the environment or to protect animals but to satisfy their own psychological needs. See the discussion of leftist psychology in the so-called "Unabomber Manifesto," *Industrial Society and Its Future*.

The foregoing notwithstanding, I speculate that among people who carry out illegal actions in defense of the environment (*not* among animal-rights activists), the stated goals of at least a significant minority do coincide roughly with their real goals. I base this conjecture on the fact that there are very good reasons, connected with the welfare of all human beings, for protecting our environment. The system's response to environmental problems has been feeble at best, so it is only to be expected that some people should grow sufficiently worried, frustrated, or angry to become "extremists" in defense of the environment.

I would also speculate that the people who work "in the field," that is, the people who repeatedly take the risk of engaging personally in illegal actions, have (on average) a stronger commitment to accomplishing practical results and are less interested in ideology than are activists who adopt primarily political methods. A relative lack of interest in ideology would suggest a more genuine commitment to defending the environment; people seeking mainly to satisfy their own psychological needs would be more likely to develop elaborate ideological rationalizations.

(b) You ask where I "see things going for the environmental and animal-rights movements." Here I assume you are referring not to the legal, conventional movements as represented for example by the Wilderness Society, the Sierra Club, or the Humane Society, but to the extreme movements represented by ELF and ALF.

I don't have any detailed knowledge of these movements, and even if I did I wouldn't venture to make any *specific* predictions about their future. In general terms I predict that these movements will never accomplish anything substantial. The extreme environmental movement may contribute to some palliation of modern society's abuse of the environment, but will not have a decisive effect. The extreme animal-rights movement probably will succeed only to the extent that a tendency toward more humane treatment of animals may already by [sic] predetermined by powerful social trends in modern society. There certainly is in our society a long-term trend in the direction of a more compassionate attitude toward animals. Even conservatives advocate more humane treatment of animals. See George F. Will's column in *Newsweek*, 7/18/05, page 66. It's true that there are economic forces that push in the opposite direction, and I suppose it's conceivable, though not likely, that the extreme animal-rights movement might tilt the balance in favor of humane treatment and against economic incentives for ruthless exploitation of animals. But even if this happens it will not be of decisive importance for the future of the world.

I should add at this point that I'm not particularly interested in animal rights. Of course, I do not like to know, for example, that many chickens spend their lives in cages so small that the birds can't even turn around, but this is not a matter of special concern to me. As I've already implied, I don't think the question of animal rights will be of much significance for the overall development of modern society in the years to come.

So, in summary, I see the environmental and animal-rights movements as futile, at least with respect to any issues that are of fundamental importance for the future of the world. As I indicated at the beginning of this letter, *the* fundamental issue is the survival or collapse of technological civilization.

(c) You ask whether I see any hope for the extreme environmental and animal rights movements. No, I do not. The reason why I see the futility of these movements as incurable is that they are under the domination of what the Unabomber Manifesto calls "the left," or what some others have called "the adversary culture." (See Paul Hollander's book, *The Survival of the Adversary Culture*). Roughly, "the left" comprises people who are fixated on such issues as racism, sexism, neocolonialism, gay rights, animal rights, indigenous people's rights, etc., etc. These people like to think of themselves as rebels or revolutionaries, but they wouldn't really want to overturn the existing structure of society. They have in fact achieved a relatively comfortable adjustment to the present society, which allows them to satisfy their psychological needs by playing at rebellion as long as they stay within certain limits (of course, not all of them do so), and as long as they espouse causes that are consistent with the well-being of technological society. Unquestionably, technological society is benefited by the suppression of racism, sexism, homophobia, etc., and by moderate measures for protection of the environment. On the other hand, if technological civilization collapses, many, many people will die, and the survivors will have to live under conditions that will seem exceedingly harsh to those accustomed to the soft life of modern society. In the struggle for survival, no one will care about the leftists' favorite issues, such as gender equality, kindness to animals, or the right of homosexuals to marry.

Thus the leftists would have nothing to gain, and a great deal to lose, through the collapse of technological civilization, and most leftists— even including many of those who like to *talk* about such a collapse, would not actually want to see technological civilization break down. ("When the old order begins to fall apart, many of the vociferous men of words, who prayed so long for the day, are in a funk. The first glimpse of the face of anarchy frightens them out of their wits." Eric Hoffer, *The True Believer*). Furthermore, the values of the left are essentially the soft values of modern society: women, homosexuals, and animals are to be protected, poor people are to be cared for, workers are to be given easy conditions and decent wages, etc., etc. A movement dominated by these soft values could never take the frankly brutal and reckless measures needed to bring down the technoindustrial system, nor would such a movement be prepared to accept the harsh consequences of the collapse of the system.

No doubt there are some individuals, and possibly even whole factions in the environmental/animal rights movement who genuinely do want to see the collapse of technological civilization, who would be willing to accept the frightening consequences of such a collapse, and might even be prepared to take the brutal measures needed to bring it about. But scattered individuals and small factions cannot constitute an effective revolutionary force as long as they remain part of a movement that is dominated by the left and its values.

The revolutionary pretensions of the left are good for a laugh. What isn't so funny is the fact that the existence of the left serves to impede the emergence of a *real* revolutionary movement. Leftists love causes— *any* causes, as long as they don't have a specifically right-wing character. So as soon as any movement of resistance begins to form, leftists come swarming to it in droves until the movement becomes swamped with leftists, is absorbed into the "adversary culture," and is thereby rendered ineffectual. The history of Earth First! provides a nice example of this phenomenon. Martha F. Lee has documented the process in her book, *Earth First!: Environmental Apocalypse*.

Thus, those who are seriously interested in saving wild nature must rigorously separate themselves from the left—that includes separating themselves from ELF, ALF, the green anarchists, the anarchoprimitivists, and so forth—and they must form a new movement of their own, which will have to take measures to exclude leftists. The new movement will need to discard the soft values of the left and adopt hard values. It will have to place the highest value on courage, skill, effort, endurance—and on freedom, but not the pampered freedom of the modern man or woman to whom society gives a long leash. Instead, the movement must value the self-reliant freedom of the rugged survivalist, and it will have to *glory* in the hard life to be expected following the dissolution of technological civilization.

(d) You ask how, "ultimately," I see things ending up. I think I've answered that question already: If technological civilization breaks down in the relatively near future, then much will be saved. But if technological civilization lasts too long, then, when it does eventually break down, there will be nothing left to save.

2. (a) You ask how I became interested in the animal-rights/ environmental movement. As I've already made clear, I'm not interested in the animal rights/environmental movement, except to the extent that I view it as an adversary to be resisted.

(b) You ask about my "personal background (education, family, political beliefs, influences, etc.)" Education: B.A., mathematics, Harvard, 1962. Ph.D., mathematics, University of Michigan, 1967. Family: working-class to lower middle-class. Political beliefs: If the term "politics" is construed in a narrow sense, then I'm not interested in politics. If the term is more broadly construed, then my political beliefs are those that have already been outlined in this letter. Influences: No comment.

3. (a) You are perhaps a wee bit careless in telling your respondents that their opinions about "illegal direct actions" "may be freely expressed" and are "protected by the First Amendment." Expressions of opinion about illegal action are protected by the First Amendment only if they do not constitute actual *incitement* of illegal action. See *Yates v. United States*, 354 U.S. 298, 313-334 (1957); *Nowak v. United States*, 356 U.S. 660, 666-67 (1958); *Kingsley Corp. v. Regents of U. of N.Y.*, 360 U.S. 684, 689 (1959); *Scales v. United States*, 367 U.S. 203 (1961); *Noto v. United States*, 367 U.S. 290, 297-98 (1961); *Carroll v. Commissioners of Princess Anne*, 393 U.S. 175, 180 (1968); *Hess v. Indiana*, 414 U.S. 105, 108-09 (1973); *Ashcroft v. Free Speech Coalition*, 535 U.S., 234, 253 (2002). The line between incitement and protected expression of opinion about illegal action is difficult to define precisely, and it won't be surprising if some of the opinions expressed by your respondents constitute, in the eyes of some people, incitement of illegal action.

Here I will be very careful to avoid incitement, and will stay well within the area protected by the First Amendment.

(b) You ask whether "illegal actions are an acceptable way of trying to change behaviors relating to the environment and nonhuman animals"; I doubt that illegal direct actions, on the scale currently practiced, are highly effective in changing behaviors related to the environment and nonhuman animals. I do think that illegal direct actions may turn out to be a necessary part of a revolutionary program designed to bring down technological civilization.

(c) You ask how I would justify actions that are against the law. Law is a code of behavior designed to preserve the structure of a given society. If one believes that a society should *not* be preserved, then one has no reason to obey its laws—provided that one is willing to accept the personal risk involved in breaking the law.[18]

Support for Illegal Direct Actions and Problems within the Movements

Should public and private efforts fail to end radical environmental and animal rights activities, internal divisions and discontent within those movements certainly threaten their future. In the preceding section Leslie James Pickering and Theodore Kaczynski provided detailed and cogent analyses as to why radical environmentalism is failing. Divisions within both the animal rights and radical environmental movements will seriously limit their successes, as arguments over theory, strategy, and tactics persist. Mainstream animal welfare and animal rights people see PETA and ALF as detrimental to their cause, while nasty splits like the one witnessed in Earth First! exemplify major disagreements over movement direction. Some activists I spoke to informally complained of egos and personalities becoming more important than the animals or the environment. Both Craig Rosebraugh[19] and philosophy professor and activist Steven Best[20] noted the problem of a lack of dedication among many activists, whose motivation often amounts to little more than teen angst. One highly dedicated activist, who asked that I not reveal his/her identity, believes that the feminist faction in the animal rights movement is especially counterproductive.

The level of support for radical direct actions in the broader mainstream animal rights and environmental movements is of critical importance and may well determine whether the radical agendas precipitate real changes in societal behavior. In fact, persons who identify with mass movements like animal rights and environmentalism are a diverse lot; very few of them actually engage in criminal activities, and many openly denounce criminal actions. In fact, existing surveys indicate that the majority of animal rights and environmental activists do not favor violence or property destruction. Most people, even within the movements, see little justification for radical direct actions and view protests, demonstrations, hunger strikes, boycotts, and media campaigns as more effective in the long term than acts of economic sabotage and violence.[21]

I sought to explore this issue further by attending two conferences popular among mainstream members of the movements. On September 24, 2005, I attended the "Green Festival," a two-day environmental conference held at the Washington, D.C., Convention Center. With an agenda promoting "sustainable economy, ecological balance, and social justice," the event featured 350 exhibits and 125 speakers, including Congressman Dennis Kucinich (D-OH).

I administered the following brief written survey to every fourth person standing in the conference registration line. Approximately two to three thousand people attended the conference that day. The results of my survey follow.[22]

1. Do you believe that entire eco-systems will be lost and many parts of the world will become uninhabitable in the near future?

Strongly Agree:	24.7%
Agree:	49.8%
Disagree:	16.5%
Strongly Disagree:	3.2%
Don't Know	6.2%

2. Significant improvements in global environmental health can be achieved through legitimate actions such as media campaigns, lobbying, and appropriate legislation.

Strongly Agree	32.3%
Agree	55.2%
Disagree	6.3%
Strongly Disagree	2%
Don't Know	4.2%

3. Acts of criminality such as civil disobedience, trespass, and tree-spiking are reasonable ways to bring attention to environmental issues and prevent environmental harm.

Strongly Agree	13.4%
Agree	32.3%
Disagree	25.8%
Strongly Disagree	19.4%
Don't Know	8.6%

4. Destruction of property, including arson, is a reasonable way to fight those institutions that cause significant environmental harm.

Strongly Agree	3.1%
Agree	9.4%
Disagree	31.2%
Strongly Disagree	51%
Don't Know	5.2%

5. Harming human beings is never an option, even if it would mean preventing serious environmental harm.

Strongly Agree	52.1%
Agree	27.1%
Disagree	12.5%
Strongly Disagree	4.2%
Don't Know	4.2%

As can be seen, the respondents were quite optimistic about the possibility of bringing about significant improvements in the environment through legal means (87.5% agreeing or strongly agreeing that lobbying and other methods can work). The respondents were about evenly split on whether relatively minor criminal acts such as civil disobedience and tree spiking were appropriate, while there was little support for arson or the harming of human beings (although about one in ten would support arson, and about one in five either didn't know or disagreed that harming humans to prevent environmental harm was never an option).

On October 15, 2005, I attended a PETA conference in Toronto called "Helping Animals 101." The conference consisted of two days of films and talks presented by PETA staff. Topics ranged from philosophical discussions of animal rights to preparing vegan meals. Talks on community activism and "How to Organize a Demo" were coupled with a march on the Japanese embassy building in Toronto to protest a seal slaughter and another demonstration at a Kentucky Fried Chicken outlet. Approximately two hundred people attended the conference (a disproportionate number were college-age females), which I believe is appropriately described as an outreach-recruitment-education vehicle for the PETA organization. I administered a brief written survey to willing participants in the lobby of the hotel where the conference was held and to marchers en route to the Japanese embassy.[23] Results from the twenty-three respondents follow.

1. The use of animals for any reason (food, clothing, research experiments, entertainment) should be completely stopped.

Strongly Agree	73.9%
Agree	26.1%

2. Nonviolent acts of criminality (such as breaking into facilities and freeing lab animals) is a reasonable thing to do in order to prevent animal suffering.

Strongly Agree	54.5%
Agree	36.4%
Disagree	9%

3. Criminal acts such as arson (where there is no intent to harm a human being, but a person might be unintentionally harmed) are reasonable things to do in order to prevent animal suffering.

Strongly Agree	8.7%
Agree	30.4%
Disagree	26.1%
Strongly Disagree	30.4%
Don't Know	4.3%

4. Threatening to do violence to human beings is a reasonable way to prevent animal suffering.

Strongly Agree	4.3%
Agree	8.7%
Disagree	30.4%
Strongly Disagree	56.5%

5. Physical violence against human beings is a reasonable way to prevent animal suffering.

Strongly Agree	4.8%
Agree	4.8%
Disagree	28.5%
Strongly Disagree	57.1%
Don't Know	4.8%

6. "Lower life forms" such as fish, insects, and other invertebrates have rights, and are deserving of moral consideration.

Strongly Agree	72.7%
Agree	27.3%

The respondents were quite uniform in their ideological beliefs, expressing agreement for the goal of ending all animal exploitation and the notion of rights for even lower life forms. Surprisingly, a significant

minority (almost 40%) expressed support for arson, and an overwhelming majority (over 90%) supported nonviolent criminal actions such as
breaking into laboratories to free animals. However, there was very little
support for either violence or threats of violence against human beings.

Overall, while there was modest support for less serious crimes involving little or no threat of harm to humans, both sets of responses indicate
that mainstream activists do not support actions intended to harm humans.

The General Public

If there is a general lack of support in the movements themselves for
radical direct action, the general public's view of illegal actions is certainly far worse. Those who burn down buildings and physically attack
scientists have an insurmountable image problem with average citizens.

Kimberly D. Elsbach and Robert I. Sutton studied the Earth First!
method of dealing with negative criticism and described a four-step process the group used to manage bad publicity arising from illegal acts such
as tree spiking. In the first step, called "institutional conformity," group
practices mirror those of legitimate corporations, using spokespersons
and press releases to portray the movement or action as legitimate (the
researchers noted that sometimes Earth First! overshot its mark by
describing itself as "non-violent and peaceful," a statement legitimate
organizations do not need to make). In the second step, called "decoupling," the group seeks to separate legitimate organizational practices
from the illegal actions taken by underground members. This is achieved
through the use of independent affinity groups or anonymous individuals who carry out illegal actions but are not formally linked to the organization. In the third step, "impression management," institutional
conformity and decoupling increase overall credibility and pave the way
for impression management techniques such as making justifications for
illegal actions. Once justifications are made, the final stage involves shift-
ing attention to the positive outcomes of illegal actions (in this case, presumably, the end of animal exploitation and the preservation of the
environment).[24] The most obvious examples of this process in the present
study are the relationships between PETA and ALF, and between the
aboveground nonprofit group Stop Huntingdon Animal Cruelty (SHAC)
and the underground activists who carry out attacks against Huntingdon
Life Sciences. In both examples aboveground spokespersons walk a tight-
rope between legitimizing their organization and defending illegal
behavior. Ultimately, movement icons like Ingrid Newkirk come across as
duplicitous at best: decoupling is never achieved, the notion of separation
is a fiction, and no one is fooled.

In his study of "leaderless resistance," Garfinkel states that, while the
strategy can effectively thwart law enforcement, it is essentially an admis-
sion of failure—a last-ditch effort to keep the struggle alive. Moreover,

such a choice of tactics indicates a lack of public support for the group's ideology.[25]

The fundamental dilemma, and the reason animal liberation and radical environmentalism are doomed to fail, is expressed well, once again, by Eric Hoffer:

> Those who would transform a nation or the world cannot do so by breeding and captaining discontent or by demonstrating the reasonableness and desirability of the intended changes or by coercing people into a new way of life. They must know how to kindle and fan an extravagant hope.[26]

Most people oppose undue animal suffering, and few favor the wanton destruction of the natural world. But still fewer will accept the premise that a guinea pig has moral value equivalent to that of a child. Saving the environment is fine, so long as there's rocks in the scotch, iPods on demand, and enough chicken McNuggets to go around. Radical environmentalism and rights for animals is a tough sell, and few people are buying.

One Remote but Very Scary Possibility

One very real danger is that as underground radicals become marginalized and isolated from other members of their own movement, the process of progressive radicalization will produce more violent activists, including so-called lone wolves bent on generating significant human casualties. In his study of leaderless resistance, Garfinkel states that violent underground cells are unlikely to moderate over time, and the resistance movement could easily devolve into anarchistic acts of violence by individuals without any concrete political objective—angry loners, petty criminals, and copycats who, being powerless, merely seek to subvert a more powerful opponent (what sociobiologists call "cultural resistance").[27] Paradoxically, as ELF, ALF, and other underground groups ultimately fail, there will remain a fringe of the fringe, a mere handful of individuals, who may become far more dangerous.

Craig "Critter" Marshall, convicted of torching a car dealership in Eugene, Oregon, was quoted in the *New York Times*: "The problem is, we've gone too far already. There's no easy solution. For life to survive as we know it, millions of people are going to have to die. It's sad, but it's true."[28] Earth First! cofounder Dave Foreman has said, "Humanity is the cancer of nature. . . . The optimum human population of Earth is zero."[29] In an article from *Wild Earth*, he adds that "if you'll give the idea a chance, you might agree that the extinction of homo sapiens would mean survival for millions if not billions of other Earth-dwelling species."[30]

Just prior to the September 2001 terrorist attacks upon the United States, staff at the Center for Strategic and International Studies compiled a threat assessment concerning weapons of mass destruction. In their report they included four possible scenarios, one of which described a hypothetical "very bad day" following a biological weapons terrorist attack:

No signs or symptoms of an attack manifested themselves during the incubation period following the covert release of a biological agent. The first cases of the illness occur among those with the weakest immune systems: children, elderly, AIDS patients, and patients undergoing chemotherapy. These victims visit their primary care physicians with complaints akin to the flu. Primary care physicians, seeing nothing unusual in either the symptoms or the number of complaints, prescribe over-the-counter medicine, and send the initial victims home to rest. As the biological weapons produce person-to-person disease contagion, the victims infect their family and friends.

As cases mount in number and seriousness, and as odd symptoms manifest themselves, physicians begin to contact fellow physicians and local public health departments. Samples are flown to the nearest laboratory and subsequently to the Centers for Disease Control and Prevention (CDC) laboratory in Atlanta for diagnostic tests. The CDC determines the sample to be a genetically altered strain of smallpox.

The time lag between testing the first patients and diagnosing the cause of their illness allows the disease to spread further. Victims, and people believing themselves to be ill, crowd the hospitals. This depletes the supply of beds and equipment. Hoarding of medication by medical staffs across the country increases sharply. Antivirals are flown into the region but, without a distribution mechanism in place, fail to reach the public. The spread of the disease exponentially complicates the efforts of the CDC and public health officials to trace the origin of the disease. And the use of experimental antiviral agents introduce a host of complicated and novel issues—such as how to obtain informed consent (for use) from recipients and how to administer the agent to large numbers (particularly intravenously).

Containment of the epidemic is the top priority. Yet the public health and health care communities are unable to work together. The antiquated communications facilities of the public health officials break down under the strain. And, despite pre-existing policies such as the Federal Response Plan and Presidential Decision Directive 39, relationships "on the ground" between the FBI, the public health community, or the governor, and emergency responders, are ad hoc.

Widespread illness in the community results in significant shortages of personnel, thereby disrupting critical services including telecommunications, electric power, and air traffic control. The rapid spread of the disease causes officials to consider containment and community isolation as the first line of defense. Command, control, and communications prove inadequate. And it is not clear who is in charge.

In the end, a quarantine is instituted, but it is too late. Public health, law enforcement, and emergency response personnel are ill prepared to implement such an untested measure. Public health officials mishandle the announcement of the quarantine, sparking panic in outlying communities and causing thousands to flee. Pressured by their own fearful populations, governors of the surrounding states deploy the National Guard to prevent citizens from the infected state from entering. Unable to enter surrounding states, while unwilling to return to their homes, thousands of citizens become refugees. Civil order collapses.[31]

One study in 1972 concluded that an anthrax spore attack on New York City (anthrax has a downwind range of 20 kilometers) could cause 600,000 deaths, and that one pound of *salmonella typhi* or *Clostridium botulinum* in a reservoir would be just as effective as *ten tons* of cyanide. Biological agents are relatively easy to manufacture (relative to nuclear or chemical weapons), are inexpensive, and are difficult to detect once deployed. While experts disagree on the technical skills required to produce biological weapons (some say a second-year biology student could grow lethal weapons in the kitchen; others argue that a graduate-level scientist would need a bacteriology lab), it is true some seed cultures can easily be stolen from labs or even purchased by mail order from commercial firms. On the other hand, deployment could be difficult, as germs have a limited lifespan and are greatly affected by factors such as wind and temperature, let alone the detonation of a bomb.[32] To date there have been no large-scale biological attacks by terrorists, but the threat does exist.

What if a dedicated deep ecologist managed to acquire a "superflu," perhaps a new virus engineered in a bio-weapons lab (scientists recently re-created the 1918 flu virus that killed millions worldwide)—a strain that is highly infectious, moves fast, and is fatal in over half of all cases? Even if *Homo sapiens* were not wiped out entirely, such a global event would be enough to precipitate a collapse of "technological civilization"—a remote eventuality perhaps, but certainly not beyond the realm of possibility. And like the Aum Shinrikyo cult (the terrorists who deployed sarin gas and killed eleven people in the Tokyo subway in 1995),[33] there undoubtedly exists a handful of radical environmental and animal liberation activists who would not hesitate to destroy humankind in order to save the planet and its non-human inhabitants.

Radical Environmental and Animal Liberation Groups

Activists Working for Animal Rights
Animal Action Group
Animal Action League
Animal Avengers
Animal Avengers for Fur-Bearing Animals
Animal Defense League
Animal Liberation Action Foundation
Animal Liberation Front
Animal Liberation Victoria
Animal Rights Action
Animal Rights Calls
Animal Rights Militia
Animal S.O.S.
Animals Court of Justice
Animals Now
Arizona Phantom
Badgers Unknown
Band of Mercy (UK)
Band of Mercy (USA)
Barry Horne Brigade
Bye Bye Egg Industry
Cathedral Forest Action Group (EF!)
Cedar River Action Group (EF!)
Chicken McHappy
Clever Foxes
Coalition to Save the Preserves
Commando Helen Steel

Crustacean Liberation Front
David Organization
Direct Action
Djurens Hamnare
Dyrenes Frigjurings Front (DDF)
Earth First!
Earth Liberation Army
Earth Liberation Front (ELF)
Earth Night Action Group (EF!)
Eco-Commando Force 70
Eco-Raiders
Electronic Civil Disobedience
Enraged Bambis
Evan Mecham Ecoterrorist International Conspiracy (EMITIC)
F.A.R.M.
Farm Freedom Fighters
Farm Sanctuary
Feuesalamander
Forest Cleaning
Forever Free
Free Fish
Friends of Animals
Fund for Animals
Gateway to Hell
Greenpeace
Guardian Apes
Healthy Genetic Future
Human Animal Liberation Front
Hunt Retribution Squad
Justice and Action for Animals and Ecological Liberation
Justice Department
Justice for Animals
Last Chance for Animals
Lawn Liberation Front
Leadfree Forest
Meat Free Mission
Menehune
Militant Vegans
Ministry of Forest Defense
Nighttime Gardeners
Operation Wild Horse
Organization for the Liberation of Animals
Paint Panthers
PBFPF and the Swamp Fox
People for the Ethical Treatment of Animals (PETA)

People of the Earth
People's Brigade for a Healthy Genetic Future
Petaluma Pruners
Pirates for Animal Liberation
Poultry Liberation Organization
Primarily Primates
Quick Martens
Radical Wolves
Reclaim the Seeds
Red Lobster
Rescue Rangers
Santa and His Elves
Save the Newchurch Guinea Pigs
Scottish National Liberation Army
Sea Shepherd Conservation Society
Socialist Committee for the Protection of Animals
Stop Huntingdon Animal Cruelty (SHAC)
Students Against in Vivo Experiments and Dissection
Students Campaign for Animal Rights
Students United Protesting
SUPPRESS
The Black Elk
The Color of Autumn
The Fox
The Frogs
The Happily Celebrating Witches and Wizards
The Radical Vegetarians
The Voice of the Forest
The Wild Minks
Tierschutz Front
True Friends
Undersea Railroad
United Animal Rights Coalition
Urban Gorillas
Vegan Action League
Vegan Action Network
Vegan Front
Vegan Revolution
Vegan Supremacy
VIVA
Werewolves
Western Wildlife Unit (ALF)Animal Liberation Action Foundation
Yedi Knights

Congressional Hearing Statements

Barry M. Sabin,
Chief Counterterrorism Section,
Criminal Division, Department of Justice,
*Concerning Stop Huntingdon Animal Cruelty (SHAC)
and Other Animal Rights Extremists,*
testimony given before the Senate Committee
on the Environment and Public Works,
109th Cong., 1st sess.,
October 26, 2005.

Mr. Chairman, members of the Committee, thank you for providing me the opportunity to appear here today and testify before you concerning the Department of Justice's efforts to investigate and prosecute entities and individuals who commit criminal acts in the name of animal rights. In that regard, I will seek to address some of the strengths and limitations of the laws that presently provide the means by which we investigate and prosecute animal rights extremist matters. These investigations are an important part of the mission of the Department of Justice to protect the American people and our institutions from acts and threats of violence.

As you know, counterterrorism is the number one priority of the Department of Justice. As such, we remain dedicated to the task of protecting the American people from violence and the threat of violence posed by terrorism while at the same time protecting the First Amendment rights and other civil liberties guaranteed to all Americans in the Constitution. In protecting America and Americans from the threat of terrorism, though, we recognize that the threat to the American people comes not only from extremists overseas, but also from extremists located within our borders.

In order to ensure that the Department has all the necessary investigatory tools, legal authorities and appropriate penalties, the Department supports amending Title 18, United States Code, Section 43 to include economic disruption to animal enterprises and threats of death and serious bodily injury to associated persons. The proposed modifications provide a clear and constitutional framework for timely, effectively and justly addressing prohibited criminal conduct that will ensure that victims' rights are respected and preserved.

Justice Department Efforts to Combat Domestic Extremists

Mindful of incidents such as the 1995 bombing of the Alfred P. Murrah Federal Building in Oklahoma City, the United States government is resolved to address the use of violence by Americans, against other Americans, for the purpose of coercing the government or intimidating civilians in furtherance of political or social goals. The Department of Justice has had numerous recent successes in combating those Americans who commit acts of domestic terrorism. Working in a task force approach with our state and local partners, we have sought to timely share information across the nation to prevent incidents from occurring. These Joint Task Forces have sought to use all available investigatory tools, including undercover operations and informants, as well as all available criminal statutes, such as interstate stalking and explosives statutes, to disrupt violent groups and marshal compelling evidence to bring them to justice.

For example, in the past year the Department has prosecuted white supremacists who have used or threatened to use violence against other Americans. In November, 2004, in the District of Nevada, former Aryan Nations official Steve Holten pleaded guilty to sending threatening messages to employees of several local newspapers, as well as state government employees. On February 25, 2005, in the Western District of Pennsylvania, Ku Klux Klan leader David Wayne Hull was sentenced to 12 years in prison for unlawfully teaching a government informant how to construct an improvised explosive device. Matthew Hale—formerly the leader of the World Church of the Creator—was sentenced on April 6, 2005, to serve 40 years in prison for, among other things, soliciting the murder of a federal district court judge in the Northern District of Illinois. On August 30, 2005, neo-Nazi skinhead Scan Gillespie—who videotaped himself fire-bombing a synagogue—was sentenced to 39 years in prison in the Western District of Oklahoma.

The Department has also prosecuted other extremists who used or threatened to use explosives to commit acts of violence. On July 18, 2005, Eric Rudolph was sentenced to life in prison for the bombing of an abortion clinic in Birmingham, Alabama, as well as a night club and Centennial Park in Atlanta, Georgia. On September 12, 2005, Gale William Nettles was convicted of conspiring to blow up the Dirksen Federal Building in Chicago, Illinois. On September 22, 2005, former Jewish Defense League leader, Earl Krugel, was sentenced to twenty years in prison for carrying an explosive device as part of a conspiracy to injure or impede a United States Congressman and damage a mosque.

Similarly, the Department has also made progress in prosecuting animal rights and environmental extremists who have violated federal law. On November 19, 2004, in the Central District of California, William Cottrell was convicted for the arson of a car dealership in West Covina, California, as well as numerous sport utility vehicles. In the Western District of Wisconsin, Peter Young pleaded guilty on September 2, 2005, to violations of the Animal Enterprise Protection Act arising from his activities in 1997 in Wisconsin and other states. Earlier this month, on October 14, 2005, environmental extremist Ryan Lewis, and two associates, pleaded guilty in the Eastern District of California to arson and attempted arson of several partially completed homes under construction.

The Threat Posed by SHAC and Other Animal Rights Extremists

As this Committee well knows, animal rights extremists have not hesitated to use violence to further their social and political goals. In those cases where individuals have used improvised incendiary or explosive devices, federal prosecutors are well-equipped to prosecute and punish such individuals using the tools provided in Title 18, United States Code, section 844.

Domestic violence by animal rights extremists is not limited, however, to the use of arson and the use of explosives. As Mr. Lewis has described in his testimony, Stop Huntingdon Animal Cruelty (or SHAC) and other animal rights extremist organizations and entities are engaging in a campaign of criminal conduct which is calculated to aggressively intimidate and harass those whom it identifies as targets. In pursuit of its goal of closing the animal testing operations of Huntington Life Science (HLS), SHAC's campaign has included a wide variety of "direct action" techniques specifically designed to coerce the subjects of those efforts while avoiding an effective law enforcement response. Harassment of other businesses, and the employees of those businesses, vandalism of property belonging to individuals whose only offense is working for a company that does business with HLS, or, even worse, publication of private information about such individuals, their spouses and even their young children, are only some of the techniques used by SHAC and like-minded persons to coerce and intimidate companies and individuals. With every perceived success, SHAC emboldens other extremist organizations to act similarly. The personal and economic consequences of this campaign have been, and will continue to be, significant.

Tools for the Prosecution of SHAC and Similar Groups and Individuals

In the past, this kind of criminal conduct was prosecuted as a violation of the Hobbs Act, codified in section 1951 of Title 18 of the United States Code. In *Scheidler v. National Organization for Women*, however, the

United States Supreme Court held that, in order to commit the extortion that is the gravamen of a Hobbs Act violation, a defendant must actually "obtain" property—that is, he or she must take a tangible thing of value from his or her victim. The Supreme Court specifically rejected the notion that a Hobbs Act violation was committed by a person or entity who, like SHAC, acts to deprive the victim of the free exercise of his or her property rights. Thus, while conduct similar to SHAC's campaign was previously investigated and prosecuted as Hobbs Act violations, after the *Scheidler* decision in 2003, that option was no longer available to federal prosecutors.

On the other hand, the Animal Enterprise Protection Act, codified at section 43 of Title 18, is still an important tool for prosecutors seeking to combat animal rights extremists. This statute was passed in 1992 primarily to address the problem of those who physically intruded upon the property of entities who tested or otherwise used animals in order to damage the property belonging to the animal enterprise. Originally established as a misdemeanor, the statute's penalties have been enhanced by amendments in 1996 and 2002.

The Department has used Section 43 to charge SHAC and seven individual defendants in 537 U.S. 393, 123 S. Ct. 1057, 154 L.Ed.2d 991 (2003) federal district court in New Jersey. The indictment alleges that the defendants conspired to engage in "direct action" activities, which was described by SHAC to involve activities that "operate outside the confines of the legal system." The indictment further alleges that the SHAC Website posted what it termed the "top twenty terror tactics" that could be taken against companies or individuals.

The six-count superseding indictment alleges violations of interstate stalking, in violation of Title 18, United States Code, Section 2261 A, and conspiracy to utilize a telecommunications device to abuse, threaten and harass persons, in violation of Title 47, United States Code, Section 223(a)(l)(c). The charges are pending and a trial is scheduled for February, 2006.

While section 43 is an important tool for prosecutors, SHAC and other animal rights extremists have recognized limits and ambiguities in the statute and have tailored their campaign to exploit them. While the Department is confident that some of SHAC's conduct violates this statute in its current form, amendment of the statute to make clear and unequivocal the application of the statute to recent trends in animal rights extremism will enhance the effectiveness of the Department's response to this domestic threat.

Proposed Amendment of Title 18, United States Code, Section 43

Accordingly, the Department supports Senator Inhofe's effort to amend the Animal Enterprise Protection Act in order to address several gaps in the law that keep prosecutors from using it in the most effective manner possible.

First, the statute's definition of the type of "animal enterprise" that it protects is not broad enough to include some of the entities that are now targeted by SHAC and other animal rights extremists. These include pet stores and even animal shelters. The threat posed to individuals associated with such organizations is no less significant than the threat that gave rise to the original statute. Senator Inhofe's proposal would expand the definition of "animal enterprise" so that these types of victims are also clearly included within the scope of the statute.

Second, the statute's use of the phrase "physical disruption" to describe the conduct it proscribes unnecessarily suggests that it covers a narrow scope of conduct tantamount to trespass. In that regard, the statute permits the argument that it does not cover actions by SHAC or other animal rights extremists taken not against an animal enterprise, but against those entities that choose to do business with an animal enterprise. While careful parsing of the language of the statute makes clear that this is not the case, lack of clarity threatens effective use of the statute. Senator Inhofe's proposal avoids this ambiguity by focusing instead on "economic disruption" (that is, business losses) and "economic damage" (that is, physical property damage) resulting from the threats or property damage that it would proscribe. In doing so, it would more effectively protect animal enterprises from the criminal conduct in which animal rights extremists like SHAC currently engage.

Third, Senator Inhofe's proposal would include this type of criminal conduct as a predicate for seeking electronic surveillance authority. Participants in the animal rights extremist movement exercise excellent tradecraft, and are very security conscious. Animal rights extremists have made extensive use of the internet for communications and have relied upon electronic mail and other communications media to interact. These communications are occurring on a national level, and electronic surveillance provides law enforcement authorities a timely and effective means for capturing and sharing information. Law enforcement personnel should not be restricted from proactively seeking approval from a federal district court judge to capture probative evidence that would assist their criminal investigations.

Fourth, in its current form, the statute fails to address clearly the consequences of a campaign of vandalism and harassment directed against individuals—as opposed to the animal enterprise itself. Senator Inhofe's proposal would remedy this ambiguity by clearly stating that committing the proscribed conduct against an individual, including an employee of an animal enterprise (or of an entity with a relationship with an animal enterprise), is equally illegal.

Finally, Senator Inhofe's proposal provides a range of penalties including imprisonment, fines and restitution that are tailored to reflect the nature and severity of the criminal conduct. This broad range of penalties will enable the government to effectively and appropriately charge the accused with a crime commensurate with the accused's criminal conduct and to seek punishment reflecting that degree of culpability.

Viewed in its entirety, the changes in Senator Inhofe's proposal would empower prosecutors with a more effective tool to meet the challenges now posed by animal rights extremists. I strongly encourage the Committee to endorse this proposal.

Protecting the Victims

It is important to underscore that this Congress and the Justice Department have taken significant steps to assist and protect victims of crime. The Justice For All Act, passed with overwhelming bipartisan support one year ago (Title 18, United States Code, Section 3771), and the Attorney General Guidelines on Victim and Witness Assistance, as revised in May, 2005, recognize the rights of crime victims and the importance of reasonable protections for victims from defendants, or those persons acting in concert with or at the behest of suspected offenders. Senator Inhofe's proposed legislation seeks to build upon this foundation. The criminal conduct of animal rights extremists is directed against individuals and companies in order to intentionally place these victims in reasonable fear of death or serious bodily injury. These victims suffer—often mentally, physically, and monetarily—when extremists threaten them, damage their property and affect their livelihood. This is not First Amendment protected speech, but rather criminal conduct that is within the traditional realm of statutes prohibiting threats, violence, or injury to innocent victims.

Respecting the First Amendment

In seeking to meet the challenge of these changing forms of criminal conduct by animal rights extremists, the Department is acutely aware of the importance of protecting the First Amendment rights of those who protest any cause they believe right, including the testing and other use of animals. Let me be clear: The Department does not seek to prosecute those who enter the arena of debate seeking to persuade their government or private businesses and individuals of the merit of their viewpoints, and this proposal would not—indeed, could not—criminalize such protected activity. We seek to prosecute criminal conduct, including conduct that places a person in reasonable fear of death or serious bodily injury.

The First Amendment is not a license for the use or threatened use of violence, or for the commission of other crimes. Even if these crimes are politically motivated—even if they are committed as a form of protest— Congress is empowered to prohibit the conduct it deems offensive without running afoul of the First Amendment. Those who cross the line from free speech to criminal conduct should be prosecuted and, if convicted, they should be punished appropriately. As it has done in other contexts, Congress must give prosecutors the tools to do so fairly and effectively.

Conclusion

Prior Congressional action has provided law enforcement and prosecutors with a solid framework within which to pursue the goal of prevention and disruption of violent extremism within our borders. We in the Justice Department have more work to do to eliminate this dangerous threat, and we urge you in Congress to continue to build upon and enhance the legal tools needed to accomplish our mutual goals.

Mr. Chairman, thank you for your leadership on this issue and again for inviting us here and providing us the opportunity to discuss how the statutes are being used consistent with our Constitutional values—to fight violent extremism within our criminal justice system. We would also like to thank this Committee for its continued leadership and support. Together, we will continue our efforts to secure justice and defeat those who would harm this country.

John Lewis,
Deputy Assistant Director,
Federal Bureau of Investigation,
Oversight on Eco-terrorism specifically examining the Earth Liberation Front ("ELF") and the Animal Liberation Front ("ALF"), statement given to the Senate Committee on Environment and Public Works, 109th Cong., 1st sess., May 18, 2005.

Good morning Chairman Inhofe, Ranking Member Jeffords, and members of the Committee. I am pleased to have the opportunity to appear today and to discuss the threat posed by animal rights extremists and eco-terrorists in this country, as well as the measures the FBI and its partners are taking to address this threat.

One of today's most serious domestic terrorism threats come from special interest extremist movements such as the Animal Liberation Front (ALF), the Earth Liberation Front (ELF), and Stop Huntingdon Animal Cruelty (SHAC) campaign. Adherents to these movements aim to resolve specific issues by using criminal "direct action" against individuals or companies believed to be abusing or exploiting animals or the environment.

"Direct action" is often criminal activity that destroys property or causes economic loss to a targeted company. Traditional targets have ranged from, but have not been limited to, research laboratories to restaurants, fur farmers to forestry services. Extremists have used arson, bombings, theft, animal releases, vandalism, and office takeovers to achieve their goals.

The distinctions between constitutionally protected advocacy and violent, criminal activity are extremely important to recognize, and law enforcement officials should be solely concerned with those individuals who pursue animal rights or environmental protection through force, violence, or criminal activity. Law enforcement only becomes involved when volatile talk turns into criminal activity. Unfortunately, the FBI has seen a significant amount of such criminal activity. From January 1990 to June 2004, animal and environmental rights extremists have claimed credit for more than 1,200 criminal incidents, resulting in millions of dollars in damage and monetary loss.

While most animal rights and eco-extremists have refrained from violence targeting human life, the FBI has observed troubling signs that this is changing. We have seen an escalation in violent rhetoric and tactics. One extremist recently said, "If someone is killing, on a regular basis, thousands of animals, and if that person can only be stopped in one way by the use of violence, then it is certainly a morally justifiable solution."

Attacks are also growing in frequency and size. Harassing phone calls and vandalism now co-exist with improvised explosive devices and personal threats to employees. ELF's target list has expanded to include sports utility vehicle dealerships and new home developers. We believe these trends will persist, particularly within the environmental movement, as extremists continue to combat what they perceive as "urban sprawl."

Preventing such criminal activity has become increasingly difficult, in large part because extremists in these movements are very knowledgeable about the letter of the law and the limits of law enforcement. Moreover, they are highly autonomous. Lists of targets and instructions on making incendiary devices are posted on the Internet, but criminal incidents are carried out by individuals or small groups acting unilaterally. Criminal activity by animal rights extremists and eco-terrorists in particular requires relatively minor amounts of equipment and minimal funding. Extremists of these movements adhere to strict security measures in both their communications and their operations.

The FBI has developed a strong response to domestic terrorism threats. Together with our partners, we are working to detect, disrupt, and dismantle the animal rights and environmental extremist movements that are involved in criminal activity.

Our efforts are headed by a headquarters-based team of national intelligence analysts, program managers, and seasoned field agents. We draw on the resources of our Terrorist Financing Operations Section to support field investigations into domestic terrorism, just as we do for international terrorism investigations. We also draw upon our expertise in the area of communication analysis to provide investigative direction.

Second, we have strengthened our intelligence capabilities. Since 2003, we have disseminated sixty-four raw intelligence reports to our partners pertaining to animal rights extremism and eco-terrorism activity. In addition, since 2004 we have disseminated nineteen strategic intelligence assessments to our federal, state and local counterparts. And we have developed an intelligence requirement set for animal rights/eco-terrorism, enabling us to better collect, analyze, and share information.

Finally, we have strengthened our partnerships. We have combined our expertise and resources with those of our federal, state and local law enforcement partners nationwide through our 103 Joint Terrorism Task Forces. We have increased training for JTTF members, and have strong liaison with foreign law enforcement agencies.

Our challenges are significant, but so are our successes. Currently, thirty-five FBI offices have over 150 pending investigations associated with animal rights/eco-terrorist activities. Since the beginning of 2004, the FBI and its partners have made a number of high-profile arrests of individuals involved with animal rights extremism or eco-terrorism. These arrests have led to several successful prosecutions.

Let me give you a brief snapshot of our recent successes:

In 2005:

- An individual who had been a fugitive, was arrested and charged with two counts of Animal Enterprise Terrorism for a series of animal releases at mink farms in 1997;
- Three individuals were arrested for a series of arsons and attempted arsons of construction sites in California; and
- One individual was arrested for the 2003 arson of a McDonald's in Seattle.

In 2004:

- Two individuals were arrested for arson on the campus of Brigham Young University in Utah;
- Seven individuals associated with SHAG were arrested in New Jersey, California, and Washington State;
- An individual was arrested and indicted for arsons of logging and construction equipment;
- William Cottrell was indicted and convicted last month in California for conspiracy to commit arson, seven counts of arson; and
- Two individuals were arrested in Virginia during an attempt to firebomb a car dealership.

These are just some of our many accomplishments, but we have much more work ahead of us. One of our greatest challenges has been the lack of federal criminal statutes to address multi-state campaigns of intimidation, threats, and damage designed to shut down legitimate businesses.

On the legislative front, we are interested in working with you to examine federal criminal statutes, specifically 18 USC 43, "Animal Enterprise Terrorism." The statute provides a framework for the prosecution of animal rights extremists, but in practice, it does not cover many of the criminal acts that extremists have committed.

Additionally, the statute only applies to criminal acts committed by animal rights extremists, but does not address criminal activity related to eco-terrorism.

Therefore, the existing statutes may need refinements to make them more applicable to current animal rights/eco-extremist actions and to give law enforcement more effective means to bring criminals to justice.

Investigating and preventing animal rights extremism and eco-terrorism is one of the FBI's highest domestic terrorism priorities. We are committed to working with our partners to disrupt and dismantle these movements, and to bring to justice those who commit crime in the name of animal or environmental rights. Chairman Inhofe and Members of the Committee, I appreciate the opportunity to discuss the challenges we face and the ways we can overcome them. I would be happy to answer any questions you may have.

Thank you.

Jerry Vlasak, MD,
statement given to the Senate Committee
on Environment and Public Works,
109th Cong., 1st sess.,
October 26, 2005

I. Introductory remarks

Good afternoon, gentleman, my name is Dr. Jerry Vlasak. I am a practicing trauma surgeon, but more importantly for today's purpose, I am a Press Officer with the North American Animal Liberation Press Office. I am also a former vivisector.

The stated purpose of the Animal Liberation Press Office is: to communicate the actions, strategies, philosophy and history of the underground animal liberation movement to the media and the public, and that's what I hope to do here today.

The actions of underground activists who care enough about animals to speak out in no uncertain terms, and at times to risk their own lives and freedom, have a message that is most urgent and one that deserves to be heard and understood. Often underground animal liberation speech and actions either go unreported in the media or are uncritically vilified as "violent" or "terrorist", with no attention paid to the needless and senseless suffering that industries and individuals gratuitously inflict on animals. The Press Office seeks to clarify the motivation and nature of underground actions taken in defense of animals.

II. HLS

Huntingdon Life Sciences (HLS) is the largest contract testing lab in Europe, and operates facilities in the UK and New Jersey. They kill 500 animals a day. HLS will test anything for anybody. They carry out experiments which involve poisoning animals with household products, pesticides, drugs, herbicides, food colorings and additives, sweeteners and genetically modified organisms, oven cleaner, and makeup.

HLS has been infiltrated and exposed five times in recent years by journalists, animal rights campaigners and members of the public; each time evidence of animal abuse and staff incompetence has been uncovered. A 1999 inspection of their Occold (UK) facility by the Good Laboratory Practice Monitoring Authority revealed forty-one deficiencies, including errors in standard operating procedures, training issues, record keeping, quality assurance, equipment, labeling and facilities. 520 violations of the UK Good Laboratory Practices Act were documented in an expose by the Daily Press (UK) in 2000. They are the only UK laboratory to ever have their license revoked by the government. In East Millstone, NJ in 1997, an investigator from the People for the Ethical Treatment of Animals brought information to light that forced Huntingdon to plead guilty to animal cruelty violations and pay a $50,000 fine.

III. SHAC

The campaign Stop Huntingdon Animal Cruelty (SHAC) was set up at the end of 1999. In what has become an international campaign in more than eighteen countries, a campaign that knows no limit to the creativity and length to which many demonstrators will go, SHAC has brought HLS to the brink of financial ruin. It is important to realize that SHAC is not one group, or hierarchical entity, but an ideologically aligned group consisting of thousands of people who gather in various groups to protest the atrocities perpetrated by HLS. While some like SHAG USA are incorporated, above ground non-profit organizations, who engage in legal demonstrations, legal boycotts and legal leafleting/education of the public, other groups are just individuals loosely knit. It is ridiculous to think that SHAG USA and SHAG UK is one group with a top-down organization that controls all activities worldwide.

IV. NYSE De-listing

On September 7, 2005 HLS was due to begin trading on the NYSE under the symbol LSR. Moments before trading was to begin, and with HLS executives on the stock exchange floor to celebrate, the listing was cancelled without comment. There was no direct or indirect reference or mention of animal rights action. Did NYSE president Catherine Kinney halt the listing because she had just realized the financial temerity of HLS, or did she decide that a company as debased and cruel as HLS should not be associated with her exchange? The New York Stock Exchange's reluctance to admit the lab is understandable, as the company hides their financial details from public scrutiny. Currently HLS stock still trades on the OTCBB under the symbol LSRI. It was de-listed from the London Stock Exchange in 2002; the company reincorporated in Maryland and underwent a reverse 5:1 stock split. It's split-adjusted price today is a bit under $2.00 per share. Chairman of the Board and CEO Andrew Baker owns 27% of the stock, and in June fronted the company another $43 million in a leaseback offer giving him personal ownership of the company's land, buildings and equipment, which he leases back to them. Even after that massive infusion of cash, HLS still reports a whopping $75.9 million debt. A $50 million bond is payable in mid 2006. No commercial bank or insurance company is willing to do business with HLS, and at least twenty-five market makers have thus far refused to deal in their stock. HLS has not paid a dividend in many years, two of its directors are third-world based and have no experience in the field, and its annual shareholders meetings are held secretly in Panama. Hundreds of customers and suppliers have cancelled their contracts with HLS, choosing not to do business with a company dealing in the torture and killing of defenseless animals. Is this the kind of business that belongs on any stock exchange? In the last two weeks, HLS share price has gone into a downfall, as company after company sheds their stock from their portfolios. More than a million shares have been divested, as companies are informed about the vile business carried out by HLS. One company, Awad, stated that had they known about the cruelty at HLS, they probably would have never invested in them.

Oct. 20, 2005-WASHINGTON MUTUAL SELLS OFF 188,430 OF THEIR SHARES IN HLS!
Oct. 19, 2005-ROYCE & ASSOC. SELL OFF 120,000 SHARES!
Oct. 19, 2005-THOMSON, HORSTMANN & BRYANT, INC SELL OFF 123,500 SHARES!
Oct. 18, 2005-CORTINA SELLS OFF THEIR 165,000 LSRI SHARES!
Oct. 13, 2005-AWAD SELLS OFF THEIR 250,000 SHARES IN LSRI!
Oct. 12, 2005-GREENVILLE CAPITAL MANAGEMENT SELLS OFF THEIR 251,000 SHARES IN LSRI!

V. About the Animal Liberation Movement

By their accusations against SHAG and the ALF, some are trying to disguise where the real violence exists, and not the violence of extensional self-defense, but the real violence, of Huntingdon laboratories. Other activists watch all this, and become embittered and frustrated until they begin utilizing more radical... [At this point, a portion of Vlasak's statement was missing from the website posted by the Senate Committee on the Environment and Public Works.]

VI. CCF

When it met in May of this year to discuss "animal enterprise terrorism", this committee heard from David Martosko, director of research for a lobbyist group called Center for Consumer Freedom (CCF). The Center for Consumer Freedom, formerly known as the Guest Choice Network, was set up by one Richard Berman with a $600,000 "donation" from tobacco company Philip Morris. Berman arranges for large sums of corporate money to find its way into non-profit societies of which he is the executive director. He then hires his own company as a consultant to these nonprofit groups. Of the millions of dollars "donated" by Philip Morris between the years 1995 and 1998, 49 percent to 79 percent went directly to Berman or Berman &Co. On November 16, 2004, Citizens for Responsibility and Ethics in Washington (CREW) filed a complaint with the Internal Revenue Service alleging that CCF has violated its tax-exempt status. The complaint alleges that CCF engaged in prohibited electioneering, made substantial payments to the founder of the organization, Richard Berman, and to Berman's wholly owned for profit entity Berman & Co., and engaged in activities with no charitable purpose. CREW executive director Melanie Sloan told Forbes magazine, "It doesn't seem to me that someone should get a tax deduction while they're writing public relations memos about how people should be able to smoke in restaurants."

VII. Summation

Each of the witnesses that have testified before me have their own financial interests at stake in the continued oppression, torture and murder of non-human animals by HLS. HLS is only one representative of the Global Vivisection Complex, an outdated, inefficient and wasteful entity whose time has come and gone. What are the major medical breakthroughs in the areas of cancer research, HIV/AIDS treatments, Parkinson's or other debilitating diseases has LSR's work been at the forefront of? According to recent opinion polls, only 13% of the public have confidence or trust in the Pharmaceutical industry, ranking amongst the likes of big tobacco, the oil industry, and insurance companies (Harris Poll published in July of 2005). In August of 2005, Opinion Research Corporation International of Princeton, New Jersey found that 67% of the U.S. would rather donate to medical research that does not involve animal experimentation.

In the 21st century, there is absolutely no need to torture and kill non-human animals to advance human medicine. The majority of physicians in the UK, according to a recent poll, are against animal experimentation and feel it is not necessary for medical research. Here in the U.S., there are thousands of physicians like myself who realize there is no need to kill animals in order to help humans, the vast majority of whom get sick and die because of preventable lifestyle variables such as diet, smoking, drugs and environmental toxins. In a country where 45 million people do without reliable access to ANY medical care, there is no reason to waste hundreds of millions of dollars testing drugs and procedures on non-human animals. In a world where 20,000 children are dying from lack of access to clean water each week worldwide, there is no reason to waste hundreds of millions of dollars testing drugs and procedures on non-human animals.

Huntingdon is the poster child for the abhorrent, unnecessary and wasteful industry that not only murders millions of innocent, suffering animals, but dooms countless humans to their own unnecessary suffering as scarce health-care dollars are wasted on useless animal research and testing.

Craig Rosebraugh,
Former Press Officer,
Earth Liberation Front,
Ecoterrorism and Lawlessness on the National Forests,
testimony given before the House Committee on Resources,
Subcommittee on Forests and Forest Health,
107th Congress, 2nd Session,
February 12, 2002

When a long train of abuses and usurpations, pursuing invariably the same object, evinces a design to reduce [the people] under absolute despotism, it is their right, it is their duty, to throw off such government, and to provide new guards for their future security. The oppressed should rebel, and they will continue to rebel and raise disturbance until their civil rights are fully restored to them and all partial distinctions, exclusions and incapacitations are removed.

—Thomas Jefferson, 1776

On April 15, 1972, I came into this world as a child of two wonderful parents living in Portland, Oregon. Growing up in the Pacific Northwestern region of the United States, I had the privilege of easy access to the natural world. Much of my childhood was spent in the fields and forested areas behind our home, playing and experiencing life in my time of innocence. I had no knowledge of societal problems, especially those pertaining to the natural environment.

Throughout my childhood and adolescent years, the education I received from my parents, schools, popular media and culture instilled in me a pride for my country, for my government, and everything the United States represented. I was taught about the great American history, our Constitution, Bill of Rights, and our legacy of being at the forefront of democracy and freedom. I considered myself to be just an average boy taking an active part in the popular American pastimes of competitive sports, consumer culture, and existing within a classic representation of the standard, middle-class suburban lifestyle.

Upon graduating from high school, I became exposed to new forms of education and ideas. Resulting from my exposure to people from differing socio-economic backgrounds and beginning college, I found my horizons beginning to widen. For the first time in my life, I was presented with the notion of political and social conflict coupled with the various issues contained within both categories. It was alarming yet, at the same time, invigorating as I began to feel passion burn within me.

George Bush, Sr. had just thrust the United States into what became known as the Gulf War. Now, as I was raised with a certain absolutist support of my country and government, my first inclination was to wave the stars and stripes and support unconditionally this noble pursuit of "promoting democracy and freedom" in the "less fortunate" and "uncivilized" lands. Yet, as I began to look further into the matter, I found myself asking questions such as why are we there? Why are we killing civilians? What is the true motive behind the conflict? After extensive research, I came to the logical and truthful conclusion that natural resources and regional power were the primary motives.

As news from independent sources slowly filtered out, I became increasingly horrified at the slaughter of Iraqi civilians by the U.S. military. With NO WAR FOR OIL as my personal guiding statement, I joined the local anti-war protests and movement existing in Portland, Oregon. Little did I realize that this first political activity would lead me to a life of devotion to true justice and real freedom.

While my anti-war involvement progressed, I also began to understand the disastrous relationship our modern society has with the many animal nations. Out of an interest inspired both by independent reading and through early college courses, I became involved with a local animal advocacy organization. At first, I attended meetings to hear the numerous arguments for the rights of animals and further my own education. The more I learned, the more compelled I felt to involve myself fully in working for animal protection. My activities went from merely attending meetings, rallies, and protests to organizing them. Of all the issues I had learned about during the six years I spent with that organization, I focused the majority of my time, research, and interest on fighting against the use of animals in biomedical and scientific experimentation.

While a great percentage of the public in the United States had been convinced that animal research progressed and continues to improve human health, I soon realized that this myth was not only untruthful and single sided, but the work of a slick public relations campaign by the pharmaceutical industry in coordination with federal agencies such as the National Institutes of Health. I also learned that just like the factory farm industry, the use of animals for human entertainment and for the fashion industry, animal experimentation was motivated first and foremost by profits. Furthermore, I learned how the government of the United States not only economically supports these various institutions of exploitation and slaughter, but how it continues to perpetuate and politically support the dangerous lie that animal research saves human lives. My support for various governmental policies was slowly fading.

And then memories of innocence were torn away. In the early 1990s, I learned that the lush natural acreage I used to play in as a child had been sold to a development firm. It intended to bulldoze the entire area and create a virtual community of homes for the upper middle class to wealthy. Within two years, the land as I knew it was no more. The visual reminder I used to appreciate, the one that would take me back to the years when the fields and trees were my playground, was stolen by a development corporation who saw more value in the land as luxurious houses than for its natural beauty and life.

I remember asking myself, what would happen to the various wildlife who made the area their home for so many years? Where would the deer, coyotes, skunks, wild cats, mice, raccoons, opossums, and others go? It was obvious that the developers had not even considered these questions. Rather, it appeared, the main pursuit of the corporation was working towards building incredibly large homes as close as possible to one another for maximum financial gain.

As the 1990s progressed, I became increasingly aware of the relationship between social and political problems in the United States. No single issue was truly independent but rather was affected by many others. In my work with the local animal advocacy organization, I realized that exploitation and destruction at the hands of human domination over animals also involved much more. Economics, politics, sociology, psychology, anthropology, science, religion, and other disciplines all played a significant role in understanding this unhealthy and unbalanced relationship between humans and other animals. But, by far the most important realization I made was that the problems facing animals, the problems facing the natural environment, and those affecting humans all came from a primary source. Understanding this crucial connection, I co-founded a non-profit organization in 1996 dedicated to educating the public on this fundamental realization.

During the mid-1990s, through continued formal and informal education, I also began to understand that the history I had learned growing up was only one story of many. I gained insight into the fact that everything I had learned about the origins of the United States of America had been purely from the viewpoint of the colonists and European settlers. Thus, the history I was taught was from the Perspective of the privileged white man, which not only told a mere fraction of the story, but also provided an extreme amount of misinformation as well.

I was never taught that the origins of this country were based upon murder, exploitation, and ultimate genocide. My teachers neglected to mention the fact that the white European settlers nearly annihilated the various indigenous peoples who had existed on this land for ages. Instead, I was taught about Thanksgiving and Columbus Day. I bought into this version of American history so much that I vividly recall my excitement over creating a paper model of one of Columbus' ships years ago.

No one ever seemed to provide the insight to me that the settlers, immediately upon their arrival, immediately enslaved the natives, and forced them to work and assist the European powers in their quest for gold and spices. Likewise, I failed to ever have access to a true African-American history that began when blacks were captured and shipped as property to this land to work as slaves for white men.

While I was taught about the so-called "Great American Revolution," it was never mentioned that this war for independence against the European powers only served and benefited the privileged white male. Of course, all white men were privileged to some degree; however, many were enslaved initially just like the natives and blacks. Women, natives, blacks, and, to a limited degree, poor whites were considered property, bought, sold, and owned by the affluent white hierarchy.

In school, my teachers did explain to me the importance of the U.S. Constitution and the Bill of Rights and how our forefathers drew up these documents to serve the people. This, I learned, was the foundation of our supposed great democracy. Yet, in reality, these items were created by the white power structure and only served to benefit the privileged members of white society. Women, blacks, natives, and poor white men still were not enfranchised nor had any accessibility to self-determination and freedom. Land ownership—a notion completely foreign and absurd to most of the indigenous—became a deciding factor of power and privilege for white men. Those without land lacked the opportunity for the vote, for ultimate power and respect.

As more and more settlers pushed westward through the country, the government committed endless treaty breaches and violations, stealing land that whites had allotted to the indigenous. Perhaps one of the most disturbing facts was that these original agreements made between various indigenous nations and the United States government were supposed to have international standing. Each of the indigenous populations was recognized at the time each document was signed as being a sovereign nation and, yet, the U.S. government still exerted its power and domination to steal land for eventual development and drainage of resources. This genocide against the varied Native American nations by the United States continues today with innocent people such as Leonard Pettier being imprisoned for years simply due to the government's perception of him as a political threat. Free Leonard Peltier!

On July 4 annually, U.S. citizens celebrate the founding of our country, most either blatantly forgetting or ignorant of the true issues surrounding that date. The fact that the United States as a nation systematically committed mass genocide against the indigenous of these lands, to catastrophic extremities, is certainly no cause for celebration. Rather, it should be a time for mourning, for remembrance, and, most of all for education of our children so we are not doomed to repeat the mistakes of the past.

The plight of blacks and women throughout U.S. history, although perhaps not as overtly catastrophic, still constituted outright mass murder, enslavement, exploitation, and objectification. Early on, white European settlers found that natives were much more difficult to enslave and manage due to their ability to maintain at least partial elements of their cultures. When blacks began to first arrive on slave ships, chained in the darkness below the decks, white settlers theorized they would make better slaves because they would be further removed from their cultures. Thus, the enslavement of blacks began in this land and would, in its overt form, last for a couple hundred years. During this time and well beyond, blacks were considered property to be bought, sold, traded, used, and disposed of at will.

Even after the abolitionist movement, which began in the 1820s, blacks continued to be considered second-rate citizens, restricted from voting and experiencing the free life which whites were accustomed. When the modern U.S. civil rights movement began in the 1940s, it took some twenty years of constant hardship and struggle to achieve some reform in the fascist policies of the United States. Even though blacks "won" the right to vote and exist in desegregated zones, there still was an absence of overall freedom, never any actual resemblance of equality. Today, the saga continues. While African Americans have made incredible progress in obtaining certain rights and privileges, there continues to be a more hidden, underlying discrimination that is every bit as potent. We can see a clear example by taking an honest look at the prison industrial complex and understanding who continues to be enslaved in mass to make that industry financially viable. Free Mumia Abu Jamal! Free the Move 9! Free all the political prisoners in the United States!

A similar and equally unfortunate history has and continues to haunt women in U.S. society. Also once considered property, women were not even able to vote in this country until the 1920s. Even after, they continued to be faced with a patriarchal society consisting of white men in power. While women have made many wonderful advances for themselves, they still exist today in the United States under that same sexist and patriarchal society. A quick glance at the profiles of the federal government as well as top CEOs from U.S. corporations fully illustrates this reality.

When I co-founded the non-profit organization in Portland, Oregon, in 1996, I was becoming more aware that the similarities in the human, environmental, and animal advocacy movements stemmed from this rich U.S. history, not of glory, freedom and democracy, but of oppression in its sickest forms. I began to also realize that just as the U.S. white male power structure put itself on a pedestal above everyone else, it also maintained that attitude toward the natural environment and the various animal nations existing within it. As a society, we have continuously acted towards these natural life forms as though we owned them, therefore giving us the right to do whatever we wanted and could do to them.

Particularly, with the advent of the industrial revolution in the United States, the destruction of the natural world took a sharp turn for the worse. The attitude, more so than ever, turned to one of profits at any cost and a major shift from sustainable living to stockpiling for economic benefit. This focus on stockpiling and industrial productivity caused hardship on communities, forcing local crafters and laborers to be driven out of business by overly competitive industries. Additionally, with this new focus on sacrificing sustainable living for financial gain, natural resources were in greater demand than ever. Semi-automatic to automatic machinery, production lines, the automobile, the roadway system, suburbs, and the breakup of small, fairly self-sufficient communities all came about, at least in part, due to the industrial revolution. This unhealthy and deadly transgression of course was supported and promoted by the U.S. government, always eager to see growth in the domestic economy.

All of this set the stage for the threatening shortage of natural resources and the massive environmental pollution and destruction present today in the United States. In cities such as Los Angeles, Detroit, and Houston, the air and soil pollution levels are so extreme people have suffered and continue to face deadly health problems. Waterways throughout the country, including the Columbia Slough in my backyard, are so polluted from industries it is recommended that humans don't even expose themselves to the moisture let alone drink unfiltered, unbottled water. The necessary and crucial forests of the Pacific Northwestern region of the country have been systematically destroyed by corporations such as Boise Cascade, Willamette Industries, and others within the timber industry whose sole motive is profits regardless of the expense to the health of an ecosystem. In Northern California, the sacred old growths, dreamlike in appearance, taking your breath away at first glance, have been continuously threatened and cut by greedy corporations such as Pacific Lumber/Maxxam. The same has occurred and still is a reality in states including Washington, Oregon, Idaho, and Colorado.

The first National Forests were established in the United States more than a century ago. One hundred fifty-five of them exist today spread across 191 million acres. Over the years, the forest products industry has decimated publicly owned National Forests in this country, leaving a horrendous trail of clearcuts and logging roads. Commercial logging has been responsible for annihilating nearly all of the nation's old growth forests, draining nutrients from the soil, washing topsoil into streams, destroying wildlife habitat, and creating an increase in the incidence and severity of forest fires. Only an estimated 4 percent of old growth forests in the United States are remaining.

The National Forests in the United States contain far more than just trees. In fact, more than 3,000 species of fish and wildlife, in addition to 10,000 plant species, have their habitat within the National Forests. This includes at least 230 endangered plant and animal species. All of these life forms co-exist symbiotically to naturally create the rich and healthy ecosystems needed for life to exist on this planet.

The benefits of a healthy forest cannot be overrated. Healthy forests purify drinking water, provide fresh clean air to breathe, stabilize hillsides, and prevent floods. Hillsides clearcut or destroyed by logging roads lose their ability to absorb heavy rainfall. If no trees exist to soak up moisture with roots to hold the soil, water flows freely down slopes, creating muddy streams, polluting drinking water, strengthening floods, and causing dangerous mudslides. Instead of valuing trees and forests for being necessary providers of life, the U.S. Forest Service and commercial logging interests have decimated these precious ecosystems.

The timber corporations argue that today in the United States more forests exist than perhaps at any time in the last century or more. It doesn't take a forestry specialist to realize that monoculture tree farms— in which one species of tree, often times non-native to the area, is grown in mass in a small area for maximum production do not equate to a healthy forest. Healthy forests are made up of diverse ecosystems consisting of many native plant and animal species. These healthy ecosystems are what grant humans and all other life forms on the planet with the ability to live. Without clean air, clean water, and healthy soil, life on this planet will cease to exist. There is an overwhelming battery of evidence that conclusively shows that we are already well on our path toward massive planetary destruction.

The popular environmental movement in the United States, which arguably began in the 1960s, has failed to produce the necessary protection needed to ensure that life on this planet will continue to survive. This is largely due to the fact that the movement has primarily consisted of tactics sanctioned by the very power structure that is benefiting economically from the destruction of the natural world. While a few minor successes in this country should be noted, the overwhelming constant trend has been the increasingly speedy liquidation of natural resources and annihilation of the environment.

The state sanctioned tactics, that is, those approved by the U.S. government and the status quo and predominantly legal in nature, rarely, if ever, actually challenge or positively change the very entities that are responsible for oppression, exploitation, and, in this case, environmental destruction. Throughout the history of the United States, a striking amount of evidence indicates that it wasn't until efforts strayed beyond the state sanctioned that social change ever progressed. In the abolitionist movement, the Underground Railroad, public educational campaigns, in addition to slave revolts, forced the federal government to act. With the Suffragettes in the United States, individuals such as Alice Paul acting with various forms of civil disobedience added to the more mainstream efforts to successfully demand the vote for women. Any labor historian will assert that in addition to the organizing of the workplace, strikes, riots, and protests dramatically assisted in producing more tolerable work standards. The progress of the civil rights movement was primarily founded upon the massive illegal civil disobedience campaigns against segregation and disenfranchisement. Likewise, the true pressure from the Vietnam anti-war movement in this country only came after illegal activities such as civil disobedience and beyond were implemented. Perhaps the most obvious, yet often overlooked, historical example of this notion supporting the importance of illegal activity as a tool for positive, lasting change, came just prior to our war for independence. Our educational systems in the United States glorify the Boston Tea Party while simultaneously failing to recognize and admit that the dumping of tea was perhaps one of the most famous early examples of politically motivated property destruction.

In the mid-1990s, individuals angry and disillusioned with the failing efforts to protect the natural environment through state sanctioned means, began taking illegal action. At first, nonviolent civil disobedience was implemented, followed by sporadic cases of nonviolent property destruction. In November 1997, an anonymous communique was issued by a group called the Earth Liberation Front claiming responsibility for their first-ever action in North America.

Immediately, the label of ecoterrorism appeared in news stories describing the actions of the Earth Liberation Front. Where exactly this label originated is open for debate, but all indications point to the federal government of the United States in coordination with industry and sympathetic mass media. Whatever the truth may be regarding the source of this term, one thing is for certain: the decision to attach this label to illegal actions taken for environmental protection was very conscious and deliberate. Why? The need for the U.S. federal government to control and mold public opinion through the power of propaganda to ensure an absence of threat is crucial. If information about illegal actions taken to protect the natural environment were presented openly to the public without biased interpretation, the opportunity would exist for citizens to make up their own minds about the legitimacy of the tactic, target, and movement. By attaching a label such as "terrorism" to the activities of groups such as the Earth Liberation Front, the public is left with little choice but to give into their preconceived notions negatively associated with that term. For many in this country, including myself, information about terrorism came from schools and popular culture. Most often times, the definition of terrorism was overtly racist associated frequently in movies and on television shows with Arabs and the others our government told us were threatening. Terrorism usually is connected with violence, with politically motivated physical harm to humans.

Yet, in the history of the Earth Liberation Front, both in North America and abroad in Europe, no one has ever been injured by the group's many actions. This is not a mere coincidence, but rather a deliberate decision that illustrates the true motivation behind the covert organization. Simply put and most fundamentally, the goal of the Earth Liberation Front is to save life. The group takes actions directly against the property of those who are engaged in massive planetary destruction in order for all of us to survive. This noble pursuit does not constitute terrorism, but rather seeks to abolish it.

A major hypocrisy exists when the U.S. government labels an organization such as the Earth Liberation Front a terrorist group while simultaneously failing to acknowledge its own terrorist history. In fact, the U.S. government by far has been the most extreme terrorist organization in planetary history. Some, but nowhere near all, of the examples of domestic terrorism were discussed earlier in this writing. Yet, further proof can be found by taking a glimpse at the foreign policy record of the United States even as recently as from the 1950s.

In Guatemala (1953–1990s) the CIA organized a coup that overthrew the democratically elected government led by Jacobo Arbenz. This began some forty years of death squads, torture, disappearances, mass executions, totaling well over 100,000 victims. The U.S. government apparently didn't want Guatemala's social democracy spreading to other countries in Latin America.

In the Middle East (1956–1958) the United States twice tried to overthrow the Syrian government. Additionally, the U.S. government landed 14,000 troops to purportedly keep the peace in Lebanon and to stop any opposition to the U.S.-supported Lebanese government. The U.S. government also conspired to overthrow or assassinate Nasser of Egypt.

During the same time, in Indonesia (1957–1958), the CIA tried to manipulate elections and plotted the assassination of Sukarno, then the Indonesian leader. The CIA also assisted in waging a full-scale war against the government of Indonesia. All of this action was taken because Sukarno refused to take a hard-line stand against communism.

From 1953 to 1964, the U.S. government targeted Cheddi Jagan, then the leader of British Guiana, out of a fear he might have built a successful example of an alternative model to the capitalist society. The U.S. government, aided by Britain, organized general strikes and spread misinformation, finally forcing Jagan out of power in 1964.

In Cambodia (1955–1973), Prince Sihanouk was severely targeted by the U.S. government. This targeting included assassination attempts and the unpublicized carpet bombings of 1969 to 1970. The U.S. government finally succeeded in overthrowing Sihanouk in a 1970 coup.

The examples continue. From 1960 through 1965, the United States intervened in Congo/Zaire. After Patrice Lumumba became Congo's first Prime Minister following independence gained from Belgium, he was assassinated in 1961 at the request of Dwight Eisennower. During the same time in Brazil (1961–1964), President Joao Goulart was overthrown in a military coup, which involved the United States. Again, the alleged reasoning for U.S. participation amounted to a fear of communism or, more importantly, anything that threatened this country's way of life. In the Dominican Republic (1963–1966), the United States sent in 23,000 troops to help stop a coup which aimed at restoring power to Juan Bosch, an individual the U.S. government feared had socialist leanings.

Of course, no one should forget about Cuba. When Fidel Castro came to power in 1959, the United States immediately sought to put another government in place, prompting some forty years of terrorist attacks, bombings, a full-scale military invasion, sanctions, embargoes, isolations, and assassinations.

In Chile, the U.S. government sabotaged Salvador Allende's electoral campaign in 1964. In 1970, the U.S. government failed to do so and tried for years later to destabilize the Allende government particularly by building up military hostility. In September 1973, the U.S.-supported military overthrew the government with Allende dying in the process. Some 3,000 people were executed and thousands more were tortured or disappeared. In Greece during the same period (1964–1974), the United States backed a military coup that led to martial law, censorship, arrests, beatings, torture, and killings. In the first month, more than 8,000 people died. All of this was executed with equipment supplied by the United States.

Back in Indonesia in 1965, fears of communism led the United States to back multiple coup attempts, which resulted in a horrendous massacre against communists. During this time the U.S. embassy compiled lists of communist operatives, as many as 5,000 names, and turned them over to the Army. The Army would then hunt down and kill those on the list.

The U.S. Government also has had its dirty hands connected to East Timor (1975 to present). In December 1975, Indonesia invaded East Timor using U.S. weapons. By 1989, Indonesia had slaughtered 200,000 people out of a population between 600,000 and 700,000.

In Nicaragua (1978–1989), when the Sandinistas overthrew the Somoza dictatorship in 1978, the U.S. government immediately became involved. President Carter attempted diplomatic and economic forms of sabotage while President Reagan put the Contras to work. For eight years, backed by the United States, the Contra's waged war on the people of Nicaragua.

Continuing on with Grenada (1979–1984), the United States intervened to stop a 1979 coup led by Maurice Bishop and his followers. The United States invaded Grenada in October 1983, killing 400 citizens of Grenada and eighty-four Cubans. Of course the Libya example (1981–1989) must be mentioned. In the 1980s, the United States shot down two Libyan planes in what Libya regarded as its air space. The United States also dropped bombs on the country killing more than people including Qaddafi's daughter. Yet that wasn't enough as the U.S. government engaged in other attempts to eradicate Qaddafi. This included a fierce misinformation campaign, economic sanctions, and blaming Libya for being responsible for the Pan Am flight 103 bombing without any sound evidence. The U.S. government, also in 1989, bombed Panama, leaving some 15,000 people homeless in Panama City. Thousands of people died and even more were wounded.

Prior to the October 7, 2001, invasion of Afghanistan by the United States, the U.S. government had intervened there from 1979 to 1992. During the late 1970s and most of the 1980s, the U.S. government spent billions of dollars waging a war on a progressive Afghani government, merely because that government was backed by the Soviet Union. More than one million people died, three million were disabled, and five million became refugees.

In El Salvador (1980–1992), the United States supported the government, which engaged in electoral fraud and the murder of hundreds of protesters and strikers. These dissidents, who had been trying to work within the system, took to using guns and declared a civil war in 1980. The U.S. government played an active role in trying to stop the uprising. When it was over in 1992, 75,000 civilians had been killed and the United States had spent six billion dollars.

In Haiti, from 1987 through 1994, the United States supported the Duvalier family dictatorship. During this time, the CIA worked intimately with death squads, torturers, and drug traffickers. Yugoslavia must also be mentioned, as no one should ever forget the United States' responsibility for bombing that country into annihilation.

In the early 1990s, the U.S. government continuously bombed Iraq for more than forty days and nights. One hundred seventy-seven million pounds of bombs fell during this time on the people of Iraq. The remaining uranium deposits from weapons resulted in massive birth defects and incidences of cancer. Between 1990 and 1995, the United States was directly responsible for killing more than 500,000 Iraqi children under the age of five due to economic sanctions. Additionally, due to these sanctions, coupled with the continuous U.S. bombing that has occurred on Iraq since the Gulf War, more than 1.5 million innocent Iraqi people have been killed.

These few examples since 1950 of U.S.-sponsored and organized terrorism are horrendous, and, unfortunately, these massive murderous tactics continue today. On October 7, 2001 the U.S. government began a full-scale military invasion of Afghanistan without even providing a shred of factual evidence linking Osama Bin Laden or Al Qaida to the attacks in this country on September 11. To date, well over 4,000 innocent Afghani civilians have been killed by the U.S. government in this massive genocidal campaign. All along, U.S. government officials have claimed to possess concrete evidence proving the guilt of both Bin Laden and Al Qaida, but repeatedly said they cannot release this "proof as doing so may endanger the lives of U.S. military personnel. This simply makes no sense, as there could not be any justifiable threat to U.S. personnel if they weren't already in inexcusable positions, violating the sovereignty of internationally recognized nations.

The Taliban, which the United States help put into power in 1994, have stated repeatedly to the U.S. government and the world that it would hand over Bin Laden to an international court if the United States provided proof of his guilt. The United States refused and instead claimed the Taliban was not cooperating and was therefore harboring terrorists.

Can you imagine what would have happened if, prior to September 11, 2001, a structure in Kabul were bombed and the Taliban immediately suspected CIA director George Tenet as the prime suspect? Would the United States hand over Tenet to the Taliban if requested if there was not substantial evidence provided of his guilt? Even if the Taliban supplied any shred of evidence, the United States still would refuse to hand over Tenet or any privileged citizen to an international court because the United States does not abide by them or agree to them. Regardless, the U.S. government believes that it has the right to provide no evidence of Bin Laden's or Al Qaida's guilt to the Taliban or the world before launching a massive genocidal campaign against Afghanistan civilians.

The true motives and the identities of those involved both in September 11, 2001 and October 7, 2001 are known only to a select few in power. However, evidence does exist in media sources as mainstream as the BBC (reported on September 18, 2001) that suggests the U.S. government was planning a military invasion of Afghanistan to oust the Taliban as early as March 2001. Furthermore, the intended deadline for the invasion was set for not later than October of the same year. The October 7, 2001, invasion by the United States into Afghanistan appears to have been right on schedule.

This war against terrorism, otherwise known as Operation Enduring Freedom, is the latest example of U.S.-based terrorism and imperialism. It is clear that the events of September 11, 2001, were used as a chance for the U.S. government to invade Afghanistan, to attempt to increase U.S. regional and global power in addition to open up the much-sought-after oil reserves in the Middle East and Central Asia. The bonus, of course, was that this mission has given the United States the opportunity to target and attempt to annihilate any anti-U.S. sentiment within that region. As the war against terrorism expands, so does the possibility of more U.S. military bases and more security for the global economic powers.

If the U.S. government is truly concerned with eradicating terrorism in the world, then that effort must begin with abolishing U.S. imperialism. Members of this governing body, both in the House and Senate as well as those who hold positions in the executive branch, constitute the largest group of terrorists and terrorist representatives currently threatening life on this planet. The only true service this horrific organization supplies is to the upper classes and corporate elite.

As an innocent child, I used to have faith in my government and pride in my country. Today I have no pride, no faith, only embarrassment, anger, and frustration. There are definite and substantiated reasons why the U.S. government is not only disliked but hated by populations in many nations around the globe. The outrage and anger is justified due to the history of U.S. domestic and foreign policies.

Here in the United States, the growth of the empire, of capitalism, and of industry, has meant greater discrepancies between the wealthy and poor, a continued rise in the number of those considered to be a threat to the system, as well as irreversible harm done to the environment and life on the planet. Corporations in the United States literally get away with murder, facing little or no repercussions due to their legal structures. The

U.S. government, which sleeps in the same bed as U.S. corporations, serves to ensure that the "business as usual" policies of imperialism can continue with as little friction as possible. Anyone questioning the mere logic of this genocidal culture and governing policy is considered a dissident and, more often than not, shipped off to one of the fastest growing industries of all, the prison industrial complex.

Internationally, U.S. policies have amounted to the same, often times worse, forms of violence. As I demonstrated herein with examples since 1950, the foreign policy track record has included genocide, assassinations, exploitation, military action, and destruction. Disguised as promoting or protecting freedom and democracy, U.S. foreign policies aim to directly control and conquer, while gaining power, finances, and resources.

U.S. imperialism is a disease, one that continues to grow and become more powerful and dangerous. It needs to be stopped. One of the chief weapons used by those protecting the imperialist policies of the United States is a slick, believable propaganda campaign designed to ensure U.S. citizens do not question or threaten the "American way of life." Perhaps the strongest factor in this campaign is the phenomenon of capitalism. By creating a consumer demand for products, corporations, greatly aided by the U.S. government, can effectively influence people's dreams, desires, wants, and life plans. The very American Dream promoted throughout the world is that anyone can come to the United States, work hard, and become happy and financially secure. Through the use of the propaganda campaign designed, promoted, and transmitted by the U.S. ruling class, people are nearly coerced into adopting unhealthy desires for, often times, unreachable, unneeded, and dangerous consumer goods. Through impressive societal mind control, the belief that obtaining consumer products will equal security and happiness has spread across the United States, and much of the planet at this point, like some extreme plague. The fact that the policies of the United States murder people on a daily basis is unseen, forgotten, or ignored, as every effort is made by people to fit into the artificial model life manufactured by the ruling elite.

A universal effort needs to be made to understand the importance and execution of abolishing U.S. imperialism. This by no way refers to simply engaging in reformist efforts, rather, a complete societal and political revolution will need to occur before real justice and freedom become a reality. The answer does not lie in trying to fix one specific problem or work on one individual issue, but rather the entire pie needs to be targeted, every last piece looked upon as a mere representation of the whole.

If the people of the United States, who the government is supposed to represent, are actually serious about creating a nation of peace, freedom, and justice, then there must be a serious effort made, by any means necessary, to abolish imperialism and U.S. governmental terrorism. The daily murder and destruction caused by this political organization is very real, and so the campaign by the people to stop it must be equally as potent.

I have been told by many people in the United States to love America or leave it. I love this land and the truly compassionate people within it. I therefore feel I not only have a right, but also an obligation, to stay within this land and work for positive societal and political change for all.

I was asked originally if I would voluntarily testify before the House Subcommittee on Forests and Forest Health at a hearing focused on "ecoterrorism." I declined in a written statement. U.S. Marshals then subpoenaed me on October 31, 2001 to testify at this hearing on February 12, 2002, against my will. Is this hearing a forum to discuss the threats facing the health of the natural environment, specifically the forests? No, clearly there is not even the remotest interest in this subject from the U.S. government or industry. The goal of this hearing is to discuss methodologies to improve the failed attempts law enforcement have made since the mid-1990s in catching and prosecuting individuals and organizations who take non-violent, illegal direct action to stop the destruction of the natural environment. I have no interest in this cause or this hearing. In fact, I consider it a farce.

Since 1997, the U.S. government has issued me seven grand jury subpoenas, raided my home and work twice, stealing hundreds of items of property, and, on many occasions, sent federal agents to follow and question me. After this effort, which has lasted nearly five years, federal agents have yet to obtain any information from me to aid their investigations. As I have never been charged with one crime related to these so-called ecoterrorist organizations or their activities, the constant harassment by the federal government constitutes a serious infringement on my Constitutional right to freedom of speech. This Congressional Subcommittee hearing appears to be no different, harassing and targeting me for simply voicing my ideological support for those involved in environmental protection.

I fully praise those individuals who take direct action, by any means necessary, to stop the destruction of the natural world and threats to all life. They are the heroes, risking their freedom and lives so that we as a species as well as all life forms can continue to exist on the planet. In a country so fixated on monetary wealth and power, these brave environmental advocates are engaging in some of the most selfless activities possible.

It is my sincere desire that organizations such as the Earth Liberation Front continue to grow and prosper in the United States. In fact, more organizations, using similar tactics and strategies, need to be established to directly focus on U.S. imperialism and the U.S. government itself. For, as long as the quest for monetary gain continues to be the predominant value within U.S. society, human, animal, and environmental exploitation, destruction, and murder will continue to be a reality. This drive for profits at any cost needs to be fiercely targeted, and those responsible for the massive injustices punished. If there is any real concern for justice, freedom, and, at least, a resemblance of a true democracy, this revolutionary ideal must become a reality. ALL POWER TO THE PEOPLE. LONG LIVE THE EARTH LIBERATION FRONT. LONG LIVE THE ANIMAL LIBERATION FRONT. LONG LIVE ALL THE SPARKS ATTEMPTING TO IGNITE THE REVOLUTION. SOONER OR LATER THE SPARKS WILL TURN INTO A FLAME!

William Green,
Animal Rights: Activism vs. Criminality,
testimony given before the
Senate Committee on the Judiciary,
108th Congress, 2nd Session,
May 18, 2004

Introduction and Overview

Mr. Chairman, Members of the Committee, I appreciate the opportunity to appear before you today to present Chiron Corporation's perspective on the growing movement of animal terrorism in this country. I am William Green, Senior Vice President and General Counsel of Chiron Corporation. Chiron is a biotechnology company headquartered in Emeryville, California. Since it was founded in 1981, Chiron has sought to improve human health by developing new and innovative products to prevent and treat diseases such as cancer, HIV, influenza, cystic fibrosis, meningitis and hepatitis. We have manufacturing or management facilities in several states, including California, Washington, Pennsylvania, and New Jersey, and also in international locations, principally in the United Kingdom, Germany and Italy.

We discover and develop new approaches to human health. Sound science and the applicable laws and regulations required in the U.S. and in every developed country in the world mandate testing in humans and on animal models before drugs can be approved to justify and validate our efforts to develop these life-saving products. Our own animal care and use program in the United States is accredited by the American Association for the Accreditation of Laboratory Animal Care (AAALAC) and registered with the United States Department of Agriculture. We also maintain an Assurance Statement with the Office of Laboratory Animal Welfare, Department of Health and Human Services. Additional information regarding the regulation of Chiron's animal research is provided in Addendum I. We draw the Committee's attention to this information as it is important to understanding the crux of the issue we bring before you today on two levels—first, we are victims of a sustained campaign of intimidation, harassment and extortion that we have endured at the hands of animal rights extremists; and second, that campaign is cloaked in a more subtle and more intimidating mantle of assault on an entity with which we have only remote contact.

Over the last twelve months, Chiron Corporation and its employees have been the target of a persistent and sometimes violent campaign by animal rights extremists orchestrated, we believe, by SHAG USA. The campaign has cost us significant time and resources to defend ourselves; resources that we believe would have been better invested in our research efforts. We present an overview of our experience to this Committee in the belief that it establishes a compelling basis for the Committee to amend the Criminal Code. Simply put, if human health care research is to continue, society must be able to effectively control and prevent the kinds of conduct now being directed against such research. As the law presently stands, tools are insufficient. As a consequence, Chiron and its employees have paid, and so have many other research entities. Ultimately, the public pays, in increased costs or worse, diminished health care. We believe that the Animal Enterprise Act must be updated to ensure that individuals and companies are protected and drug development is fostered.

I would like to address four issues in my statement today.

1. Animal terrorism activities directed toward Chiron Corporation by Stop Huntingdon Animal Cruelty (aka SHAC).
2. Details of terrorist activities targeting specific employees of Chiron Corporation.
3. The threat of ongoing animal terrorism that we believe exists for Chiron Corporation.
4. Chiron's thoughts and recommendations on gaps in the Criminal Code as they relate to these animal terrorist activities.

Overview of Chiron

Founded in 1981, Chiron is a pioneer in the biotech industry. As a result of its research programs, Chiron has grown to $1.8 billion in revenue in 2003. We market more than fifty products worldwide to detect, prevent and treat diseases.

Chiron is a leader in the fight to eliminate polio from the face of the earth. We are a major producer of vaccines to UNICEF and public institutions. We have contributed 30 million polio vaccine doses to the Polio Global Eradication Initiative and look forward to a time when all children can live without threat from this crippling disease. The polio vaccine is possible because of animal research. Absent that research, the vaccine would have been impossible to develop.

Among Chiron's many contributions to medicine was the discovery of the hepatitis C virus. Chiron scientists labored for years before identifying and sequencing the virus. That accomplishment led directly to tests that have dramatically improved the safety of the blood supply. An estimated 165 hepatitis C infections from blood transfusions are prevented daily in the U.S. because of Chiron's achievement.

The lives saved by those tests and the polio cases prevented by our vaccines are just two examples of Chiron's powerful contribution to global public health. Those contributions are possible in part because of animal research. The same can be said of every pharmaceutical treatment on the market. Without animal research, we would never have seen the tremendous advances in human health that we have enjoyed over the past decades. If animal rights extremists succeed in their efforts, it will have a devastating effect on human health.

SHAC Background

SHAC is an acronym for Stop Huntingdon Animal Cruelty. SHAC's stated immediate intention is to put a specific research company, Huntingdon Life Sciences ("HLS"), out of business because SHAC believes that HLS' work is cruel to animals. (See Addendum II). SHAC runs an extremist campaign of intimidation and harassment directed at HLS, but also at entities doing business with HLS (tertiary targets) in an effort to isolate and ultimately destroy HLS. SHAC appears to believe that it is morally wrong for human beings to test drugs on animals, regardless of the benefits to humans. Its primary long-term goal is the complete elimination of animal testing in all contexts, without regard to the negative impact this would have on drug development and improvements in medical care.

Its campaign against companies like Chiron Corporation established a new tactic for animal extremists intent on hindering or halting medical research and innovation. Rather than acting directly against a research facility or institution, which is an "entity" that the Congress of the United States has protected through the Animal Enterprise Protection Act of 1992, SHAC USA extremists now direct many of their harassing, threatening and menacing activities toward the people that work in our company, as well as their family members, in the communities where they live: at their homes, at their schools, and in the places where they engage in volunteer or leisure activities.

Chiron has no current contracts with HLS, and no plans to use HLS in the future. Yet, SHAC's web page boldly proclaims that Chiron is a 'Target" of its "campaign" to shut HLS down. As a direct result, the company and its employees have been subjected to a relentless stream of terrorist activities. SHAC tactics are expressly aimed at achieving this goal.

Chiron's Experience as a SHAC Targeted Company

Activities Targeting Chiron Employees

Chiron became a target of SHAC USA approximately a year ago. In April 2003, the SHAC USA website published a "diary" written by Michelle Rokke, an animal rights activist, who worked undercover at HLS in the 1990s. Rokke's diary accused HLS of abusing laboratory animals in connection with research it conducted in 1997 on behalf of Chiron. The SHAC USA website created a section devoted to Chiron that prominently states: "Chiron Kills Puppies At Huntingdon Life Sciences."

The SHAC USA website is the center of its campaign. The site issues calls to action, coordinates the attacks, targets our individual employees and reports, often erroneously, the consequence of extremist's activities. The website has published personal information of Chiron employees and encouraged extremists to harass and intimidate them. After various incidents occur, the SHAC USA website publishes mocking reports of the incidents, often ending with warnings that the harassment will continue until the employee quits or Chiron severs all ties with HLS. The website repeatedly drives home its message by warning employees that "We know where you live!" The SHAC USA website also makes available tactics and resources for the extremists to continue their activities against Chiron.

Less than a month after Chiron was first singled out on the SHAC USA website, overt acts of harassment began against Chiron and its employees. These attacks have been ongoing and unrelenting. Our employees have been targeted in California, New Jersey, Washington, the United Kingdom and the Netherlands. The tactics are numerous, but all of them are meant to harass and intimidate.

Extremists have made harassing phone calls and sent harassing emails to employees at work and at their homes. The extremists have set up fake Internet advertisements (such as soliciting sexual services) with employees' phone numbers to encourage strangers to harass the employees. Several employees have had their financial information misappropriated, resulting in fraudulent credit card charges. One employee received a death threat. SHAC USA also sent a letter to a scientific research conference threatening acts of violence if a Chiron employee was permitted to speak at the conference. Extremists also threatened to disrupt a conference for high school girls in Washington if a Chiron employee was allowed to participate.

SHAC USA's most chilling tactic is the so-called "home visit." Groups of extremists assemble at a targeted employee's house, often in the middle of the night. The extremists are often clad in black clothes and ski masks to increase the intimidation. They shout obscenities at employees through bullhorns, pound on doors and windows, and scatter leaflets around the neighborhood. These home visits are often accompanied by acts of vandalism and trespass. The groups of extremists repeated these visits to the same employees over a period of months.

On the night of May 12, 2003, Chiron employees around the San Francisco Bay Area received "home visits" from groups of extremists. SHAC USA published on its website and in its newsletters the names of targeted Chiron employees, their home addresses, phone numbers, email addresses and names of spouses and children. The home visits continued against Bay Area employees on a weekly basis through August 2003. These incidents were regularly celebrated on the SHAC USA website.

Beginning in August 2003, SHAC USA also began targeting Chiron's office in Seattle, Washington. Groups of extremists showed up at the Seattle office, harassing and threatening employees as they entered and left work and home visits to Chiron employees in Seattle started. Later in 2003 and continuing into 2004, SHAC USA has repeatedly attacked a Chiron employee in New Jersey.

Specific Activities Undertaken by SHAC USA Targeting Chiron Employees

As Chiron's General Counsel, I also have received harassing phone calls and "home visits," as well as harassment of my family. Let me describe to you in detail how some other Chiron's employees, representing a range of levels within the company, have been victimized by SHAC USA's activities. In order to protect the personal safety of these individuals, we are not identifying them by name.

Employee A: This employee has been subject to repeated incidents of harassment and intimidation. Groups of extremists have assembled at her home on at least seven occasions, including in the middle of the night. The extremists have shouted obscenities at her in front of her children and other neighborhood children. They have blocked her driveway, preventing her family from returning home. They shouted at her husband and children as they entered their house. SHAC USA extremists have scrawled slogans on her driveway and littered the neighborhood with leaflets accusing her of being a "puppy killer." On one occasion, extremists began taking photographs of her through her dining room window as she talked on the telephone.

This employee and her family have received obscene and harassing phone calls. They have been subscribed to over $3,000 in fraudulent magazine subscriptions. Her husband's work email has been repeatedly used to enroll him in catalogue distribution lists and to request company prospectuses.

Extremists have also attempted to disrupt a sports group to which this employee belongs. They assembled at one outing of the group, shouting at members through bullhorns and encouraging them to kick this employee out of the group. The group's email group began receiving spam emails from SHAC USA denouncing the employee, and personal information on group members was published on SHAC USA's website. At least one member of the sports group began receiving late night, harassing phone calls.

This employee and her family have had to change the way they live. They have retained personal security. They limit the amount of time they spend away from home. The family's children have been traumatized. Their younger child now has trouble sleeping and is very nervous when his parents aren't home.

Employee B: This employee has also been subject to repeated harassment. Groups of extremists have assembled at her home in the middle of the night on numerous occasions, shouting through bullhorns and setting off screeching personal alarms to wake her and her family from their sleep. They have littered her neighborhood with leaflets containing her picture and personal information. On one occasion, the extremists smeared animal feces on the front and rear entrances to her house; threw mangled stuffed animals on her yard; and spray-painted slogans such as "puppy killer" and "drop HLS" on her front walkway. On another occasion, these same slogans were etched onto the windows of her car with permanent etching fluid. This employee has also received harassing phone calls at home and had her phone number used to place fake Internet advertisements. Employee B has never been involved in animal experiments.

Employee C: This employee has never been involved in animal testing, but still has received numerous "home visits." On May 12, 2003, at the beginning of SHAC USA's campaign against Chiron, extremists dumped a substance subsequently identified as butyric acid on his front steps, leaving an overwhelming stench resembling vomit. The incident was particularly threatening as the substance was originally unknown to those responding to the attack and presumed to be toxic. As a result, the cleanup was hampered and cost increased. It ultimately cost thousands of dollars to remove the odor, which still lingers at the property. This employee has received numerous harassing and obscene phone calls, and his home phone number was used to request sexual services on the Internet. SHAC USA's website published the names and email addresses this employee' spouse and children, encouraging extremists to harass them as well. They began receiving harassing emails. This employee has retained personal security.

Employee D: This employee has been subject to repeated late-night home visits by groups of extremists. The extremists screamed through bullhorns, pounded on her front door, rang her doorbell, and shouted obscenities. The employee's family, including three young children, were awakened and scared. The employee has also received numerous harassing phone calls and messages at home, had her address posted on the Internet in false advertisements, and had her picture and personal information placed on leaflets accusing her of murdering animals. This employee has also been forced to retain personal security. Again, Employee D is not involved with any animal testing for Chiron.

Employee E: This employee became a target at the beginning of this year after SHAC USA published his picture and home information on its website. Groups of extremists have visited his home on at least four occasions. Since this employee travels extensively for his work, these home visits often occur when his wife and children are home alone. On one occasion, they drove up and down the employee's street in a truck with a giant television screen on the rear of the vehicle, displaying extremely graphic images of animals being mutilated. Other extremists shouted at the employee through bullhorns and scattered leaflets with his personal information around the neighborhood. The SHAC USA website reported this incident and warned: "2004 is going to be one hell of a long year for [the employee], now that we know where he is. If you can't join us on future demos—please be sure to get in touch with [the employee] on your own." On other occasions, the extremists have assembled in the early morning hours shouting obscenities and threats. For instance, one individual made reference to the Chiron bombing and implied it could happen at this employee's home. Another individual shouted, "Security won't protect you during the day [employee's name]. Not everything happens at night." On another occasion, after a neighbor complained to the protestors that children were sleeping, a protestor exposed his genitals and told the neighbor to perform a sexual act on him. As a result of these actions, the employee has been forced to retain security to protect his home and family. Like other SHAC USA targets, Employee E has never been involved in animal testing.

Employee F: This employee has had his personal checking account number posted on SHAC USA's website. This forced him to cancel the checking account, close a related credit card account, review all transactions made on his checking account, review his credit history for acts of fraud, and make good all outstanding checks. The SHAC USA website also threatened to send animal feces in the mail and warned that he would be harassed in the coming year. In January 2004, SHAC USA extremists assembled at his house shouting through bullhorns. The employee was forced to flee his home with his autistic son, who would have been severely traumatized by the loud noises.

August 2003 Bombing at Chiron

Two pipe bombs exploded on the company's campus on August 28, 2003. The blast shattered the glass doors and windows in the entrance and foyer. Among the debris, police officers found pieces of a kitchen timer and other plastic components. Within five minutes, a second explosive device was found but before the bomb squad arrived, the second device also detonated. It was extremely fortunate that no one was injured. Timing a second explosive device to detonate shortly after the first would seem to be a technique calculated to attack security personnel and police officers responding to the first explosion.

The following day, SHAC USA's website posted a link to a statement issued by a previously unknown group calling itself The Revolutionary Cells." That statement took credit for the bombing at Chiron and made death threats against its employees: "This is the endgame for the animal killers and if you choose to stand with them you will be dealt with accordingly. There will be no quarter given, no more half measures taken. You might be able to protect your buildings, but can you protect the homes of every employee?" SHAC USA also published its own press release regarding the bombings stating that the bombings were "part of a global assault on the customers of HLS." SHAC USA's president, Kevin Kjonaas, was quoted as saying that the bombings "against

Chiron mark a drastic escalation in severity. . . . If I were Chiron, I would be very worried."

SHAC USA sought to compound the terror effects of the bombing to intimidate Chiron and its employees. On August 31, 2003, SHAC USA flooded Chiron email accounts with the suggestion that thousands of emails would "take their minds off last Thursday's firework show." In a demonstration against Chiron in New York City, persons affiliated with SHAC USA carried signs stating, "Invest in Chiron & Make a Bang for Your Buck!" and "HLS and Chiron Are Always a Blast!" Extremists in Seattle left a note at Chiron's offices that read: "Chiron is going out with a bang." The SHAC USA newsletter crowed that "Chiron is starting to shake like a California quake" and that "[t]he campaign to close Huntingdon is being fought with 'exploding' new tactics."

About a month after the Chiron bombing, a second company in the San Francisco Bay Area, Shaklee Corporation—a subsidiary of another SHAC USA target, Yamanouchi Consumer, Inc.—was bombed. The FBI has said that the device used in the Shaklee bombing was nearly identical to the devices used in the Chiron bombing. After the blast at Shaklee, SHAC USA again posted a link to a statement issued by "The Revolutionary Cells" making death threats against Chiron employees. The statement singled out Chiron Chairman Sean Lance and contained a direct threat of future violence against him and Chiron's employees: "Hey Sean Lance, and the rest of the Chiron team, how are you sleeping? You never know when your house, your car even, might go boom. Who knows, that new car in the parking lot may be packed with explosives. Or maybe it will be a shot in the dark."

Although SHAC USA has carefully avoided taking responsibility for the bombings, there is reason to believe that SHAC USA and Kevin Kjonaas closely orchestrate the terrorists who claim to be The Revolutionary Cells. On October 5, 2003, a federal arrest warrant was issued in the Northern District of California for Daniel Andreas San Diego. The FBI believes that Mr. San Diego was involved in the Chiron and Shaklee bombings and has charged him with maliciously damaging and destroying property by means of explosives.

Other SHAC Tactics Directed Against Chiron Corporation

Beyond the attacks on our employees and the bombing of our headquarters, Chiron has been subjected to repeated attempts to disrupt our business, steal confidential information and prevent us from carrying out our mission to improve health globally. One tactic employed by extremists on multiple occasions has been to flood the company with mass faxes and emails. SHAC USA sponsors so-called "Electronic Civil Disobedience" in which extremists attempt to knock out a company's internet server by targeting it with repeated spam emails. These efforts include: sending spam emails to employees at their work email addresses. Over 4,000 emails, sent on numerous occasions and often generated by automatic computer programs threatened to overload our computer systems. These emails were sent using the techniques of hackers.

The mass emails and faxes are just one tactic employed by extremists to try to shut down business. There are others, just as destructive which have also been directed against Chiron, including:

"Phone blockades," in which extremists make numerous repeat phone calls to a targeted company to tie up its phone lines.

Instructions on the SHAC USA website on how to infiltrate targeted companies, including Chiron, by fraudulently posing as job applicants. The goal is to infiltrate a company to obtain confidential information.

Fake phone calls from individuals designed to trick employees into revealing confidential information.

"Black faxes" of over 1, 000 facsimile pages designed to use up a fax machine's ink, potentially resulting in the loss of critical business communications.

SHAC USA's Threat of Ongoing Terrorism Against Chiron

SHAC USA has made it clear that the harassment and intimidation against the Company and its employees will not stop until Chiron disavows any intention ever to use HLS. Thus, our employees live with SHAC USA's ongoing threats hanging over their heads. After the incidents of harassment occur against Chiron employees, the SHAC USA website regularly reports on the actions. From April 2003 to February 2004, Chiron employees have been the target of ongoing threats, examples of which are included below.

"Until Chiron stops doing business with Huntingdon Life Sciences we will be a constant voice for the 500 animals who die inside their walls everyday. We know who you are, we know what you look like, and best of all we know where you live!"

"[Names of employee and spouse], it will only get worse from here. With every day that goes by and every animal that is tortured and murdered inside HLS, our anger and vengeance grows. We will not stop until the walls of HLS are turned to rubble. . . We will not stop until HLS is shut down and we will take you with them as long as you are part of the suffering."

"Prepare yourself Chiron because this is only the beginning. As long as you continue to act as a customer for HLS you will be exposed in your neighborhoods and communities. We know how you make your money, and we know where you live! Drop HLSI"

"It's a simple equation. Stop doing business with Huntingdon Life Sciences. Until you do we will be watching you. We will invite ourselves over to your homes and into your private lives. Do you really want the spotlight on you Chiron?"

"Quit doing business with Huntingdon Life Sciences Chiron. You're not getting any sleep and your neighbors are growing weary of your presence. Your personal information is all over your neighborhood. You have to be wondering what's next. . . well guess what? We're just getting warmed up!"

"[Name of employee], if you are interested in sleeping through the night, stop supporting HLS (and maybe those bags under your eyes will go away too)."

"Don't worry [name of employee], there will be more and more visits to come. Quit your job!"

"If only she would stop her gross killing spree, and then wouldn't have to worry about us being there every step she takes. . ."

"We hope you don't think we are going away Chiron. Until you sever all ties with HLS, we will be a permanent part of your life. Until Next Time!" "We're just getting started Chiron!"

Notes

1 Introduction: Criminality in the Environmental and Animal Rights Movements

1. House Committee on the Judiciary, *Acts of Ecoterrorism by Radical Environmental Organizations: Hearing before the Subcommittee on Crime,* 105th Cong., 2nd sess., 1998; House Committee on Resources, *Ecoterrorism and Lawlessness on the National Forests: Oversight Hearing before the Subcommittee on Forests and Forest Health,* 107th Cong., 2nd sess., 2002;. Senate Committee on the Judiciary, *Animal Rights: Activism vs. Criminality,* 108th Cong., 2nd sess., 2004; Senate Committee on Environment and Public Works, *Oversight on Ecoterrorism Specifically Examining the Earth Liberation Front (ELF) and the Animal Liberation Front (ALF),* 109th Cong., 1st sess., 2005.
2. Lee, *Earth First!,* 96.
3. Beirich and Moser, "From Push to Shove," http://www.splcenter.org/intelligenceproject/ip-4w3.html.
4. Law Enforcement Agency Resource Network,"Ecoterrorism," http://www.adl.org/learn/ext_us/Ecoterrorism.asp?LEARN_subCat=Extremism_ in_ America&xpicked=4&item=eco.
5. Ibid.
6. Beirich and Moser, "From Push to Shove," http:/www.splcenter.org/intelligenceproject/ip-4w3.html.
7. Manes, *Green Rage,* 175.
8. Oliver, *Animal Rights, 205.*
9. Ibid.
10. Manes, *Green Rage.*
11. Ibid.
12. Lee, *Earth First!.*
13. Ibid.
14. Earth Liberation Front, "Meet the ELF," http://earthliberationfront.com/about/.

15. Ibid.
16. Earth Liberation Front, "Diary of Actions and Chronology," http://www.earthliberationfront.com (accessed Nov. 15, 2004).
17. Ibid.
18. Oliver, 1999; Animal Liberation Front, *2001 Direct Action Report,* http://www.wlfa.org/interactive/features/pdf/ALF2001Report.pdf.
19. Ibid.
20. Countless sources discuss the definition of terrorism, but the specifics of that debate will not be explored here. Readers may wish to see Laqueur, *The New Terrorism.*
21. Conklin, *Criminology.*
22. Oliver, *Animal Rights.*

2 History and Philosophy of Radical Environmentalism

1. Long, *Ecoterrorism,* 11.
2. Ibid., 11.
3. Ibid.
4. Lee, *Earth First!,* 25.
5. Switzer, *Environmental Activism.*
6. Lee, *Earth First!;* Long, *Ecoterrorism;* Switzer, *Environmental Activism.*
7. Long, *Ecoterrorism;* Switzer, *Environmental Activism.*
8. Long, *Ecoterrorism.*
9. Lee, *Earth First!.*
10. Long, *Ecoterrorism;* Switzer, *Environmental Activism.*
11. Long, *Ecoterrorism;* Switzer, *Environmental Activism.*
12. Switzer, *Environmental Activism.*
13. Ibid.
14. Manes, *Green Rage;* Long, *Ecoterrorism.*
15. Manes, *Green Rage;* Long, *Ecoterrorism.*
16. Long, *Ecoterrorism.*
17. Long, *Ecoterrorism,* 26.
18. Long, *Ecoterrorism;* Egan, "From Spikes to Bombs."
19. Long, *Ecoterrorism;* Manes, *Green Rage;* Egan, "From Spikes to Bombs."
20. Long, *Ecoterrorism,* 19.
21. Long, *Ecoterrorism.*
22. Long, *Ecoterrorism,* 28.
23. Long, *Ecoterrorism,* 28.
24. Long, *Ecoterrorism;* Lee, *Earth First!.*
25. Disentangling and explaining the various theoretical perspectives that have developed into the body of literature called environmental philosophy is well beyond the scope of this work. Environmental philosophers have found a natural home in the varied perspectives of postmodernism, where deconstructing basic assumptions about human-environmental relations is a central effort of the intellectual environmental wing. Interested readers

should see Zimmerman et al., *Environmental Philosophy* and Zimmerman, *Contesting Earth's Future*. Eco-feminism is a distinct branch of environmental philosophy that sees the present environmental crisis as a direct result of patriarchy. Readers interested in the large and growing body of ecofeminist literature would do well to start with Merchant, *Radical Ecology*; various essays contained in Zimmerman et al., *Environmental Philosophy*, should also be useful.

26. Deep ecology consists of a broad and growing body of academic literature. Readers interested in this subject matter should see Naess, *Ecology, Community and Lifestyle*; Devall and Sessions, *Deep Ecology*; Drengson and Inoue, *The Deep Ecology Movement*; and Barnhill and Gottlieb, *Deep Ecology and World Religions*.

27. Naess, "The Deep Ecological Movement," in Zimmerman et al., *Environmental Philosophy*, 189.

28. Barnhill and Gottlieb, *Deep Ecology and World Religions*; Drengson and Inoue, *The Deep Ecology Movement*; Long, *Ecoterrorism*.

29. Naess, *Ecology, Community and Lifestyle*; Devall and Sessions, *Deep Ecology*; Barnhill and Gottlieb, *Deep Ecology and World Religions*. The underlying philosophy of animal rights, discussed in Chapter 3, also contains a millennial component. Noted animal rights philosopher Tom Regan believes that "those who respect the rights of animals are embarked on a journey back to Eden—a journey back to proper love for God's creation." Michael Fox, vice president of the Humane Society of the United States, says that "the dawning of a New Eden is to come," and that animal rights involves "the restoration, dressing, and keeping of the Garden of Eden: Paradesia." Similarly, PETA president Ingrid Newkirk foresees "a world where the lion will lie down with the lamb, where man will live in harmony with nature, where, when two animals fight, human beings will intervene." That animal rights theology compliments deep ecology is unmistakable. The religious-millenarian-utopian overtones are obvious as well. Quotes from Oliver, *Animal Rights*, 7.

30. Lee, *Earth First!*; Long, *Ecoterrorism*.

3 History and Philosophy of the Animal Rights Movement

1. Masters Evans, *Animal Rights*.

2. Finsen and Finsen, *The Animal Rights Movement*; Masters Evans, *Animal Rights*.

3. Finsen and Finsen, *The Animal Rights Movement*; Masters Evans, *Animal Rights*.

4. Masters Evans, *Animal Rights*, 20.

5. Masters Evans, *Animal Rights*.

6. Singer, *Animal Liberation*, 206–7.

7. Singer, *Animal Liberation*; Finsen and Finsen, *The Animal Rights Movement*; Masters Evans, *Animal Rights*.

8. Embodied in the work of Jeremy Bentham and John Stuart Mill, utilitarianism requires that "right" actions be governed by the maximization of positive outcomes and the minimization of negative outcomes for concerned parties. Extending moral consideration to non-human animals greatly complicates the formulation of right actions and requires a deep change in how humans think

about their relationship to other life forms. See Bentham, *Principles of Morals and Legislation*; Mill, *Utilitarianism*.

9. Frey, *Interests and Rights*; Carruthers, *The Animals Issue*.

10. Singer, *Animal Liberation*; Dombrowski, *Babies and Beasts*.

11. Singer, *Animal Liberation*.

12. Finsen and Finsen, *The Animal Rights Movement*. There is in fact a large and growing body of literature dealing with the topic of animal rights. Readers interested in delving into the finer philosophical arguments would do well to start with Pluhar, *Beyond Prejudice*; Sunstein and Nussbaum, *Animal*; Regan, *Empty Cages*; and Nibert, *Animal Rights, Human Rights*.

13. Regan, *The Case for Animal Rights*; Regan, *Animal Rights, Human Wrongs*.

14. Finsen and Finsen, *The Animal Rights Movement*, 3.

15. Readers interested in the animal rights-deep ecology debate should refer to Zimmerman et al., *Environmental Philosophy*.

16. Masters Evans, *Animal Rights*, 25.

17. Masters Evans, *Animal Rights*.

18. Finsen and Finsen, *The Animal Rights Movement*.

19. Ibid.

20. Ibid.

21. Finsen and Finsen, *The Animal Rights Movement*; Jasper and Nelkin, *The Animal Rights Crusade*; Guither, *Animal Rights*.

22. Finsen and Finsen, *The Animal Rights Movement*; Jasper and Nelkin, *The Animal Rights Crusade*.

23. Finsen and Finsen, *The Animal Rights Movement*.

24. Finsen and Finsen, *The Animal Rights Movement*; Guither, *Animal Rights*; Jasper and Nelkin, *The Animal Rights Crusade*.

25. Ibid.

26. Ibid.

27. Ibid.

28. Finsen and Finsen, *The Animal Rights Movement*, 51.

29. While the hardcore anti-vivisectionists viewed the collaboration of the humane organizations as a sell out, it must be noted that despite the failure of bringing about the more ambitious goal of ending vivisection, the mainstream humane movement did manage to lobby successfully for more humane treatment of animals as pets, food products, and experimental subjects. For example, by 1907 every U.S. state had enacted a broad range of anti-cruelty statutes. Finsen and Finsen, *The Animal Rights Movement*.

30. Finsen and Finsen, *The Animal Rights Movement*.

31. Ibid.

32. Guither, *Animal Rights*; Finsen and Finsen, *The Animal Rights Movement*; Masters Evans, Animal Rights.

33. Finsen and Finsen, *The Animal Rights Movement*; Jasper and Nelkin, *The Animal Rights Crusade*.

34. Finsen and Finsen, *The Animal Rights Movement*; Jasper and Nelkin, *The Animal Rights Crusade*.

35. CE: Finsen and Finsen, *The Animal Rights Movement*; Jasper and Nelkin, *The Animal Rights Crusade.*

36. Finsen and Finsen, *The Animal Rights Movement*; Guillermo, *Monkey Business.*

37. Yount, *Animal Rights.*

38. Ibid.

39. Guither, *Animal Rights*; Jasper and Nelkin, *The Animal Rights Crusade*; Finsen and Finsen, *The Animal Rights Movement*; Yount, *Animal Rights.*

40. Ibid.

41. Singer, *Animal Liberation.*

42. Regan, *The Case for Animal Rights.*

43. Finsen and Finsen, *The Animal Rights Movement*; Yount, *Animal Rights.*

44. Law Enforcement Agency Resource Network, "Ecoterrorism," http://www.adl.org/learn/ext_us/Ecoterrorism.asp?LEARN_subCat=Extremism_in_America&xpicked=4&item=eco.

45. Oliver, *Animal Rights.*

46. Oliver, *Animal Rights,* 97.

47. Singer, *Animal Liberation.*

4 Animal Rights Criminality

1. Oliver, *Animal Rights,* 7.

2. Beirich and Moser. "From Push to Shove," http:/www.splcenter.org/intelligenceproject/ip-4w3.html.

3. Warner, "The Siege of Darley Oaks Farm," http://www.animalliberationfront.com/ALFront/Actions-UK/DarleyOaks.htm.

4. Senate Committee on the Environment and Public Works, *Oversight on Ecoterrorism,* Testimony of David Martosko, 109th Cong., 1st sess., 2005.

5. Senate Committee on the Environment and Public Works. *Concerning Stop Huntingdon Animal Cruelty,* Hearing statements, 109th Cong., 1st sess., 2005.

6. Molland, "Thirty Years of Direct Action"; Animal Liberation Front, "History of the Hunt Saboteurs," http://www.animalliberationfront.com/ALFront/Actions-UK/HSA/.

7. Finsen and Finsen, *The Animal Rights Movement*; Stoner and Perlstein, "Implementing 'Justice,'" 90–133.

8. Finsen and Finsen, *The Animal Rights Movement*; Stoner and Perlstein, "Implementing 'Justice'"; Stallwood, "A Personal Overview of Direct Action"; Guither, *Animal Rights*; Yount, *Animal Rights*; U.S. Justice Department, *Report to Congress,* http://www.cdfe.org/doj_report.htm; Law Enforcement Agency Resource Network. "Ecoterrorism," http://www.adl.org/learn/ext_us/Ecoterrorism.asp?LEARN_subCat=Extremism_in_America&xpicked=4&item=eco.

9. Stoner and Perlstein, "Implementing 'Justice'"; Senate Committee on the Judiciary, *Animal Rights,* 108th Cong., 2nd sess., 2004; U.S. Justice Department, *Report to Congress,* http://www.cdfe.org/doj_report.htm.

10. Guither, *Animal Rights.*

11. Guither, *Animal Rights*; Stoner and Perlstein, "Implementing 'Justice.'"

12. "ALF A,B,C's," http://www.directaction.info/library_abcs.htm.

13. Stoner and Perlstein, "Implementing 'Justice.'"

14. Workman, *PETA Files.*

15. Ibid.

16. Animal Liberation Front, "Diary," http://www.animalliberationfront.org; Brown, "Animal Rights Campaigners," http://www.animalliberationfront.com/ALFront/Actions-UK/OsfordProt.htm; Senate Committee on the Environment and Public Works, *Oversight on Ecoterrorism,* Testimony of David Vitter and David Skorton, 109th Cong., 1st sess., 2005.

17. A biography of Barry Horne can be found at http://barryhorne.org/.

18. U.S. Justice Department, *Report to Congress,* http://www.cdfe.org/doj_report.htm.

19. Senate Committee on the Environment and Public Works, *Oversight on Ecoterrorism,* Statements given by Bradley Campbell, John Lewis, and Carson Carroll, 109th Cong., 1st sess., 2005.

20. Animal Liberation Front, "Animal Rights Militia Fact Sheet," http://www.animalliberationfront.com/ALFront/Actions-UK/alfarm.htm; Wikipedia, "Animal Rights Militia," http://en.wikipedia.org/wiki/Animal_Rights_Militia; Beirich and Moser. "From Push to Shove," http:/www.splcenter.org/intelligenceproject/ip-4w3.html.

21. Wikipedia, "Justice Department (animal rights)," http://en.wikipedia.org/wiki/Justice_Department_(animal_rights); Beirich and Moser. "From Push to Shove," http://www.splcenter.org/intelligenceproject/ip-4w3.html.

22. Wikipedia, "Stop Huntingdon Animal Cruelty," http://en.wikipedia.org/wiki/SHAC; "SHAC History," http://www.shac.net/SHAC.who.html; Senate Committee on the Environment and Public Works, *Oversight on Ecoterrorism,* Hearing Statements, 109th Cong., 1st sess., 2005; Senate Committee on the Environment and Public Works, *Concerning Stop Huntingdon Animal Cruelty,* Hearing statements, 109th Cong., 1st sess., 2005; Senate Committee on the Judiciary, *Animal Rights,* Hearing statements, 108th Cong., 2d sess., 2004.

23. Wikipedia, "Stop Huntingdon Animal Cruelty," http://en.wikipedia.org/wiki/SHAC; Senate Committee on the Environment and Public Works, *Concerning Stop Huntingdon Animal Cruelty,* Hearing statements, 109th Cong., 1st sess., 2005; Beirich and Moser. "From Push to Shove," http://www.splcenter.org/intelligenceproject/ip-4w3.html.

24. Senate Committee on the Judiciary, *Animal Rights,* Testimony of Mr. William Green, 108th Cong., 2d sess., 2004.

25. Law Enforcement Agency Resource Network. "Ecoterrorism," http://www.adl.org/learn/ext_us/Ecoterrorism.asp?LEARN_subCat=Extremism_in_America&xpicked=4&item=eco.

26. Foundation for Biomedical Research, "Violent and Illegal Activity by Animal Activists is Escalating," http://www.fbresearch.org/animal-activism/violence.htm.

27. Law Enforcement Agency Resource Network. "Ecoterrorism," http://www.adl.org/learn/ext_us/Ecoterrorism.asp?LEARN_subCat=Extremism_in_America&xpicked=4&item=eco.

28. Senate Committee on Environment and Public Works, *Concerning Stop Huntingdon Animal Cruelty,* Statement given by John Lewis, 109th Cong., 1st sess., 2005.

29. Senate Committee on Environment and Public Works, *Concerning Stop Huntingdon Animal Cruelty,* Statement given by Skip Boruchin, 109th Cong., 1st sess., 2005.

30. Wikipedia, "Stop Huntingdon Animal Cruelty," http://en.wikipedia.org/wiki/SHAC.

31. Garfinkel, "Leaderless Resistance Today," http://www.firstmonday.org/issues/issue8_3/Garfinkel/index.html.

32. Beirich and Moser. "From Push to Shove," http://www.splcenter.org/intelligenceproject/ip-4w3.html.

33. Committee on the Judiciary, *Animal Rights,* Hearing statements, 108th Cong., 2d sess., 2004, 10; Law Enforcement Agency Resource Network. "Ecoterrorism," http://www.adl.org/learn/ext_us/Ecoterrorism.asp?LEARN_subCat=Extremism_in_America&xpicked=4&item=eco; Senate Committee on the Environment and Public Works, *Oversight on Ecoterrorism,* Testimony of David Martosko, 109th Cong., 1st sess., 2005.

34. Senate Committee on Environment and Public Works, *Concerning Stop Huntingdon Animal Cruelty,* Statement given by John Lewis, 109th Cong., 1st sess., 2005.

35. Wikipedia, "Stop Huntingdon Animal Cruelty," http://en.wikipedia.org/wiki/SHAC.

36. Wikipedia, "Stop Huntingdon Animal Cruelty," http://en.wikipeidia.org/wiki/SHAC.

37. West, "Animal Rights Activists in New Wave of Attacks," http://www.animalliberationfront.com/ALFront/Actions-UK/ALFCambridge.htm.

38. Wikipedia, "Stop Huntingdon Animal Cruelty," http://en.wikipedia.org/wiki/SHAC; Senate Committee on the Environment and Public Works, *Concerning Stop Huntingdon Animal Cruelty (SHAC),* Hearing statements, 109th Cong., 1st sess., 2005.

39. Stop Huntingdon Animal Cruelty, "SHAC Global," http://www.shac.net/SHAC/global.html.

40. Senate Committee on the Environment and Public Works, *Concerning Stop Huntingdon Animal Cruelty (SHAC),* Hearing statements, 109th Cong., 1st sess., 2005.

41. Oliver, *Animal Rights,* 116.

42. Guither, *Animal Rights;* Oliver, *Animal Rights,* 115.

43. Senate Committee on the Environment and Public Works, *Oversight on Ecoterrorism,* Testimony of David Martosko, 109th Cong., 1st sess., 2005.

44. Senate Committee on the Environment and Public Works, *Oversight on Ecoterrorism,* Testimony of David Martosko, 109th Cong., 1st sess., 2005; Workman, *PETA files.*

45. Workman, *PETA Files.*

46. Arnold, "Undue Influence," http://www.undueinfluence.com/peta.htm; Oliver, *Animal Rights;* Workman, *PETA Files;* Senate Committee on the

Environment and Public Works, *Oversight on Ecoterrorism,* Testimony of David
Martosko, 109th Cong., 1st sess., 2005.

47. Workman, *PETA Files*; Senate Committee on the Environment and Public
    Works, *Oversight on Ecoterrorism,* Testimony of David Martosko, 109th Cong.,
    1st sess., 2005; House Committee on Resources, Subcommittee on Forests and
    Forest Health, *Ecoterrorism and Lawlessness,* 107th Cong., 2nd sess., 2002;
    Associated Press, "PETA Calls Attack a New Breed of McCarthyism," http://
    www.cdfe.org/peta_responds.htm; Center for the Defense of Free Enterprise,
    Letter to Ingrid Newkirk from Rep. Scott McInnis, March 4, 2002, http://
    www.cdfe.org/mcinnis_peta_letter.htm; Center for the Defense of Free
    Enterprise, "Has PETA Funneled More Money to Domestic Terrorist
    Groups?" http://www.cdfe.org/petarantsnews.htm, May 1, 2002; a letter
    submitted for the record to the McInnis Committee by Jeffrey S. Kerr, counsel
    for the PETA Foundation, March 14, 2002—the letter was included in the
    hearing record, and includes information concerning campaign contributions
    to McInnis from entities known to oppose PETA.

48. Oliver, *Animal Rights,* 122.

49. Oliver, *Animal Rights*; Workman, *PETA Files*; Arnold, "Undue Influence,"
    http://www.undueinfluence.com/peta.htm.

50. Center for the Defense of Free Enterprise, Letter to IRS Commissioner Charles
    O. Rossotti, http://www.undueinfluence.com/ewg_complaint.htm.

51. Gazette Mail (Charleston, WV), January 15, 1989, cited in Oliver, *Animal
    Rights,* 207.

52. Carnell, "Debunking the Animal Rights Movement," November 16, 2001,
    http://www.animalrights.net/articles/2001/000229.html.

53. Workman, *PETA Files.*

54. Oliver, *Animal Rights,* 124.

55. Workman, *PETA Files*; Center for the Defense of Free Enterprise, Letter to IRS
    Commissioner Charles O. Rossotti, http://www.undueinfluence.com/ewg_
    complaint.htm.

56. Workman, *PETA Files*; Oliver, *Animal Rights*; Center for the Defense of Free
    Enterprise, Letter to IRS Commissioner Charles O. Rossotti, http://www.
    undueinfluence.com/ewg_complaint.htm; Government's Sentencing
    Memorandum, *U.S. v. Coronado,* No. 1:93-CR-116.

57. Center for the Defense of Free Enterprise, Letter to IRS Commissioner Charles
    O. Rossotti, http://www.undueinfluence.com/ewg_complaint.htm;
    Workman, *PETA Files.*

58. Workman, *PETA Files.*

59. Senate Committee on the Environment and Public Works, *Oversight on
    Ecoterrorism,* Testimony of David Martosko, 109th Cong., 1st sess., 2005. PETA
    president Ingrid Newkirk herself chronicled early ALF activities in the United
    States in her book *Free the Animals! The Amazing True Story of the Animal
    Liberation Front.* In Newkirk's account, a single female activist, "Valerie," is
    largely credited with initiating and organizing ALF liberations in the United
    States. Intimate details in the book have led some to surmise that Newkirk is
    "Valerie." Either way, Newkirk's account demonstrates that she, and PETA,
    possess inside knowledge concerning illegal ALF activities, further

supporting the notion that PETA and ALF are not distinct and separate entities.

60. Law Enforcement Agency Resource Network. "Ecoterrorism," http://www. adl.org/learn/ext_us/Ecoterrorism.asp?LEARN_subCat=Extremism_in_ America&xpicked=4&item=eco.

61. On November 13, 2005, *Sixty Minutes* aired an interview with Vlasak in which, speaking literally, not hypothetically, he explicitly endorsed the murder of research scientists. When pressed about whether he supported the killing of scientists, Vlasak said that if people refused to desist from exploiting animals, then they should be stopped by "whatever means necessary."

5 Criminality in the Radical Environmental Movement

1. Lee, *Earth First!*.

2. For a detailed, sympathetic view of Earth First!, see Zakin, *Coyotes and Town Dogs;* see also, Manes, *Green Rage*. The best neutral, scholarly account of Earth First! remains Lee's *Earth First!*.

3. Bron Raymond Taylor notes that Earth First! ideology contains both political and religious themes. Rejecting organized religion, most Earth First!ers rely on a "radical ecological consciousness" embodied in their recognition of the "sacredness and interconnectedness of all life." In his analysis, Taylor demonstrates the spiritual and reverent connection Earth First!ers have with the natural world, and the explicit religious themes that grow out of this relationship. Mother Earth, or Gaia, is God. And although Taylor observes elements of Taoism, Buddhism, Hinduism, witchcraft, and pagan earth-worship in the movement, the most important influence is American Indian spirituality. When Earth First! split along ideological lines some ten years after its formation, Dave Foreman derisively referred to the mix of pagan mysticism, eco-feminism, and other New Age influences in the movement as the "woo-woo" factor. For more on Earth First!'s spiritual dimensions, see Taylor, "Religion and Politics." For a broader look at similar environmental movements, see Taylor, *Resistance Movements*.

4. Lee, *Earth First!*, 32.

5. Lee, *Earth First!*

6. Ibid.

7. Lee, *Earth First!*, 39.

8. Lee, *Earth First!*.

9. Lee, *Earth First!*, 40.

10. Lee, *Earth First!*.

11. Ibid.; Zakin, *Coyotes and Town Dogs;* Manes, *Green Rage*.

12. Manes, *Green Rage*, 235.

13. Lee, *Earth First!*, 74.

14. Lee, *Earth First!*, 53.

15. Lee, *Earth First!;* Manes, *Green Rage*.

16. Lee, *Earth First!;* Manes, *Green Rage*.

17. Lee, *Earth First!*.

18. Ibid.

19. Ibid.

20. Ibid. Earth First! founders Dave Foreman, Howie Wolke, and Bart Koehler remained active in the environmental movement despite their departure. Foreman, free on probation, went on to edit a new journal, *Wild America,* and established the Wildlands Project, devoted to ecosystem recovery in North America.

21. Ibid., 133.

22. Long, *Ecoterrorism.*

23. "Earth First!," http://www.activistcash.com/organization_overview.cfm.

24. Earth First! homepage at http://www.earthfirst.org. Additional EF! affiliates include Alachua EF!, Allegheny EF!, Bay Area EF!, Big Bend EF!, Boundary Waters EF!, Buffalo Trace EF!, Croatan EF!, Dallas EF!, East Texas EF!, EF! Austin, French Broad EF!, Gainseville/Ichetucknee EF!, Houston EF!, Kalmiopsis EF!, Katuah EF!/River Faction, Katuah EF!/Tennessee Valley Faction, Katuah Foothills EF!, Kekionga EF!, Lake Erie EF!, Lake Worthless EF!, Loon Antics EF! Love Canal EF!, Madison EF!, Maine EF!, OFF!, Olympia EF!/Cascadia Defense Network, Peninsular Ranges EF!, Phoenix EF!, Red Gate EF!, San Juan EF!, Santa Cruz EF!/EF! Radio, Seattle EF!, Shawnee EF! Sonoma County EF!, Teewinot EF!, Tucson EF!, Two Rivers EF!, Uwharrie EarthFirst!, Wild Rockies EF!/Wild Rockies Review, Yellowstone EF! List accessed at http://www.activistcash.com/organization_overview.cfm.

25. http://www.activistcash.com/organization_overview.cfm.

26. http://www.earthfirst.org/issues.htm; http://www.earthfirst.org/ about.htm; http://www.earthfirstjournal.org/AboutEF.shtml.

27. Ibid.

28. Earth First!, "Snitches get Stitches," http://www.earthfirstjournal.org/ articles.php?a=672; Earth First!, "The War this Time," http://www. earthfirstjournal.org/articles.php?a=668; Earth First!, "Most Wanted Ecoterrorists: The Biotechnology Industry," http://www.earthfirstjournal. org/articles.php?a=713.

29. http://www.activistcash.com/organization_overview.cfm.

30. Ron Arnold reports that environmental defectors have claimed that the formation of Earth First! was in fact a calculated move by the Sierra Club and the Wilderness Society for the purpose of making their views seem more reasonable. The allegation is that the groups offered to fund Foreman for up to ten years in the running of a more radical group. Foreman himself provides some support for the story, stating in a *Smithsonian* article, "We thought it would have been useful to have a group to take a tougher position than the Sierra Club or the Wilderness Society . . . it [EF] could be sort of secretly controlled by the mainstream and trotted out at hearings to make the Sierra Club or Wilderness Society look more moderate," http://www.activistcash. com/organization_overview.cfm.

31. An earlier group calling itself Environmental Life Force used the ELF acronym in the late 1970s. Throughout 1977 the original ELF perpetrated a variety of criminal acts, including placing timed fire bombs underneath crop dusters in Salinas, California, shooting out windows in the home of future

U.S. Senator Dianne Feinstein, as well as other "armed actions" in California and in the corporate headquarters of a paper company in Oregon City, Oregon. This ELF disbanded in 1978 after the arrest and conviction of founding member John Hanna. Wikipedia, "Earth Liberation Front," http://en.wikipedia.org/wiki/Earth_Liberation_Front.

32. Stoner and Perlstein, "Implementing 'Justice'," 93.

33. Ibid. In one sense, it may be appropriate to say that the ELF existed from the very beginning of Earth First!—it was simply those activists in the EF! movement that crossed the line from protest and civil disobedience to active monkey wrenching and property destruction. In the mid-1990s, wishing to legitimize EF! and make it appear more reasonable, the Earth First!ers who carried out large-scale monkey wrenching simply began to call themselves the ELF.

34. Animal Liberation Front, "Frequently Asked Questions," http://www.animalliberationfront.com/ALFront/ELF/elf_faq.pdf.

35. Stoner and Perlstein, "Implementing 'Justice.'"

36. Animal Liberation Front, "Frequently Asked Questions," http://www.animalliberationfront.com/ALFront/ELF/elf_faq.pdf.

37. Ibid.

38. Arnold, *Ecoterror*; Rosebraugh, *Burning Rage.*

39. Rosebraugh, *Burning Rage,* 20.

40. Earth Liberation Front, "Meet the ELF," http://www.earthliberationfront.com/about/; House Committee on Resources, Subcommittee on Forests and Forest Health, *Ecoterrorism and Lawlessness,* 107th Cong., 2nd sess., 2002.

41. Rosebraugh, *Burning Rage,* 60.

42. NAELFPO, "Frequently Asked Questions," 11, http://www.animalliberationfront.com/ALFront/ELF/elf_faq.pdf.

43. The Law Enforcement Agency Resource Network, "Ecoterrorism," http://www.adl.org/learn/ext_us/Ecoterrorism.asp?LEARN_subCat=Extremism_in_America&xpicked=4&item=eco.

44. Law Enforcement Agency Resource Network. "Ecoterrorism," http://www.adl.org/learn/ext_us/Ecoterrorism.asp?LEARN_subCat=Extremism_in_America&xpicked=4&item=eco. An additional statement read, "In pursuance of justice, freedom, and equal consideration for all innocent life across the board, segments of this global revolutionary movement are no longer limiting their revolutionary potential by adhering to a flawed, inconsistent, non-violent ideology." Audrey Hudson, "ELF Admits to Arson," http://www.washtimes.com, September 10, 2002.

45. Law Enforcement Agency Resource Network. "Ecoterrorism," http://www.adl.org/learn/ext_us/Ecoterrorism.asp?LEARN_subCat=Extremism_in_America&xpicked=4&item=eco.

46. http://www.arissa.org; Law Enforcement Agency Resource Network, "Ecoterrorism," http://www.adl.org/learn/ext_us/Ecoterrorism.asp?LEARN_subCat=Extremism_in_America&xpicked=4&item=eco.

47. Law Enforcement Agency Resource Network. "Ecoterrorism," http://www.adl.org/learn/ext_us/Ecoterrorism.asp?LEARN_subCat=Extremism_in_America&xpicked=4&item=eco. See also statement of Craig Rosebraugh and written responses to committee questions, Committee on Resources.

6 Structure and Modus Operandi of Radical Movements

1. Garfinkel, "Leaderless Resistance Today," http://www.firstmonday.org. Beam himself acknowledged a debt to one Colonel Ulius Louis Amoss, a U.S. intelligence officer fearful of a communist takeover in the United States in the early 1960s.
2. Munro, *Confronting Cruelty*, 98.
3. Eyerman and Jamieson, *Social Movements*.
4. Munro, *Confronting Cruelty*.
5. Best and Nocella II, *Terrorists or Freedom Fighters*.
6. Center for the Defense of Free Enterprise, *Report to Congress*, http://www.cdfe.org/doj_report.htm.
7. Arnold, *Ecoterror*.
8. U.S. Justice Department, *Report to Congress*.
9. Oliver, *Animal Rights*.
10. Animal Liberation Front, *The ALF Primer*, http://www.animalliberation.net/library/alprimer.html.
11. Animal Liberation Front, *The ALF Primer*, http://www.animalliberation.net/library/alprimer.html, 5.
12. Animal Liberation Front, *The ALF Primer*, http://www.animalliberation.net/library/alprimer.html,10–11.
13. U.S. Justice Department, *Report to Congress*.

7 A Profile of Eco-Warriors and Animal Liberationists

1. Foreman, "Violence and Earth First!" 4.
2. Steven Best, telephone interview with author, December 15, 2005. Best corroborated my suspicions on this point, noting the number of activists who had little direction and apparently just wanted to "break shit."
3. See Hoffer, *The True Believer*.
4. Guither, *Animal Rights*.
5. Jamison and Lunch, "Results from Demographic, Attitudinal, and Behavioral Analysis of the Animal Rights Movement," paraphrased in Guither, *Animal Rights*, 63–72.
6. Richards, and Krannich, "The Ideology of the Animal Rights Movement," paraphrased in Guither, *Animal Rights*, 63–72.
7. Guither, *Animal Rights*, 67–71.
8. Stoner and Perlstein, "Implementing 'Justice' through Terror and Destruction."
9. Newkirk, *Free the Animals!*
10. Peter Young, personal correspondence with author, November 17, 2005.
11. For an account reconstructed by witnesses at the hearing, see http://www.supportpeter.com/111705-3.htm.
12. John Wade, personal correspondence with author, December 28, 2005.

13. Christopher McIntosh, personal correspondence with author, November 17, 2005.

14. Hoffer, *True Believer*.

15. Steven Best, telephone interview with author, December 15, 2005.

16. Ibid.

17. Festinger, *A Theory of Cognitive Dissonance*.

18. Sykes and Matza, "Techniques of Neutralization," 664–70.

19. White, *Terrorism*, 22.

20. Cooper, "What is a Terrorist," cited in White, *Terrorism*, 23.

21. Sykes and Matza's five techniques are denial of responsibility, denial of injury, denial of the victim, condemnation of the condemners, appeals to higher loyalties; others have added defense of necessity, defense of the ledger, denial of the justice or necessity of the law, claim that "everybody is doing it," and claim of entitlement. See Conklin, *Criminology*.

22. Best and Nocella II, quoting Paul Watson in "Behind the Mask," 11.

23. Ibid., 48.

24. Ibid., 21.

25. Ibid., 48.

26. Ibid.

27. Ibid.

28. Anonymous communiqué dated July 11, 2001, http://www.stopecoviolence. org/words.htm, p. 9 (accessed November 22, 2005).

29. Quote attributed to David Barbarash, ALF spokesperson, December 5, 1998, http://www.stopecoviolenc.org/words.htm, p. 5 (accessed on November 22, 2005).

30. Quote attributed to Craig Rosebraugh in the *Seattle Weekly*, April 9–15, 2003, http://www.stopecoviolence.org/words.htm, p. 7 (accessed on November 22, 2005).

31. Anonymous ELF communiqué, September 3, 2003, http://earthliberationfront. com/news/2002/090302.shtml (accessed October 24, 2003).

32. Churchill, "Illuminating the Philosophy," 3.

33. Best and Nocella II, "Behind the Mask," 12.

34. Ibid.

35. Bernstein, "Legitimizing Liberation," 101.

36. Best and Nocella II, "Behind the Mask," 14.

37. Ibid., 16.

38. Ibid., 24.

39. Ibid., 25.

40. Ibid., 26.

41. Bernstein, "Legitimizing Liberation," 101.

42. Quote attributed to SHAC USA organizer Kevin Jonas in the *Philadelphia Inquirer*, July 14, 2002, http://www.stopecoviolence.org/words.htm, p. 3 (accessed November 22, 2005).

43. Anonymous letter sent to wilderness guide outfitters in 1996, http://www. stopecoviolence.org/words.htm, p. 6 (accessed November 22, 2005).

44. Quote attributed to Mike Roselle in the Earth First Journal, Dec 1994/Jan1995, http://www.stopecoviolence.org/words.htm, p. 11 (accessed November 22, 2005).

45. Quote attributed to Gary Yourofsky, http://www.stopecoviolence.org/words.htm, p. 13 (accessed November 22, 2005).

46. Anonymous communiqué posted at Bite Back Magazine, September 17, 2005, http://www.directactioninfo/news_sept17_05.htm (accessed October 28, 2005).

47. Anonymous communiqué, September 17, 2005, http://animalliberationpressoffice.org/communiques/2005-09-13_diliberto.htm (accessed October 28, 2005).

48. Anonymous communiqué, December 27, 2004, http://animalliberationpressoffice.org/communiques/2004-12-27_comm_laas_david.htm (accessed October 28, 2005).

49. Anonymous communiqué dated April 21, 2005, http://animalliberationpressoffice.org/communiques/2005-04-21_forestHLS.htm (accessed October 28, 2005).

50. Pearlstein, *Mind of the Political Terrorist.*

51. Ibid., 7.

52. Ibid., 18.

53. Ibid., 42.

54. Hoffer, *True Believer,* 22.

55. Ibid. 3.

56. Ibid., 24.

8 The Future of Eco-Terrorism and Animal Liberation

1. An August 1993 report to Congress on "Animal Enterprise Terrorism" also noted ALF's effectiveness: "Where the direct, collateral, and indirect effects of incidents such as this are factored together, ALF's professed tactic of economic sabotage can be considered successful, and its objectives, at least towards the victimized facility, fulfilled." U.S. Justice Department, *Report to Congress,* http://*www.cdfe.org/doj_report.htm.* Guither notes that there is in fact a consensus among industry officials, government, and law enforcement that animal rights extremism in the United States has significantly affected the industries it has targeted. My point here is that the larger goals of animal liberationists and radical environmentalists are beyond the reach of the radicals. See Guither, *Animal Rights.*

2. U.S. Justice Department, *Report to Congress,* http://*www.cdfe.org/doj_report.htm;* Guither, *Animal Rights.*

3. Long, *Ecoterrorism.*

4. House Committee on the Judiciary, Subcommittee on Crime, *Acts of Ecoterrorism,* 105th Cong., 2nd sess., 1998; House Committee on Resources, Subcommittee on Forests and Forest Health, *Ecoterrorism and Lawlessness,* 107th Cong., 2nd sess., 2002; Senate Committee on the Judiciary, *Animal Rights,* Hearing statements, 108th Cong., 2nd sess., 2004; Senate Committee on

the Environment and Public Works, *Oversight on Ecoterrorism,* Hearing Statements, 109th Cong., 1st sess., 2005.

5. Animal Liberation Front, *2001 Direct Action Report,* http://www.wlfa.org/interactive/features/pdf/ALF2001Report.pdf.

6. Law Enforcement Agency Resource Network, "Ecoterrorism," http://www.adl.org/learn/ext_us/Ecoterrorism.asp?LEARN_subCat=Extremism_in_America&xpicked=4&item=eco.

7. Ibid.

8. http://www.stopecoviolence.com/words.htm#eco.

9. Best and Kahn, "Trial by Fire: The SHAC 7 and the Future of Democracy," http://www.drstevebest.org/papers/vegenvani/Shac7.php. Note: In March 2006 all seven defendants were convicted of Animal Enterprise Act violations and were facing multi-year sentences, Potter, "Green is the New Red," http://www.earthfirstjournal.org/articles.php?a=903.

10. Guither, *Animal Rights.*

11. Best, "It's War!"

12. Long, *Animal Rights.*

13. Ibid.

14. Ibid.

15. Long, *Animal Rights;* Mission statement of Arissa, http://www.arissa.org.

16. Leslie James Pickering, e-mail message to author, January 30, 2006.

17. Arnold, *Ecoterror;* Long, *Animal Rights.*

18. Theodore Kaczynski, personal correspondence with author, January 14, 2006.

19. Rosebraugh, *Burning Rage of a Dying Planet.*

20. Steven Best, interview with author, December 15, 2006.

21. Richards, "Consensus Mobilization through ideology, networks, and grievances." Also see "Animals and Social Issues Survey" in Munro, *Confronting Cruelty.*

22. Of the 97 respondents, 50 (51.5%) identified themselves as a Democrat, 13 (13.4%) were members of the Green Party, and 18 (18.5%) were Independents. Twelve of the respondents did not identify with a political party; a sprinkling identified as "other"; one identified as Republican and one as an anarchist. By far the greatest number of respondents (51%) identified themselves as white-collar/professional workers; the second largest group was students 21 (21.6%). A full 29% of attendees held a graduate degree, and another 48.5% had a four-year degree.

23. The sample comprised 18 females and 5 males, 13 were democrats, 9 identified with the green party, and 1 was an independent; 21 of 23 had at least some college.

24. Ellsbach and Sutton, "Acquiring Organizational Legitimacy through Illegitimate Actions."

25. Garfinkel, "Leaderless Resistance Today," http://www.firstmonday.org/issues/issue8_3/garfinkel/index.html.

26. Hoffer, *The True Believer,* 18.

27. Garfinkel, "Leaderless Resistance Today."

28. Marshall quoted in *The New York Times*, http://www.stopecoviolence.com/words.htm#eco.
29. Dave Foreman, quoted in *Sarasota Herald Tribune*, Jan. 17, 1998, http://www.stopecoviolence.com/words.htm#eco.
30. Foreman quoted in Arnold, *Ecoterror*, 8.
31. Cilluffo, Cardash, Lederman, *Report of the CSIS Homeland Defense Project.*
32. Laqueur, *The New Terrorism.*
33. Lifton, *Destroying the World to Save It.*

Bibliography

Abbey, Edward. *The Monkey Wrench Gang*. New York: Avon Books, 1975.

"ALF A,B,C's." *Bite Back Magazine*. http://www.directaction.info/library_abcs.htm.

Animal Liberation Front. *2001 Direct Action Report*. http://www.wlfa.org/interactive/features/pdf/ALF2001Report.pdf.

———. *The ALF Primer. http://www.animalliberation.net/library/alprimer.html.*

———. "Animal Rights Militia Fact Sheet." http://www.animalliberationfront.com/ALFront/Actions-UK/alfarm.htm.

———. "The History of the Hunt Saboteurs Association (Part 1) 1963: From Protest to Resistance." http://www.animalliberationfront.com/ALFront/Actions-UK/HSA/HSA%20-%20The%20History.htm.

Arnold, Ron. *Ecoterror: The Violent Agenda to Save Nature*. Bellevue, WA: The Free Enterprise Press, 1997.

———. "Undue Influence: PETA—People for the Ethical Treatment of Animals." http://www.undueinfluence.com/peta.htm.

Associated Press. "PETA Calls Attack a New Breed of McCarthyism." Center for the Defense of Free Enterprise. March 15, 2002. http://www.cdfe.org/peta_responds.htm.

Barnhill, David Landis, and Roger S. Gottlieb. *Deep Ecology and World Religions*. Albany, NY: State University of New York Press, 2001.

"Barry Horne, Animal Liberationist." *http://barryhorne.org/.*

Beirich, Heidi and Bob Moser. "From Push to Shove: Radical Environmental and Animal-Rights Groups Have Always Drawn the Line at Targeting Humans. Not Anymore." *Southern Poverty Law Center Report on Ecoterror*, 107 (Fall 2002). http://www.splcenter.org/intelligenceproject/ip-4w3.html.

Bentham, Jeremy. *An Introduction to the Principles of Morals and Legislation*. New York: Clarendon Press, 1996.

Bernstein, Mark. "Legitimizing Liberation." In *Terrorists or Freedom Fighters: Reflections on the Liberation of Animals*, edited by Steven Best and Anthony J. Nocella II, 93–105. New York: Lantern Books, 2004.

Best, Steven. "It's War! The Escalating Battle Between Activists and the Corporate-State Complex." In *Terrorists or Freedom Fighters: Reflections on the Liberation of Animals*, edited by Steven Best and Anthony J. Nocella II, 300–39. New York: Lantern Books, 2004.

Best, Steven, and Anthony J. Nocella II. "Behind the Mask." In *Terrorists or Freedom Fighters: Reflections on the Liberation of Animals*, edited by Steven Best and Anthony J. Nocella II, 9–63. New York: Lantern Books, 2004.

———. *Terrorists or Freedom Fighters: Reflections on the Liberation of Animals*. New York: Lantern Books, 2004.

Best, Steven, and Richard Kahn. "Trial by Fire: The SHAC 7 and the Future of Democracy." http://www.drstevebest.org/papers/vegenvani/Shac7.php.

Brown, Jonathan. "Animal Rights Campaigners Target Oxford." Animal Liberation Front. August 15, 2005. http://www.animalliberationfront.com/ALFront/Actions-UK/OsfordProt.htm.

Carnell, Brian. "Debunking the Animal Rights Movement: PETA and Animal Rights Violence." AnimalRights.Net. November 16, 2001. http://www.animalrights.net/articles/2001/000229.html.

Carruthers, Peter. *The Animals Issue: Moral Theory in Practice*. Cambridge: Cambridge University Press, 1994.

Center for the Defense of Free Enterprise. "Has PETA Funneled More Money to Domestic Terrorist Groups?" http://www.cdfe.org/petarantsnews.htm (accessed May 1, 2002).

———. Letter to Ingrid Newkirk from Rep. Scott McInnis. http://www.cdfe.org/mcinnis_peta_letter.htm (accessed March 4, 2002).

———. Letter to IRS Commissioner Charles O. Rossotti. http://www.undueinfluence.com/ewg_complaint.htm (accessed March 4, 2002).

Churchill, Ward. "Illuminating the Philosophy and Methods of Animal Liberation," In *Terrorists or Freedom Fighters: Reflections on the Liberation of Animals*, edited by Steven Best and Anthony J. Nocella II, 3. New York: Lantern Books, 2004.

Cilluffo, Frank J., Sharon L. Cardash, and Gordon N. Lederman. *A Report of the CSIS Homeland Defense Project*. Washington D.C., U.S. Government Printing Office, 2001.

Conklin, John. *Criminology*. 6th ed. Boston: Allyn and Bacon, 1998.

Cooper, H. H. A. "What is a Terrorist: A Psychological Perspective," *Legal Medical Quarterly* 1 (1977): 8–18.

Devall, Bill, and George Sessions. *Deep Ecology: Living as if Life Mattered*. Salt Lake City, UT: Gibbs Smith, 1985.

Dombroski, Daniel A. *Babies and Beasts: The Argument from Marginal Cases*. Urbana: University of Illinois Press, 1997.

Drengson, Alan, and Yuichi Inoue. *The Deep Ecology Movement: An Introductory Anthology*. Berkeley, CA: North Atlantic Books, 1995.

Earth First!, "Most Wanted Ecoterrorists: The Biotechnology Industry." *Earth First! Journal* 22 no. 5, 2002. http://www.earthfirstjournal.org/articles.php?a=713.

———, "Snitches get Stitches." *Earth First! Journal* 23 no. 5, 2003. http://www.earthfirstjournal.org/articles.php?a=672.

———, "The War this Time." *Earth First! Journal* 23 no. 5, 2003. http://www.earthfirstjournal.org/articles.php?a=668.

Earth Liberation Front. "Diary of Actions and Chronology." http://www.earthliberationfront.com (accessed Nov. 15, 2004).

———. "Meet the ELF." http://earthliberationfront.com/about/.

Egan, Sean P. "From Spikes to Bombs: The Rise of Ecoterrorism," *Studies in Conflict and Terrorism* 19 no. 1 (1996): 1–18.

Ellsbach, Kimberly D. and Robert I. Sutton. "Acquiring Organizational Legitimacy through Illegitimate Actions: A Marriage of Institutional and Impression Management Theories," *Academy of Management Journal*, 35, no. 4 (October, 1992).

Environmental Action Staff. *Ecotage!* New York: Pocket Books, 1971.

Eyerman, Ron and Andrew Jamieson. *Social Movements: A Cognitive Approach.* State College, PA: The Pennsylvania State University Press, 1991.

Festinger, Leon. *A Theory of Cognitive Dissonance.* Stanford, CA: Stanford University Press, 1957.

Finsen, Lawrence and Susan Finsen. *The Animal Rights Movement in America: From Compassion to Respect.* New York: Twayne Publishers, 1994.

Foreman, Dave. "Violence and Earth First!" *Earth First Newsletter* 2, no. 4 (1982): 4.

Foundation for Biomedical Research. "Violent and Illegal Activity by Animal Activists is Escalating." http://www.fbresearch.org/AnimalActivism/violence.htm.

Frey, Raymond Gillespie. *Interests and Rights: The Case Against Animals.* Oxford: Clarendon Press, 1980.

Garfinkel, Simson L. "Leaderless Resistance Today," *First Monday.* http://www.firstmonday.org/issues/issue8_3/Garfinkel/index.html.

Guillermo, Kathy Snow. *Monkey Business: The Disturbing Case that Launched the Animal Rights Movement.* Washington, D.C.: National Press Books, 1993.

Guither, Harold D. *Animal Rights: History and Scope of a Radical Social Movement.* Carbondale, IL.: Southern Illinois University Press, 1998.

Haywood, Bill (pseudo.) and Dave Foreman. *Ecodefense: A Field Guide to Monkeywrenching.* Tucson, AZ: Ned Ludd Books, 1985.

Hoffer, Eric. *The True Believer.* New York: Harper and Row, 1951.

Hudson, Audrey. "ELF Admits to Arson." *Washington Times*, September 10, 2002. http://www.cdfe.org/torch_usfs.htm.

Jasper, James M. and Dorothy Nelkin. *The Animal Rights Crusade.* New York: The Free Press, 1992.

Laqueur, Walter. *The New Terrorism: Fanaticism and the Arms of Mass Destruction.* New York: Oxford University Press, 1999.

Law Enforcement Agency Resource Network. "Ecoterrorism: Extremism in the Animal Rights and Environmental Movements." Anti-Defamation League.

http://www.adl.org/learn/ext_us/Ecoterrorism.asp?LEARN_subCat=
Extremism_in_America&xpicked=4&item=eco.

Lee, Martha F. *EarthFirst!: Environmental Apocalypse*. Syracuse, NY: Syracuse
University Press, 1995.

Lifton, Robert Jay. *Destroying the World to Save It: Aum Shinrikyo, Apocalyptic
Violence, and the New Global Terrorism*. New York: Henry Holt and Company,
2000.

Long, Douglas. *Ecoterrorism*. New York: Facts on File, Inc., 2004.

Manes, Christopher. *Green Rage: Radical Environmentalism and the Unmaking of
Civilization*. Boston, MA: Little, Brown and Company, 1990.

Masters Evans, Kim. *Animal Rights*. New York: Gale, 2004.

Merchant, Carolyn. *Radical Ecology: The Search for a Livable World*. New York:
Routledge, 1992.

Mill, John Stuart. *Utilitarianism*. Oxford: Oxford University Press, 1998.

Molland, Noel. "Thirty Years of Direct Action." In *Terrorists or Freedom Fighters:
Reflections on the Liberation of Animals*, edited by Steven Best and Anthony J.
Nocella II, 65–74. New York: Lantern Books, 2004.

Munro, Lyle. *Compassionate Beasts*. Westport, CT: Praeger, 2001.

———. *Confronting Cruelty: Moral Orthodoxy and the Challenge of the Animal Rights
Movement*. Leiden, The Netherlands: Brill, 2005.

NAELFPO, "Frequently Asked Questions," 11, http://www.animalliberationfront.
com/ALFront/ELF/elf_faq.pdf.

Naess, Arne. *Ecology, Community, and Lifestyle: Outline of an Ecosophy*.
Translated by David Rothenberg. Cambridge: Cambridge University
Press, 2001.

Newkirk, Ingrid. *Free the Animals! The Amazing True Story of the Animal Liberation
Front*. Chicago: The Noble Press, Inc, 1992.

Nibert, David. *Animal Rights, Human Rights: Entanglements of Oppression and
Liberation*. New York: Rowman and Littlefield, 2002.

Oliver, Daniel T. *Animal Rights: The Inhumane Crusade*. Bellevue, WA: Merril Press,
1999.

Pearlstein, Richard M. *The Mind of the Political Terrorist*. Wilmington, DE: SR
Books, 1991.

Pluhar, Evelyn B. *Beyond Prejudice: The Moral Significance of Human and Nonhuman
Animals*. Durham, NC: Duke University Press, 1995.

Potter, Will. "Green is the New Red." *The Earth First! 26* no. 4, 2006. http://www.
earthfirstjournal.org/articles.php?a=903.

Regan, Tom. *Defending Animal Rights*. Chicago: University of Illinois Press, 2001.

———. *Animal Rights, Human Wrongs*. New York: Rowman and Littlefield, 2003.

———. *Empty Cages*. New York: Rowman and Littlefield, 2004.

Richards, Rebecca. "Consensus Mobilization through Ideology, Networks, and
Grievances: A Study of the Contemporary Animal Rights Movement," PhD
diss., Utah State University, 1990.

Rosebaugh, Craig. *Burning Rage of a Dying Planet: Speaking for the Earth Liberation
Front*. New York: Lantern Books, 2004.

Rudacille, Deborah. *The Scalpel and the Butterfly: The Conflict Between Animal Research and Animal Protection*. Berkeley: University of California Press, 2001.

Scarce, Rik. *Eco-Warriors: Understanding the Radical Environmental Movement*. Chicago: The Noble Press, 1990.

"Screaming Wolf" [pseud. attributed to Sidney and Tanya Singer]. *A Declaration of War: Killing People to Save Animals and the Environment*. Grass Valley, CA: Patrick Henry Press, 1991.

Singer, Peter. *Animal Liberation*. New York: Random House, 1990.

Stallwood, Kim. "A Personal Overview of Direct Action in the United Kingdom and the United States." In *Terrorists or Freedom Fighters: Reflections on the Liberation of Animals*, edited by Steven Best and Anthony J. Nocella II, 81–90. New York: Lantern Books, 2004.

Stoner, Kelly and Gary Perlstein. "Implementing 'Justice' through Terror and Destruction: Ecoterror's Violent Agenda to Save Nature." In *Terrorism: Research, Readings, and Realities*, edited by Lynne L. Snowden and Bradley C. Whitsel, 90–134. Upper Saddle River, NJ: Prentice Hall, 2005.

Stop Huntingdon Animal Cruelty, "SHAC Global," *http://www.shac.net/SHAC/ global.html*.

———. "SHAC History" *http://www.shac.net/SHAC.who.html*.

Sunstein, Cass R. and Martha C. Nussbaum. *Animal Rights: Current Debates and New Directions*. New York: Oxford University Press, 2004.

Switzer, Jacqueline Vaughn. *Environmental Activism*. Santa Barbara, CA: ABC-CLIO, 2003.

Sykes, Gresham M., and David Matza. "Techniques of Neutralization: A Theory of Delinquency." *American Sociological Review* 22 (December 1957): 664–70.

Taylor, Bron Raymond. "The Religion and Politics of EarthFirst!" *Ecologist* 21, no. 6 (November/December 1991): 259.

———. *Ecological Resistance Movements: The Global Emergence of Radical and Popular Environmentalism*. Albany: State University of New York Press, 1995.

U.S. Congress. House. Committee on the Judiciary. Subcommittee on Crime. *Acts of Ecoterrorism by Radical Environmental Organizations*. 105th Cong., 2nd sess., June 9, 1998.

———. Committee on Resources. Subcommittee on Forests and Forest Health. *Ecoterrorism and Lawlessness on the National Forests*. 107th Cong., 2nd sess., February 12, 2002.

———. Committee on Resources. Subcommittee on Forests and Forest Health. *Ecoterrorism and Lawlessness on the National Forests*. Statement given by Craig Rosebraugh, Former Press Officer, Earth Liberation Front. 107th Cong., 2nd sess., February 12, 2002.

U.S. Congress. Senate. Committee on the Environment and Public Works. *Concerning Stop Huntingdon Animal Cruelty (SHAC) and Other Animal Rights Extremists*. Hearing statements. 109th Cong., 1st sess., October 26, 2005.

———. Committee on Environment and Public Works. *Concerning Stop Huntingdon Animal Cruelty (SHAC) and Other Animal Rights Extremists*. Statement given by Jerry Vlasak, MD. 109th Cong., 1st sess., October 26, 2005.

————. Committee on Environment and Public Works. *Concerning Stop Huntingdon Animal Cruelty (SHAC) and Other Animal Rights Extremists*. Statement given by John Lewis. 109th Cong., 1st sess., October 26, 2005.

————. Committee on Environment and Public Works. *Concerning Stop Huntingdon Animal Cruelty (SHAC) and Other Animal Rights Extremists*. Statement given by Skip Boruchin. 109th Cong., 1st sess., October 26, 2005.

————. Committee on the Environment and Public Works. *Concerning Stop Huntingdon Animal Cruelty (SHAC) and Other Animal Rights Extremists.* Testimony of Barry M. Sabin, Chief Counterterrorism Section, Criminal Division, Department of Justice. 109th Cong., 1st sess., October 26, 2005.

————. Committee on the Environment and Public Works. *Oversight on Ecoterrorism Specifically Examining the Earth Liberation Front (ELF) and the Animal Liberation Front (ALF)*. Hearing Statements. 109th Cong., 1st sess., May 18, 2005.

————. Committee on the Environment and Public Works. *Oversight on Ecoterrorism Specifically Examining the Earth Liberation Front (ELF) and the Animal Liberation Front (ALF)*. Statements given by Bradley Campbell, John Lewis, and Carson Carroll. 109th Cong., 1st sess., May 18, 2005.

————. Committee on the Environment and Public Works. *Oversight on Ecoterrorism Specifically Examining the Earth Liberation Front (ELF) and the Animal Liberation Front*. Testimony of David Martosko. 109th Cong., 1st sess., May 18, 2005.

————. Committee on the Environment and Public Works. *Oversight on Ecoterrorism Specifically Examining the Earth Liberation Front (ELF) and the Animal Liberation Front (ALF)*. Testimony of David Vitter and David Skorton. 109th Cong., 1st sess., May 18, 2005.

————. Committee on the Judiciary. *Animal Rights: Activism vs. Criminality.* Hearing statements. 108th Cong., 2nd sess., May 18, 2004.

————. Committee on the Judiciary. *Animal Rights: Activism vs. Criminality.* Testimony of Mr. William Green. 108th Cong., 2nd sess., May 18, 2004.

U.S. Department of Justice. *Report to Congress on the Extent and Effects of Domestic and International Terrorism on Animal Enterprises.*1993. Center for the Defense of Free Enterprise. *http://www.cdfe.org/doj_report.htm.*

Vlasak, Jerry. Interviewed by Ed Bradley. *Sixty Minutes*. CBS. November 13, 2005.

Warner, Adam. "The Siege of Darley Oaks Farm." Animal Liberation Front. *http://www.animalliberationfront.com/ALFront/Actions-UK/DarleyOaks.htm.*

West, Rosie Murray. "Animal Rights Activists in New Wave of Attacks." Animal Liberation Front. *http://www.animalliberationfront.com/ALFront/Actions-UK/ALFCambridge.htm.*

White, Jonathan R. *Terrorism: An Introduction*. 2nd ed. Belmont, CA: West/Wadsworth, 1998.

Wikipedia. "Animal Rights Militia." *http://en.wikipedia.org/wiki/Animal_Rights_Militia.*

————. "Earth Liberation Front," *http://en.wikipedia.org/wiki/Earth_Liberation_Front.*

————. "Justice Department (animal rights)," *http://en.wikipedia.org/wiki/Justice_Department_(animal_rights).*

————. "Stop Huntingdon Animal Cruelty," *http://en.wikipedia.org/wiki/SHAC.*

Wolfe, Cary. *Animal Rites*. Chicago: University of Chicago Press, 2003.

Workman, Dave. *PETA Files: The Dark Side of the Animal Rights Movement*. Bellevue, WA: Merril Press, 2003.

Yount, Lisa. *Animal Rights*. New York: Facts on File, 2004.

Zakin, Susan. *Coyotes and Town Dogs: EarthFirst! and the Environmental Movement*. New York: Viking Penguin, 1993.

Zimmerman, Michael E., J. Baird Callicott, George Sessions, Karen J. Warren, and John Clark. *Environmental Philosophy: From Animal Rights to Radical Ecology*. 3rd ed. Upper Saddle River, NJ: Prentice Hall, 2001.

Zimmerman, Michael E. *Contesting Earth's Future: Radical Ecology and Postmodernity*. Berkeley, CA: University of California Press, 1994.

Index

About the Author

DONALD R. LIDDICK is Associate Professor of Administration of Justice at the University of Pittsburgh, Greenburg. He is the author of *The Global Underworld* (Praeger, 2004), and other books and articles that have appeared in various journals.